COLLABORATE OR PERISH!

"Becoming more effective and succeeding is a goal most of us share. Now William Bratton and Zachary Tumin focus on the power of effective collaboration, citing real-life examples as the key to real success. Their insight together with their extremely readable story clearly and convincingly explain why 'going it alone' no longer works in our increasingly connected society."

—**LEONARD STERN**, chairman and CEO of the Hartz Group

"*Collaborate or Perish!* is a refreshing kick in the pants—a wonderful collection of real-world, 'power of the many' examples. We all need to hear the rallying cry to take action together. Bill Bratton and Zach Tumin create excitement and a new desire to get involved. They not only motivate, they provide a playbook for how." —**LT GEN TAD OELSTROM**, USAF (ret.), and director of the National Security Program, Harvard Kennedy School

"The days of a Lone Ranger approach to problem-solving are over. In today's interconnected world, the best ideas and most effective implementation come when collaboration is at the core. *Collaborate or Perish!* is chock-full of real-world examples and behind-the-scenes insights from across industries and sectors that illustrate how success comes when teams work together."

—**ELI BROAD**, founder of the Broad Foundations

"Like many New Yorkers, I love Bill Bratton. It may be that no single person had more of a role transforming New York City into the safe, welcoming city it became when he was police commissioner. *Collaborate or Perish!*, written with Zachary Tumin, captures everything that makes Bratton so special. It's built around a big vision—that true collaboration is the key to solving the world's most complex problems—but it's also grounded in incredibly specific, cool, disruptive strategies for how to make collaboration happen, and the sort of insider stories that only someone like Bratton is in a position to know. I savored every word of this book . . ." —**TONY SCHWARTZ**, author of *The Way We're Working Isn't Working* and *The Power of Full Engagement*

"In today's world, collaboration across organizational boundaries is an imperative—not only within the public sector, but between the public, private, and nonprofit sectors. In *Collaborate or Perish!*, Bill Bratton and Zach Tumin show us how it works, providing a series of lessons that spell the difference between success and failure. Not only that, they do so in entertaining fashion, with real-world stories that jump off the page. Read this book!"

—**DAVID OSBORNE**, senior partner at the Public Strategies
Group and coauthor of *Reinventing Government,*
The Price of Government, and other books.

"No effective organization is an island. Whether you're in the corporate world, the public sector, the military, or even a small business owner, Bill Bratton and Zach Tumin's guide to institutional collaboration is a game changer."

—**CYNTHIA BROWN**, publisher of American Police Beat

"In this networked, wired, 'flat' world of ours today, for some reason, America is losing its competitive edge. In *Collaborate or Perish!*, internationally renowned anti-crime expert Bill Bratton and Zach Tumin identify that reason and point the way to regaining our edge. In today's world, our individualist culture won't cut it. We've simply *got* to collaborate, if we are to survive, much less thrive. Wall Street, Main Street, and, especially, Washington, listen up!"

—**CLARK ERVIN**, director of the
Aspen Institute Homeland Security Program

"Bratton and Tumin make a convincing case that collaboration benefits not only policing, but virtually every organizational process and decision. In settings from casinos to schools, *Collaborate or Perish!* demonstrates how systematic collaboration can transform an organization."

—**THOMAS H. DAVENPORT**, President's Distinguished
Professor of IT and Management, Babson College

"Bill Bratton has proved that he knows how to get results. In New York City and Los Angeles, he brought crime down because he had a big new vision for the police—he said police must prevent crime, not just investigate after the harm has been done. And Bratton saw his job as changing the urban environment, so people would feel safe in the city and would once again trust their police. To achieve these sweeping changes, Bill looked beyond the police department and got other people and organizations involved in his mission. Zach Tumin has led the way in bringing this kind of collaborative thinking to corporate America. Together, Bill and Zach have written a book that's a road map for any organization to succeed. They tell compelling stories of what is possible when you look for partners who can help you achieve your goals." —CHUCK WEXLER, Police Executive Research Forum

"The joy of this book—yes, joy—is in seeing people run through walls: on the streets of a big city plagued by extortion rackets; submersed in a submarine that is not picking up danger signals; in a disease-control center baffled by clues to the source of a bug that is hourly threatening thousands and ruining hundreds of angry farmers; in a customs shed unable to process goods fast and safely enough; in a convoy in Iraq and Afghanistan up against the diabolical permutations of the bomb-makers. Bratton and Tumin document scores of successful resolutions of apparently insuperable complexities. The magic key, from their own experiences and others, is collaboration. Technology counts but people talking to people counts for more. . . . The rich accumulation of the lessons is valuable but entertaining too. Every copy of the book should bear a sticker: Guaranteed not to bore.
—SIR HAROLD EVANS, author of *They Made America: From the Steam Engine to the Search Engine, Two Centuries of Innovation*

"Bill Bratton and Zach Tumin reveal in this book a first-class understanding for organization and management in a variety of situations. Their theme is collaboration along with technology that provides critical information for evaluating the situation on the ground under a leadership that supplies direction and support. The lessons, based in part on Bill Bratton's own record as police commissioner of both New York and Los Angeles, shine through the pages of this book to the point where it becomes inspirational for the reader . . . An extraordinary book for anyone interested in how 'action leads to results,' as Mr. Bratton puts it. —MORT ZUCKERMAN, editor in chief of *U.S. News & World Report* and publisher of the New York *Daily News*

COLLABORATE OR PERISH!

REACHING
ACROSS
BOUNDARIES IN
A NETWORKED
WORLD

WILLIAM BRATTON

AND

ZACHARY TUMIN

CROWN
BUSINESS
NEW YORK

Library of Congress Cataloging-in-Publication Data
Bratton, William.
Collaborate or perish! : reaching across boundaries in a networked
world / William Bratton, Zachary Tumin. — 1st ed.
p.   cm.
Includes bibliographical references and index.
1. Cooperation. 2. Business networks. 3. Social networks.
4. Strategic alliances (Business) I. Tumin, Zachary. II. Title.
HD2963.B73   2012
658'.046—dc23   2011029606

ISBN 978-0-307-59239-2
eISBN 978-0-307-59242-2

Printed in the United States of America

BOOK DESIGN BY BARBARA STURMAN
JACKET DESIGN BY BASE ART CO.

2 4 6 8 10 9 7 5 3 1

First Edition

To my wife, Rikki—
"Twenty-five years and a day."
—W.B.

To my parents, Sylvia and (in loving memory) Melvin;
my wife, Laura; our children, Remy and Ben,
and Kathleen and Alexandra,
for their love and support.
—R.Z.T.

Contents

COLLABORATE
OR PERISH!

INTRODUCTION

We live in a digital age, a networked world, where the race is on to out-collaborate, out-network, and out-innovate adversaries, competitors, and even nature.

In today's networked world, virtually everyone is connected. Today, 800 million of your "friends" are on Facebook. None were there a few years ago. In five years, Google's Eric Schmidt says, Chinese-language web pages will dominate search returns. In 2011, 20 million joined Google+'s new platform in a matter of weeks. By 2020 twelve billion mobile devices will connect to the Internet. The rate of change is heart-stopping.

Plan to go it alone? Think again.

Fifty years ago the visionary Marshall McLuhan foresaw today's "global village," where it's impossible for someone in Tunisia to tweet a demonstration without someone in Cairo catching wind of revolution.

We live in a boundary age where change is fast, but none of us moves quite as fast as change. Sometimes it seems we want the fast fixes of the digital world to solve slow-moving disasters that have been with us for a long time. Dangle the right incentives in front of teachers—surely student scores will rise, won't they? Add more cops—surely crime will fall. Layer more regulation on food growers—surely our dinner tables will be safer. What, no "app" for that?

If only. Even in a networked world schools stay broken. Financial systems stay stacked, "tails I win" for rich guys and "heads you lose" for main street. Poor people die hungry and broken—from New York to Rio to Mogadishu.

Being connected is no silver bullet. Not when the move forward runs into go-it-alone, no-one-does-it-better mind-sets. Those are powerful headwinds few can take on alone.

In the networked world, no one needs to.

Where everyone is connected, the game-changer is collaboration. Reaching across boundaries, often abetted by technology that connects us all, collaboration unleashes the power of the many to do together what none can do alone.

Collaboration is about people. If it were only about technology, the one with the best toys would always win. Technology can tip change, and speed it up. But in the networked world, with change moving fast, success depends more than ever on having the right people saying "yes" and *doing* "yes."

That takes a new mind-set, one that says, "we can achieve more together than we can alone." A mind-set that looks across boundaries of departments, companies, and nations, and sees people as partners and change as opportunity, not threats.

A mind-set for collaboration.

Collaboration lets you start with a simple plan to bring two schools onto a network and within three years scale to 20,000, as Doug Hull did in Canada.

Collaboration lets you find the one farm in a million that's shipping tainted produce around the nation . . . not in months or days, but in hours, as the FDA's David Acheson and industry partners did.

When the US Navy lost its undersea advantage to espionage, Bill Johnson regained it not in five years, as admirals predicted, but in eighteen months—by collaborating with vendors and researchers on new submarine sonar that used commercially available off-the-shelf systems.

The police officers and citizens of New York and Los Angeles restored their cities after years of crime and disorder with one strategy: collaboration.

Steve Ellis moved Wells Fargo's commercial customers to the Internet and brought astounding returns to the bank—by collaborating. "Eighty percent of things we built, the ideas are our customers'; twenty percent are ours," Ellis said.

Paul O'Neill led Alcoa to record profits by rallying all Alcoans around a single vision: make it the safest workplace in the world. Collaborating, workers and executives perfected Alcoa's business processes and took its financial performance through the roof.

Claudia Costin, Rio de Janeiro's secretary of education, mobilized Rio's teachers, students, and business leaders to restore the city's schools, return the joy to teaching, and give Rio's desperately poor public school children something many thought impossible: an education. She started the collaboration on Twitter.

In the Arab Spring of 2011 millions of Egyptians led themselves through city streets and squares energized by one shared vision: "The people want . . . to overthrow . . . the regime!"

A re you *ready* to collaborate? Even if you think you are—it's not just about you. It's about the people, the technology, the platforms, the politics—everything you need to win whatever contest you're in, whether its for health and prosperity, fun and games, or safety and security.

In *Collaborate or Perish!*, we created eight tests of readiness you should know before you start.

Number One: have a vision. A vision of a better day and a better way energizes people around you. It conjures up a world others want to work toward and support; it captures their imaginations and their passion.

Number Two: right-size the way forward. Make it do-able. Deliver value fast—not all of it, but enough to prove to all: "We know how to do this."

Number Three: create a platform, a physical or virtual clearing, that collaborators can find, get to, trust, and use. That's where you share knowledge, insight, and assets, and take steps together.

Number Four: make it pay. Collaboration requires there be something in it for everyone—whether it's glory and honor, money and power, latitude and position, or a chance to do the job they showed up to do. Whatever the currency, collaboration needs to pay for those who will be with you on the journey.

Number Five: have the right people with you—from top performers to sponsors backing you and giving you cover, to everyday folks eager for change, waiting for your signal and a sense of the path they should follow.

Number Six: deliver on performance. Collaboration can promise a way better, faster, or cheaper; or more efficient, equitable, or effective. Whatever the promise, that's the performance collaboration must deliver.

Number Seven: mind your political support, stay in its headlamps, and ensure you have what you need to deliver on the promise.

Number Eight: you must have the passion and playbook to lead. Whether from above, the middle, the side, or below, leadership in a collaboration helps make it pay for everyone. You help everyone achieve together what none can accomplish alone.

As you'll discover in story after story, *Collaborate or Perish!* is nothing less than a playbook for collaboration. It offers strategies that alter the go-it-alone habit, move the mind-set, and ultimately change the culture. You will see ordinary and extraordinary men and women just like you in action, as they work to shape our world—together.

THE CASE FOR COLLABORATION

1

THE HUNT FOR TEN RED BALLOONS

On October 29, 2009, the Defense Advanced Research Projects Agency (DARPA) announced its "Network Challenge." At 10:00 a.m. on December 5, 2009, at ten locations throughout the United States, DARPA would let fly an eight-foot-diameter red weather balloon tethered to the ground. Each balloon would be readily visible from local roads and buildings—points the average person could reach. A $40,000 prize would go to the first team to accurately report the location of all ten weather balloons.

The contest was meant to replicate the challenge of trying to gather information about an adversary in an open environment. DARPA wanted to test whether ordinary folks using commonly available off-the-shelf technology and social media like Twitter or Facebook could work together—collaborate—to solve a problem that would be, in the words of one expert from the National Geospatial-Intelligence Agency, "impossible to solve by traditional intelligence gathering methods."

A team from MIT's Media Lab won. No surprise there. MIT had a slew of faculty and top graduate students, the most sophisticated equipment, and great publicity. CNN profiled them and drew attention to their cause. A Georgia Tech team placed second, for similar reasons.

Both teams competed fiercely. They put out misinformation, reporting false sightings, sent others on wild-goose chases, and bought time for themselves. Both teams wrote complex computer programs to defend themselves against such attacks.

Given their advantages, you would expect MIT and Georgia Tech to come out ahead—and they did, with a winning time under nine hours.

But what is interesting is the guy who finished in a tie for third with eight balloons, and actually led the pack for the first four hours of the competition—nineteen-year-old hacker George Hotz. Hotz heard about the contest only a couple of days before, and only an hour before it started he put up a website called Dudeitsaballoon.com.

How did he do it? His idea was based on a kind of mass collaboration.

Hotz had nearly fifty thousand followers on Twitter. They, in turn, had hundreds of thousands of followers. His plan was to mobilize them all—get thousands in the game and all those eyeballs searching for the prized red balloons. It almost worked.

Hotz was already famous in the hacker community for "jailbreaking" the Sony PlayStation and the Apple iPhone. He'd cracked their proprietary codes, and for the iPhone wrote software that let iPhone owners use it on any wireless network, not just AT&T's—much to AT&T's and Apple's chagrin and the hacker community's glee.

These legendary hacks made Hotz a star. He gained tens of thousands of Twitter followers, all of whom wanted to be the first to know what George Hotz might do next. On Twitter, they would soon find out.

On the day before the DARPA contest, Hotz—who went by his Twitter name, @geohot—tweeted his followers to stand by for a major announcement the next day. That started a buzz going in the Twitterverse and on hacker bulletin boards.

On Saturday morning @geohot tweeted his fifty thousand followers:

> 10AM EST today marks the start of a US wide scavenger hunt,
> for 10 red balloons http://bit.ly/7chum5 #dudeitsaballoon

He quickly followed up with another tweet:

> So I need your help to do two things, 1, find big red balloons,
> and 2, RT [retweet] and trend this !!!! http://bit.ly/7chum5
> #dudeitsaballoon

He included a link to his website. The hashtagged #dudeitsa balloon guaranteed that if his message got retweeted, as requested,

#dudeitsaballoon would rise to the top of the Twitter trending terms. That would amplify its effect—and call further attention to Hotz's cause.

Visitors clicking through to Hotz's website found the following message:

> **Right now you are all probably waking up to another normal Saturday. But this Saturday is not normal. In addition to planes, birds, owls, and everything else in the sky, there are 10 red balloons scattered around the United States. Starting at 10AM EST, your US government is using tax dollars to send 10 big red weather balloons into the sky. I need to know the location of those balloons.**
>
> **So if you see a big red balloon in the sky, about 8ft round, numbered 1 to 10 . . . report it here ASAP so I can win the contest.**

Hotz offered $1,000 to anyone who gave him a confirmed sighting. And he offered something that would incite any die-hard hacker.

"Seriously," Hotz wrote. "If you guys come through for me . . . I'll make you an untethered jailbreak."

"Chop chop."

Offering an untethered jailbreak to the hacker community was like dangling red meat in front of a lion. It was the gold standard of all hacks. Unlike Hotz's earlier iPhone hack, which left the iPhone tethered to software you had to run each time you started the phone, this time Hotz was promising to hack the iPhone again and create an *untethered* jailbreak. Untethered, you could use your phone just like any cell phone, on any carrier. Untethered, the iPhone would be released from its earthly moorings. It would be hacker heaven.

Word raced around hacker online sites and bulletin boards that George Hotz was offering to do an untethered jailbreak for spotting the red balloons. *We have to win this*, the hacker community buzzed. *Do it for @geohot; do it for us!*

By hour four, Hotz had four verified sightings—more than the MIT team and the Georgia Tech team. He traded two of his four sightings with one of the other front-running teams. That made six.

Eventually, the MIT and Georgia Tech teams surged ahead, but not before Hotz found eight of the ten balloons. He had done better than dozens of teams competing. It was far more than what traditional intelligence gathering could accomplish.

More than that, it showed DARPA the raw power of the Internet to foster collaboration. What George Hotz lacked in funding, institutional support, and educational credentials he made up for with digital age assets: networks of followers who, on an otherwise ordinary Saturday and with a promise of glory and gifts, he could get in the game fast. Already arrayed on trusted platforms, Hotz sent current through those networks, turned followers into partisans, and got them collaborating—in minutes. Together, they pulled off something extraordinary (and nearly won the Challenge).

RESTORING AN EMPIRE STATE OF MIND

BILL BRATTON Takes New York

As the commissioner of the New York City Police Department and the Boston Police Department, and chief of the Los Angeles Police Department, I learned about the power of collaboration across departments, agencies, and private industry early on.

In 1993, an army of squeegee people seemed to have taken over New York. At every corner and tunnel entrance in the city, you'd stop for a light and they would pounce, some filthy rag or sponge coming up to your windshield, a face and hand close behind. You could try to wave them off. Or you could try to ignore them, eyes straight ahead. Not always practical. It was sort of a mini–street corner protection racket, with the convenient charade of a spit-enhanced wipe down and a key scratch across your car's paint job if you didn't pay them for the "cleaning."

In 1993, the election for New York City mayor was on. US Attorney Rudy Giuliani was running against Mayor David Dinkins, crime, disorder—and squeegee people. You could almost make a compound noun of those terms, lumping them all together, and many voters did. The news stories were incessant, fueling what every New Yorker sensed anyway, whether they commuted by car, foot, or subway: the city was out of control.

Ten percent of New Yorkers experienced violent crime in a year. But every day 100 percent experienced the city's disorder: fare beaters and drunks on the subways, mental patients off their meds wandering the streets, prostitution operating out in the open. Long lines, high taxes, poor service. Broken neighborhoods, broken people, broken windows—a broken city.

It all fueled a sense of chaos. The *New York Post* summed it up for the incumbent, Mayor Dinkins: "Dave, Do Something!"

Too late for his mayoralty, Dinkins raised money for six thousand more cops. Too often, NYPD commissioner Ray Kelly's cops scattered the squeegee people only to see them rally to some other corner moments later.

When the dust of the November elections settled, the voters had replaced Dinkins with Giuliani; the new mayor soon replaced Kelly with me as NYPD commissioner. I had been the commissioner of the Boston Police Department and before that, in 1991, chief of the New York City Transit Police Department.

Giuliani had made a campaign promise to get rid of the squeegee guys, so I knew I needed to move quickly, continuing the work Kelly had begun. Counting heads, it turned out that the "army" of squeegee men had actually numbered about seventy-five. Well before the Internet, the blogosphere, or the Twitterverse, New York's potent tabloids had turned seventy-five sponge-and-bucket guys into a national symbol of impotent government and a city on the brink.

Persistent police work paid off. Many of the men had had prior problems with the law and couldn't afford to get arrested again. Which is exactly what we promised, and did. We stayed around long enough to break up this thriving little extortion racket that was driving the city crazy. Seemingly overnight the squeegee men were gone—though we did have in our favor thirty-eight thousand cops versus seventy-five squeegee pests.

The tactics I used to conquer that problem formed the strategy of what I hoped would be a much more ambitious effort, one aimed not just at cutting crime but at dramatically changing the quality of life in New York.

The NYPD had people bluffed, as I later wrote in my first book looking back at the time. They had the reputation as the greatest crime-fighting machine in the history of policing, but to me the big blue wall was a lot of blue smoke and a few mirrors.

They were good at responding to crime; they just weren't very good at preventing it. They weren't even trying to prevent it. They were just cleaning up around it.

The NYPD, like many departments, was "all response, all the time." The 911 dispatch system created in the 1970s had democratized policing: it was no longer "who you knew downtown." Now, any citizen could mobilize the department with a free call from a pay phone. And millions did. Police were racing across the city from call to call.

But the 911 system didn't dent crime much—the onslaught of crack, disorder, and guns in the 1980s and '90s saw to that. A single citizen could make hundreds—even thousands—of calls complaining about nuisance gangs, drugs, and prostitutes on the same corner. Officers responded every time, but nothing changed. It was like shoveling sand against the tide—the tide kept coming back.

Remember the precinct house nicknames of the time—"Fort Apache, the Bronx" or "Little House on the Prairie"? That's what American policing had become: isolated outposts, controlling little outside its four walls—or outside the cruiser. The 911 dispatch kept cops in cars, windows rolled up, AC blasting, racing to calls or on "random" patrol in between, intending to deter crime by their mere presence.

As New York City's police commissioner, I quickly set out to establish a new form of policing, one that required collaboration not only between all areas of the department, but also with other agencies and the public. My goal was to transform the city and the American police profession.

It all starts with a vision, I told the department: as good as we are, we can do better. But we can't do it alone.

The path forward—the new platform for policing New York—came to be known as CompStat.

"When have you guys ever addressed crime?" Jack Maple, my right hand at the New York Transit Police Department and now at the NYPD, was digging in. John Timoney, a twenty-five-year NYPD veteran and now my chief of department, had called Maple out for his comment to a reporter. "Those guys over there at the NYPD have given up on crime fighting," Maple had said.

Timoney pointed to this operation and that, and cited his stellar service as commander of New York's 5th Precinct on the Lower East Side. Maple would have none of it. "Your Narcotics Bureau works nine to five, Monday through Friday. The Warrant squad is off weekends. Auto crimes, off weekends. Robbery squad, off weekends. The whole place takes weekends and nights—just when the criminal element gets down to work."

And that was the problem.

To transform the city, I knew, my team and I would have to start with the NYPD. To succeed, I needed believers and doers. I screened the incoming command staff and promoted my own leaders over the heads of others—Timoney among them, and Louis Anemone, who would be chief of patrol. My inner staff was made up of long-time NYPD partisans—but commanders who were loyal to me, who understood and bought into my vision: the NYPD could do better, and this was the way.

Maple had been through this before with me when years earlier I reorganized the New York Transit Police Department. Metropolitan Transit Authority president David Gunn had told me at the time that fare beating was bleeding the MTA dry; disorder was shrinking ridership. There was brand-new capital waiting to be poured into rebuilding the subways—but the subways were out of control. He needed them tamed.

I concentrated patrols where the problem was highest, and ran high-visibility mass arrests. We were able to bring fare beating on the subways down from 170,000 per day to the point where it fell so low that the MTA stopped tracking it. Malcolm Gladwell wrote about this "tipping point" phenomenon in his book of the same name.

But I also learned something that stuck with me: many fare beaters tend to have character flaws. One in seven was wanted on a warrant or probation and parole violation. One in twenty-one carried an illegal weapon.

And that got the cops going: an arrest for fare beating wasn't just about writing a paper summons anymore. Now it was about making felony collars. And when fare beating went away, crime fell, and so, too, did the sense of disorder. And when it did, ridership returned. The MTA coffers began to fill again; the capital plan could go forward. That was the idea.

Take care of the small stuff, shake the tree for information, and you head off the big stuff. Take a fare beater or a low-level drug dealer off the street, and whatever criminal behavior he had in mind goes away with him. You can control behavior to such an extent that you can change it. That was the broken windows theory in practice.*

The same theory held on the street with regard to the NYPD. If cops restore some order on the nuisance matters, good folks start coming out, venturing that next step. The dog walkers, the everyday citizen just trying to get to work or school in one piece would bring others.

We needed to jump-start that—empower cops to deal with small stuff that mattered to communities and the serious stuff that only cops could deal with. In doing so, we'd bring communities forward to collaborate, cops would collaborate, and together we would signal that the bad guys were no longer in control. We'd bring collaboration into the sunlight.

What wasn't to like?

A lot, as it turned out. For starters, I was going to call the NYPD's bluff—tear the veil off the NYPD's and the system's so-called performance on crime and disorder.

That would take numbers—lots of numbers.

After all, you can't fix what you can't measure. You can expect what you inspect.

The first crime stats we gathered were delivered to Jack Maple in crayon. That was telling, but it wasn't the only revelation.

Maple was astounded to discover that the Patrol Borough Commands (there were eight) and the NYPD as a whole reported comprehensive crime information only several times a year, as required by the FBI's Uniform Crime Report system. That report covered, among other matters, seven major crime categories including kidnapping (barely a handful each year in New York) but no narcotics,

---

*The "broken windows" theory was articulated by George L. Kelling and James Q. Wilson in the March 1982 issue of *The Atlantic*: "Broken Windows: The Police and Neighborhood Policing. "

though there were tens of thousands of such incidents each year. And the NYPD made almost no internal use of it. The borough commands and precincts used pin maps to show crime locations in greater detail. But out in the precincts, Maple noticed there weren't many holes in the maps. No one ever moved the pins. The maps were decoration.

We didn't even have week-to-week insight into crime and disorder. That had to change.

Maple vowed that these commanders were soon going to know more than he did about their business. That would take some doing. Maple and I already knew a lot about the business. Now we were all going to learn a lot more—together.

For starters, Jack, John Miller (my deputy commissioner for public information), and I ordered pagers for ourselves and insisted that we be notified of any shooting or homicide. That meant the borough commanders would have to have the same awareness as I did—before I came asking. The same was true for the precinct commanders and the lieutenants. It would all trickle down. To stay ahead of us the commanders would need news of shootings or homicides to start its way up the chain of command even before the smoke had cleared or the body went cold.

We insisted on moving the borough commands and the precincts into the information era, with the technology to go with it—no more crayons, no more faxes, no more disks shipped by messengers as some precincts were now doing. We wanted information online and presented formally in regular large command staff meetings that I would attend and Maple would run.

"Do you know how long it will take each day to keep our crime maps current?" the commands asked Maple.

Maple knew they'd carp. "Eighteen minutes a day," he said. He'd timed it at the 75th Precinct, one of Brooklyn's busiest. "Do you think we can spend eighteen minutes to fight crime?"

New metrics captured not just the FBI crime categories but also shooting incidents and victims, gun arrests, and summons activity on quality-of-life efforts—the things that broke the back of New York. Not just the usual quarterly reports but management reports—ranking the precincts against themselves year over year, month over month, day over day—and against all other precincts.

Week after week, we called out commanders on their numbers: what was the plan to deal with complaints of drug dealing on the twentieth floor of a high-rise public housing project? "We can't get in there," commanders would tell us. "Have you worked the angles, pressured the informants, papered the rec rooms with signs, checked every address in the building for outstanding warrants? Checked the rooftops, checked for parole violators . . . ?"

Unreasonable demands, I knew, lead to reasonable results.

"You've got to know the questions to ask," Maple said. "If you don't know the questions to ask and how to ask them, you're finished."

CompStat hinged on transparency, sharing and learning, accountability—and collaboration. Chief of Patrol Louis Anemone and Maple convened each patrol borough and its precincts twice weekly for three hours at One Police Plaza, NYPD's headquarters. With me present, and occasionally DAs, the mayor, and others, Maple and Anemone grilled borough and precinct commanders relentlessly on the data and the results.

Everyone was challenged to collaborate. "What have you learned that you can teach us?" commanders were asked. "What have we learned that we can teach you?"

Many complained about rush hour traffic, making the 8:30 a.m. starts impractical. Not a problem, said Maple. He mandated they start at *7:00 a.m.* so the commanders could beat the traffic.

We made CompStat performance translate into career gains. I made personnel decisions based on who was performing—not just on who was avoiding corruption problems or keeping overtime down. Those who got the data and the challenge, and who col-laborated, rose fast. Those who didn't found themselves on slower tracks, in less high-stress locations.

We found that CompStat created a new collaboration plat-form for policing in New York—led from above, fueled from below, and calling the broad middle to account. With CompStat, policing expanded its platforms—moving from a work queue established solely by 911 dispatch to a work queue driven by where the problems were. CompStat, I told anyone who would listen, would put cops on the dots.

With my team in place, the information beginning to flow, and a CompStat process shaping up, I felt optimistic that the NYPD could return 10 percent reductions in crime year after year. That was my goal. At the off-site meeting that spring, my command staff gasped. They had never been asked to deliver more than 1 or 2 percent per year.

"That's as good as it gets," went the sentiment. "Besides, we're the NYPD: nobody does it better."

Whether anybody did it "better" or not, we were nowhere near our limits. But the world's largest police department doesn't run on improvisation. With the command staff and consultants collaborat-ing we developed eight core strategies. Everyone would be headed in the same direction. Managers and cops were empowered to bring about the change they wanted, but within an agreed-upon frame-work. Every action had to align with the plan. We gave them lati-tude, but held them accountable. That was the mantra.

Starting in early 1994, we took great pains to develop and com-municate the strategies, rolling them out one after another. The first, titled "Police Strategy No. 1: Getting Guns off the Streets of New York," had clear direction: just as with Transit's fare beaters, on every gun collar NYPD detectives were required to pursue all accomplices and seek out suppliers; they would ask everyone they arrested for any crime if they knew where guns could be acquired. The strategy would increase the highly trained plainclothes Street Crime Units.

I knew the rank and file would follow: I'd seen the internal surveys. Asked which functions their superior officers valued most, cops reported, "write summonses," "hold down overtime," "stay out of trouble." Asked which functions the cops themselves valued most, they said, "reduce crime, disorder and fear," "make gun arrests," "provide police services to people who request them."

There was a vanguard for change waiting in the rank and file, and I was determined to tap it. I slashed a layer of bureaucracy between the seventy-six precinct commanders and the eight patrol borough commanders, and gave the precinct commanders the authority to deploy cops, invent strategies, and run narcotics and vice operations. No longer were such investigations to be the province of specialized bureaus alone.

Nor did I de-emphasize fighting corruption. Soon after I arrived, dozens of officers were arrested in a multiyear, multiagency narcotics investigation we had planned a long way out. I made sure that officers wearing NYPD windbreakers were seen involved in the arrests. The next morning I went to one of the worst offending precincts—the 30th in upper Manhattan. Addressing the roll call and again at a subsequent press conference, I held up the badges of the arrested officers and announced I was retiring the badge number of every officer involved so those numbers would never again be worn in the NYPD.

Over the spring, the consultants and senior command rolled out other strategies, each intended to provide specific guidance to the precinct commanders. "Reclaiming the Public Spaces of New York"; "Curbing Youth Violence in the Schools and on the Streets"; "Driving the Drug Dealers out of New York"; "Breaking the Cycle of Domestic Violence."

Each contained targets. "Reclaiming the Public Spaces of New York" cited street prostitution, aggressive panhandlers, sales of alcohol to minors, graffiti vandalism, public urination, unlicensed peddlers, reckless bicyclists, and earsplitting noise from "boom box" cars, loud motorcycles, clubs, and spontaneous street parties. But each challenged the commands: create your own tactics. Tell us what you do. Let us learn together.

To handle the legal issues involved in this kind of enforcement, we placed thirty-four NYPD attorneys in the field commands across the city. Tools like civil forfeiture, nuisance abatement, and padlock laws would now be in the NYPD's kit.

Better policing created more work for DAs, judges, corrections, probation. The whole system had to recalibrate. Like a huge pipeline with valves and releases, the system needed to hold pressure once the NYPD started pumping through a lot of arrests that the system used to ignore. Judges didn't want to open more courtrooms; prosecutors didn't want to add more assistant district attorneys; corrections officials didn't want to handle increased populations.

In the past, the easy thing was to dismiss cases.

I was determined that that wouldn't happen this time. I worked with Mayor Giuliani to bring these other resources in the "ecosystem" in line—nothing would work without that collaboration across political, bureaucratic, and agency boundaries. Fortunately, in New York the mayor had extraordinary influence over many of these agencies.

The results, people said, were impressive: within the year major crimes were down 12 percent in New York, compared to 1 percent nationally. Robberies were down 16 percent; homicides, 20 percent; burglaries, 11 percent; gun-related deaths, 23 percent. And these gains repeated themselves the next year, in 1996, when Giuliani forced me out. The covers of major newsmagazines were giving too much credit to me and the department, and not enough to the mayor and city hall. The mayor didn't like it.

BRATTON

Still, the transformation we put into place through collaboration—through information gathering and sharing, reaching across boundaries, and a strategy that addressed murderers and squeegee guys as parts of a larger problem to be solved as one—continued for years afterward with year-over-year declines in crime. And today, New York remains one of the safest, most orderly cities in the world.

As for the squeegee guys—well, they'd always enjoyed some immunity as beggars under the Constitution's First Amendment. But NYPD lawyers found a traffic regulation that we could use—lawful, appropriate, and effective. The drill was simple: check the corners every two hours. Warn the squeegee pests they were subject to arrest and imprisonment. With that warning half drifted away. The other half got arrested—half of them having previous arrests for serious felonies or drug offenses.

Once arrested, they never returned. The squeegee guy became history—a symbol as potent in his absence as he had been in his presence.

COLLABORATION BY DESIGN

The Rally Fighter is a radically cool car. An off-road racer designed for the deserts of the American Southwest, it has eighteen inches of ground clearance, seats four, develops 435 horsepower at 5900 RPM and delivers thirty-six miles per gallon on the highway. To put that into context: a ten-year-old Jeep (when ten years ago Jeeps were actually meant to go off road) has only nine inches of ground clearance; the flagship 2012 Lexus LS460 gets twenty-four miles per gallon on the highway and develops an impressive 370 horsepower.

But the Rally Fighter was not created by Chrysler or Toyota. It was manufactured by a twelve-person company called Local Motors, Inc.

and took a mere twenty-four months to design and build. Twelve people, twenty-four months—about how long it takes the big auto companies to redesign a door handle.

To be fair, the twelve employees had some help. In fact, the car's designer, Sangho Kim, from Pasadena, California, doesn't even work for the company. He's part of the online "Local Motors community" made up of thousands of car designers, engineers, and enthusiasts from around the world. They voted for Kim's design as the desert racer they all wanted.

It's an amazing looking car: Kim used the P-51 World War II vintage Mustang fighter plane as his inspiration. With the basic design set, Local Motors gave all its fans a second-round stake: a chance to design the rest—interior, transmission coupling, and engine choice. "Here are the parameters," Local Motors told its enthusiasts. "We've got five different options. We've got six different criteria that we'd like to meet. You can pick from some pretty nice parts and players—a Ford F-150 suspension over here, a BMW engine over there if you want. Bring your collective talent to bear, and tell us what will work the best."

The first of 3,000 planned Rally Fighters rolled off the production line in late summer 2010. Price tag: about $50,000. That's not affordable for everyone, but it was an amazing accomplishment. By turning to its fan base, crowd-sourcing the design, and holding the winners high for all to see, Local Motors and its devoted followers created the Rally Fighter they all wanted in less than two years.

If a tiny company can create an entirely new kind of car through collaboration, think about the other amazing things the talents of large groups of people with vastly different skills could develop. Remember, those thousands of car enthusiasts who collaborated on the Rally Fighter weren't on Local Motors' payroll. They shared their knowledge and opinions simply because they were invited to collaborate and contribute to one of the greatest global mind-melds the auto industry had ever seen. Think of it as a potluck: Local Motors provided the platform, complete with infrastructure, rules, and gear. Thousands of enthusiasts responded, passionate for cars, thirsting to show their chops, eager to design the very best—and win.

A fine collaboration.

COLLABORATION IS THE GAME CHANGER

Collaboration in today's world is critical for companies and organizations that want to out-innovate and out-perform the competition.

Collaboration, of course, depends on information. And, thanks to today's technology, collecting data and sharing information are easier than ever. But collaboration is about much more than simply making information available. It's about action that leads to results. That means reaching across boundaries that might otherwise separate people, getting them involved and moving when you have little authority and even less say. Success requires leaders and managers and collaborators to step back and look at the whole picture rather than just one small part of it.

Collaboration takes people, platforms, incentives—hard work at first, but once you've started, easier and easier. In the end, it's all worthwhile. Done right, collaboration unleashes assets, your own as well as others'. It allows companies to reuse, recombine, and transform resources; to cut costs, improve performance, and deal with every opportunity and challenge that comes along.

In a world where everyone is connected, collaboration is the difference maker, the force multiplier, the game changer.

COLLABORATION AVERTS COLLISION

In 2009, for the first time ever, two satellites collided in space—one a commercial American spacecraft, the other a defunct Russian orbiter. The odds of that event, the *Wall Street Journal* reported, "were considered so small as to be basically unthinkable."

The task of predicting the next collision fell to the US Air Force's Jim "Crash" Blanton (yes, that's really the name he goes by). After all, although it might have been the first such calamity, with twenty-two thousand trackable objects in orbit around the earth, it surely wouldn't be the last.

"I called up some of my software guys," Crash said. "I said, 'Hey, all the tools are here. I need a different application.' Kind of like the iPhone: 'I need an app for that.' Something that runs all the time, machine-to-machine, and when it sees a potential collision, it flashes a warning: 'If you don't do something now, in seven days you're going to have a big problem.'

"My guys were salivating," Crash said. "And they had this thing done in two weeks. 'Done, here it is.'"

An impressive achievement. But four months later, with the collision debris now in permanent orbit 480 miles above the earth, Crash was still waiting for the systems security folks to certify the new application so it could sit on the network.

That's understandable: the security folks came in after the design-and-develop work was finished. They had no reason to doubt the design, but they had no reason to trust it, either. Their principal concern was protecting the network from any security threat the application might present.

That would take time to do right. They felt none of the urgency Crash and his team felt.

Now, imagine if the network of developers and systems security had collaborated right from the start, solving the security and the mission problem simultaneously, and creating a secure satellite collision system together rather than in sequence. Security staff would understand the design right from the start; designers could address security issues from day 1. Fewer handoffs, fewer fixes, less agita. Better performance.

Organizations often solve one piece first, then the next. And yet they're surprised when the pieces don't fit together. It's no surprise that collaboration right from the start can take weeks and months off the clock.

COLLABORATE OR PERISH

An unwillingness to collaborate—whether across divisions *within* an organization or among companies and other entities—can threaten even the mightiest institutions.

The biggest organizations may be the most prone to mind-sets that block collaboration.

MIND-SET #1: A "not invented here" attitude that crushes innovation. The world moves faster now than ever. Companies not open to ideas regardless of the source will be left behind.

MIND-SET #2: A "winner takes all" competition within the company. "Compete the ideas" is a common mantra for top firms everywhere. For some, though, it's devolved into "eat your young." No surprise, then, when it leads to extinction.

MIND-SET #3: A "we don't do windows here" point of view. It's not in the job description, the task order, the chairman's message? Those formal statements all serve good purposes. But too often this mind-set is used as an excuse to put blinders on. It can keep an organization's assets locked into ossified missions long after they've served their purpose, even when new opportunities strike or risks arise.

It doesn't have to be this way. There's good news for companies, industries, and agencies that lack a track record of collaboration: major players around the world have discovered that it's easier than ever to start up and get results fast.

COLLABORATION RISES FROM THE ASHES

Before Toyota stumbled badly over safety issues in 2009, it had dominated the world's auto sales. What was "Japan, Inc.'s" secret?

The answer: a relentless pursuit of quality, rapid innovation, and broad teaching of lessons learned. Most especially, a culture of collaboration fostered between workers and management, suppliers and producers—groups that in the culture of American manufacturing often regard themselves as adversaries. Here is an example:

Late one Friday night in 1997 a fire leveled Aisin Seiki Company's Factory No. 1, one of Toyota's principal suppliers of P-valves, a $5 brake part. The fire had an immediate impact on factories. Toyota kept only four hours' supply of the valves on hand; without more coming in, the automaker quickly shut down twenty of its thirty assembly lines, terminating production of fourteen thousand cars per day. It took twenty thousand parts to build each car; none would be needed until Toyota brought its plants back into production. That would take a fresh supply of P-valves.

Suppliers, distributors, utilities, truckers—everyone involved in the Japanese auto business—were threatened. One-tenth of 1 percent of Japan's national industrial output was lost every day Toyota factories were dark.

As dawn broke Saturday, February 1, with the fire still smoldering, Aisin (pronounced EYE-sin) convened its war room of executives. The fire had destroyed Aisin's 506 highly specialized jigs, drills, cutters, and milling machines. The P-valves required incredibly precise and complex machining. It would be weeks before Aisin could restore even a semblance of production.

Aisin asked for and received Toyota's help—four hundred engineers were dispatched that day to help Aisin rebuild its factory. Before the fire, Toyota factories had been in overdrive, feeding a voracious American market with record-breaking production. This could not wait.

With Toyota at its side, on Saturday afternoon Aisin mobilized its own supplier networks, convening a second war room and distributing P-valve blueprints. It asked its suppliers to set up alternative P-valve production sites, machining the parts to Aisin's specifications. Sixty-two firms responded, many already established as suppliers within the Toyota "family." New firms also responded, hoping to achieve that same lucrative status.

Few had any expertise in P-valve production. What many *did* have was experience in the Toyota ecosystem: shared problem solving, links between suppliers and producers. A culture of collaboration. They got it. They knew that everyone's fortunes were linked; everyone's reputation was on the line; everyone was in this together. A win for Toyota would be a win for all.

In the war rooms, there was no talk of intellectual property concerns, no contracts, no lawyers. If Toyota lost, everyone would lose.

Suppliers turned to one another for materials, machining, and design; together they would create new P-valves to Aisin's specifications. One supplier, Denso, sent its other manufacturing jobs to its competitors to clear its own factory floor for rush P-valve production. Others like Taiho brought thirty of its suppliers and fifty machining centers online for the valve manufacture. Toyota converted its own experimental prototype production floor to P-valve manufacture.

By Monday—two days after the fire—a small supplier, Kyoritsu Sangyo, shipped the first prototype of its P-valve to Aisin for approval. Denso followed, then Toyota, then others. Kyoritsu began volume production on Tuesday, followed by Denso, Taiho, Kayaba (another supplier), and Toyota. One week after the devastating fire, the Toyota assembly lines were coming back to life.

Toyota lost production of seventy-two thousand cars—but said later it had recouped nearly all the lost output with overtime and extra shifts. It rewarded its suppliers with a $100 million "thank you" check. Some of the large suppliers passed on the payments to their supply chain partners, and so on down the line.

Years later, MIT's Steven Spear visited an auto parts maker in Tennessee for a weeklong boot camp of Toyota "family" supply and production executives—just the sort of training for collaboration that Toyota had harvested years earlier in the Aisin fire.

The host auto parts maker took Spear aside and confessed something that was troubling him. The parts maker supplied not just Toyota but

America's Big Three auto companies. A recession had already hit; sales were off by 50 percent. But a Big Three customer had just placed a huge order for more parts than ever before and more than it could possibly use in the short term.

"As best as I can figure," the executive told Spear, "the only reason they're doing this is that on the chance *they* go into bankruptcy, they're going to get *our* parts for free."

The Big Three customer, according to Spear's account, took a view of the supplier relationship as a zero-sum game—your gain can come only at my loss. There was one pie to divide up, and it was as big as it was going to get. If you want more, you're going to have to take something off the other guy's plate. The relationship was adversarial. With that kind of go-it-alone, every-firm-for-itself mind-set, pessimistic about doing better *together,* no wonder the Big Three were struggling long before the financial crisis of 2008.

NO MORE EMPTY SHELVES

At any given time 7 percent of all US retail products are out of stock—and that number jumps to 15 percent for products on promotion. Having no brand product on the shelves is a big problem. Faced with a need and no choice, customers switch—and some never return.

The solution? Point-of-sale (POS) tracking and reporting software gives managers access not just to internal data such as order and shipment records, which can lag significantly, but to daily figures from retailers selling their products. The whole process, called "demand signal management," has been around for a while. Walmart has been working at it for years, pushing its suppliers (without much success) to use its Retail Link software.

In the past, suppliers complained that Walmart forced the system on them; they had no idea how to use the data to reduce inventory. And since suppliers got POS data from different retailers in different formats—CVS, Target, and Walgreens all reported differently—it had been hard to integrate all the information into a complete picture.

Recent technology advances have made POS tracking both easier to integrate into a business and more affordable. Ultimately, though, the technology is truly helpful only when supply chain partners collaborate. By using mountains of real-time data, combining and analyzing it with historical information, retailers and suppliers can work together to spot trends in consumer demand sooner and raise revenues for all.

Collaboration can make the pie bigger, and with it everyone's slice. What's more, fewer stock-outs and more successful promotions mean it's paying off handsomely for retailers.

Before Kimberly-Clark jumped onto Food Lion's system with its thirteen hundred stores, the paper giant suffered 18 percent stock-out rates when it ran in-store promotions. Once it adopted the demand signal regime, the companies saw those rates drop to 10 percent when it reran the promotion, and sales increased 167 percent.

The key? Collaboration across boundaries helps everyone to see and make sense of managing for the whole in a way that no one can see or make sense of alone.

PLATFORM TO A SUCCESSFUL COLLABORATION

Of course, companies and groups can have the best intentions of working together, but still stumble at their boundaries. It can be hard to cross boundaries.

Sometimes, it takes a *platform*.

Imagine this: a panel truck is headed south down Interstate 270 toward Washington, DC. As it passes through Frederick, Maryland, fifty miles north of the nation's capital, it trips a radiation sensor—part of an array of sensors laid out in belts around the capital to alert authorities of vehicles containing biological, radioactive, or chemical materials.

The truck trips another sensor at the forty-five-mile marker, and another again at forty. As it continues south, it trips more and more sensors. What might have at first been a false alarm now appears to be a potentially dangerous vehicle heading toward a highly sensitive location.

Is the threat genuine or imagined? Maybe it's a truck hauling scrap metal, granite, bananas—or even kitty litter—all of which emit isotope signals that "rad-nuke" sensors can pick up as "hot."

An urgent countdown has begun; the race is on to make sense of the data. Any delays can prove deadly. Is this a false alarm or a real threat? There are many legitimate transporters of radioactive materials on America's roadways, at its ports and to and from its storage facilities. Stop them all and commerce grinds to a halt. Let the wrong one through and you could have a cataclysm on your hands.

In the aftermath of 9/11, this was the daunting challenge faced by the US Domestic Nuclear Detection Office (DNDO): how to move data from thousands of sensors in dozens of networks around the country to analysts and scientists at Sandia National Laboratories for analysis, and get that information back to decision makers and security forces in time to stop the truck *now*, if necessary.

The problem is that different organizations own different sensor networks, and each uses different sensor technology. Moreover, each network has its own interface, captures data in its own way, and records *different* data.

The networks collided at each others' boundaries; signal traffic never made it across. Instead, it was like the old Pony Express, updated for the twenty-first century: messages traveled over a bumpy terrain of e-mail, telephone, and fax. Humans intervened at almost every handoff, writing on pads, transposing from screens, slowing the detection process, introducing errors, and adding risk. E-mail systems rejected large files (sensor data files can be huge), or treated attachments from unknown parties as security risks.

In an ideal world, machines would move data to machines by messaging—quickly, with minimal error, across the boundaries of organizations, sectors, and jurisdictions. Data would move from the badge sensor of a state trooper on the interstate, for example, to scientists at a national lab, and on to the tablet display of a Secret Service agent scrambling to move the president through a complex urban corridor out of harm's way. All in minutes, if not seconds.

In the real world, timely collaboration was next to impossible. The networks were fractured, the data unrecognizable. Everyone could see one small piece of the puzzle, but no one person could see it all or make sense of the picture.

Everyone shared a single, noble goal: thwart the terrorists. They had plenty of sophisticated technology and were more than willing to share information. What they lacked was a true collaboration strategy, or a platform all could use to see and move data.

So DNDO and other government agencies set about developing a "global nuclear detection architecture" that would give the nation a "network of networks" of sensors around the world. Technology would lay the digital rails across boundaries, giving anyone on the network a view no one could have seen alone.

First they needed a common way for all sensor networks to send their data in a standardized way over a secure web to a common location—the Joint Analysis Center. Next they needed a way to wrap the sensor message in a "metamessage" that contained all the critical information a scientist would need from the file no matter what system sent it.

Success required true collaboration among all partners who owned different radiological/nuclear ("rad-nuke") and chemical/biological ("chem-bio") sensors. And that's exactly what happened. The government brought in the partners to agree to a standard. No company or agency would have to change its own systems, but each would have to wrap their terms as agreed so all the systems could speak the same language. Meanwhile, the government built the communications backbone to ship the messages.

Everyone realized that if this collaboration worked, it would be a huge win for both industry and the nation.

In 2008, DNDO and its partners launched a pilot program. Trucks were sent through Atlanta-area weigh stations. Some carried radioactive material. If the system worked as hoped, the "hot" trucks would trip the detection alarms, causing the sensor data to be messaged at the Joint Analysis Center, and from there to the scientists at Sandia National Laboratories.

The trial was a success. By creating a platform where diverse systems could exchange data, DNDO helped all reach across boundaries and accomplish together what none could alone: take the first steps to organize the wild west of networks and sensors. With that success, analysts and scientists could evaluate the radiation threat from any weigh station anywhere in America no matter what kind of sensor, network, or location picked up the signature—all in time to act.

YES, WE CAN COLLABORATE

Even when groups or organizations share a vision, collaboration takes a conviction that it's better working together than going it alone.

Sometimes collaboration involves millions, few of whom know each other, working together toward a common purpose.

Barack Obama's campaign for president in 2008 knew it couldn't compete with those of Democratic rivals Hillary Clinton and John Edwards in the Democratic Party's traditional fund-raising platforms—hotel dinners for big party donors, union phone-call boiler rooms, local party machines. But other platforms were up for grabs.

Millions of partisans for change were already connected socially and professionally over the Internet, in chat rooms, by text messaging and e-mails. They gathered on social and work-related sites and linked to ever-expanding networks of friends of friends.

Could Obama's campaign appeal directly to these networks, energize these partisans, and unleash a global collaboration with a single goal: victory on November 4, 2008, Election Day?

The new online platforms had been used before, but not as a decisive factor in a major campaign. Bill Bradley had raised $1 million online in 1999; Howard Dean raised $15 million online in 2003. The next year, John Kerry pulled in $82 million online—a third of his entire campaign fund-raising.

Online tools were far less familiar to both major parties than traditional top-down strategies and backroom deals. Even so, working with proven campaign professionals and technology-savvy aides like Julius Genachowski, a top communications and entertainment executive; Joe Rospars, a veteran of the Dean campaign and principal of Blue State Digital, a new media consulting firm; Kevin Malover of Orbitz as chief technology officer; and Chris Hughes, a cofounder of Facebook, Obama and his advisers put the Internet at the heart of the election operation. They flipped campaign strategy on its head: a lot of donors with a few bucks replaced a few prominent donors with big bucks; instead of building content and message only from the top down, strategy was shaped at the top by pulling content from up and across the network, pulling it to the campaign website, and pushing it back out.

The collaboration turned on many hinges, none as prominent as the integration of new-media experts with traditional campaign staff. Instead of having the two sides work separately, then attempting to reconcile their different strategies, they collaborated right from the start. "The big difference this year," Joe Rospars said, comparing the Obama campaign to the Dean effort, "is not the technology, it's the coordination."

Traditional campaign tactics—knock on doors, raise money, get out the vote—still mattered. But they were quickly adapted to the new social networking technology that would soon be pushed to its limits, with extraordinary results.

Obama's e-mail list had thirteen million addresses. The campaign generated one billion e-mails in seven thousand unique messages. One million partisans signed up for Obama text messages—and received upward of twenty text messages per month. Two million created profiles on MyBarackObama.com, one of the campaign's main sites. He established "embassies" in fifteen social media "countries." Whether on Facebook, Twitter, or Myspace, Obama took pains to behave and speak like "locals." Each embassy welcomed all comers with opportunities to find like-minded souls and download easy-to-use tools for testimonials and meet-ups. Anyone could organize friends, families, and neighborhoods without waiting for permission from the candidate or his campaign.

"We're organizing ourselves," the new ethos went. "The campaign is here to help us."

The network was building the network. On Facebook alone, 3.2 million "liked" Obama.

"We generated organizing far beyond the reach of our paid staff," Joe Rospars told an audience in 2008. "We created self-organizing tools and gave someone ownership of events. Where we had no staff we gave supporters the same tools we gave our paid organizers—the ability to create events and post to the website," Rospars said. "We lowered the barriers to entry for leadership, empowering the person lowest on the totem pole to be an organizer."

That changed everything. Supporters created 35,000 volunteer groups. They planned 200,000 offline events—5 percent organized by paid staff. They wrote 400,000 blog posts, watched or made 1.2 billion minutes of YouTube videos, and produced a torrent of citizen testimonials from the far reaches of the globe. The campaign sucked these up onto barackobama.com and pushed them back out, repeatedly republishing them to bring even more people in.

The campaign's analytics team measured every move, every ad, every piece of website traffic, every e-mail campaign. They knew what worked and tweaked it.

And Obama raised money—lots and lots of money. He held traditional fund-raisers, to be sure. One with Oprah raised $2.3 million. But a week later the campaign did something online called "Dinner with Obama." For a $250 donation, your name went in a digital hat, out of which four winners were picked to have dinner with the candidate. Obama raised $2.1 million from that online raffle—and repeated it numerous times.

The network was building a *huge* network.

The total harvest staggered even Obama's own team. All in all the campaign raised $745 million—$500 million of it from online contributions by 3 million donors who made 6.5 million donations, nearly all in increments of $100 or less. Fifty-two-year-old Linnie Frank Bailey from California was typical: she gave $120.40 over two years—$10 at a time.

For Obama, the money advantage translated to a two-to-one advantage over John McCain in local TV spot advertising. Obama ran 336 field offices in battleground states. McCain: 101. Obama's campaign out-contacted voters by knocks on doors or phone calls by a margin of thirty-five to one.

From the Iowa caucuses forward, Obama's candidacy soared. Too late, Democratic challenger Senator Hillary Clinton launched a "me too" social media campaign that never caught fire. John McCain's online efforts were even sorrier.

On November 4, 2008, thirteen million Obama votes—one of every five cast—came from the ranks of online supporters. The campaign handed out the digital hammers and nails, and millions of volunteers designed and built the house. And quite a house they built: designed by the network for a network, on a platform using the Internet's fast access and collaboration-friendly configurations to emphasize the candidate's message of inclusiveness and change.

The point? To cross boundaries, collaborate right from the start, give others the digital tools needed, and let the network build the network. You'll leave the competition behind.

TRANSFORMATION THROUGH COLLABORATION

Chances are, you're already collaborating. In every cubicle, squad room, teacher's office, nurses' station, ops center, and boardroom—wherever men and women see a better way—people are eager to make the change happen.

But folks who want to make change happen are often surrounded by folks who don't get it. Some are scared or uninterested; others are pessimistic and full of their own self-importance. Those mind-sets we spoke of earlier bog everyone down. Come to folks with an idea about how to make things better and they'll peer over their glasses at you.

"Impossible," they will say. "That's outside of our organization. We don't have the resources. This is not what has been mandated. That's not how we do things."

When information and networks or human and political capital are locked down behind institutional barriers, it's time to find a fix. It's time to turn to the strategies, plans, and tactics that reach across boundaries and lead to collaboration.

We've written this book to share with you the collective insight of hundreds of top executives and managers, leaders and researchers, men and women we have worked with, collaborated with, led, and followed over forty years in our careers.

It is a book that will help you to collaborate better, and to get on with the business of transforming the world as it is into the world as it should be.

BLUE-SKY
VISION

2

ollaboration starts with a vision—a *blue-sky* vision of a better way. It's a way that's better, faster, or cheaper; or more efficient, effective, or equitable. It's the way to greater wisdom and justice, safety and wealth, health or beauty.

If you're like just about everyone else, you have an aspiration for yourself, your family, your company—whether it's buried at the bottom of your in-box or engraved on a plaque in your office; whether it's about your school or your marriage, or just a daydream you keep having—you envision a better day and a better way.

George Hotz had a vision of putting his network to work and winning the DARPA Challenge: I bet I can beat those "Joe College" boys at their high-priced game—with nothing but a few tweets and a website.

Barack Obama and his team had a vision of mobilizing millions of partisans for change—outflanking his more traditional rivals, and winning the race for the White House.

A banker might have a vision of bringing the Internet to millions of customers—and bringing millions of new customers to his bank.

An Egyptian street activist might chant, along with thousands of others in a city square, "We want . . . the regime . . . to go!"

Those are all visions. Each has a belief in the possibilities of a better way, promising better days ahead. Large or small, all collaboration begins with a blue-sky vision.

THE INTERNET COMES TO CANADA

In 1993, a financial crisis gripped Canada. Nonetheless, its leaders were determined to bring the Internet to all Canadians. Costly as it would be, staying competitive with international partners in the emerging world of e-commerce demanded it.

Doug Hull, a midlevel manager in his government's Industry Canada organization, began with a modest vision—to distribute educational materials more efficiently. As his mission expanded, Hull's vision broadened. His blue-sky vision opened more eyes and energized his networks throughout the country, adding their blue-sky vision to his. Ultimately, Hull's efforts led communities across Canada, from cities to the most rural outposts, to connect to the Internet.

In the past, Canada's central government had connected the nation's citizens. It laid the railroad rails, ran the phone lines, built the highways that tied Canadians together across five time zones, from the North Pole to the US border. Now its leaders fretted over how fast the nation could build a national Internet infrastructure. Who should pay for it? How should Canada balance competition and regulation? Could Canadians be assured of universal access at reasonable cost?

Hull had no idea how to answer these big questions. He only knew that he was paying huge amounts of money to distribute educational materials electronically over dedicated networks. With a looming budget crunch, something had to give. Switch to the Internet, a staffer advised him. It was better, faster, and cheaper.

In May 1993, Hull convened a dozen advisers from government, industry, and education to explore whether their network could support the distribution of educational materials via the Internet. The city of Ottawa said, Sure, Hull could put computers in its schools, link them to the Internet, and distribute his materials that way. But only if it cost them nothing.

Hull had no money to buy computer equipment. But he noticed twelve junked computers in his ministry's basement, rescued them, and delivered them to Ottawa's schools. He helped Ottawa hook them up to the Internet and link them by satellite to Newfoundland schools.

"Bell [Telephone] gave us some telephone lines," Hull said. "The university donated the server. We hired some students to do the engineering work and put stuff up on the web."

And so a network was born—SchoolNet—at virtually no cost to the government.

A new vision jelled for Hull: connecting more and more schools all across Canada. "I figured if it was so easy to get twelve computers into the schools, why not twelve thousand?"

There was a big "why not" waiting for Hull to smack into. Canada's federal government didn't run education—the provincial governments did. Hull's vision could spark a confrontation with the provincial governments.

As Hull's vision grew, he realized his efforts to collaborate with others had to grow with it.

So, he created another network—this one wider still. The National SchoolNet Advisory Board comprised fifty representatives from industry and all levels of government—federal, provincial, and local. Hull shared his vision of connecting schools across Canada. The board agreed to let Hull connect three hundred schools to the Internet by the end of the 1993–94 school year. Moreover, board members agreed to go into their provinces and towns to promote SchoolNet's possibilities and to help build corporate, government, and civic support. Hull's network would help build a network.

In the meantime, Hull shared his vision with other agencies in the federal government, such as Human Resources Development Canada, to get them to reallocate existing budgets, helping SchoolNet to do better, faster, and cheaper what the agencies had to do anyway. Hull negotiated bulk network and equipment deals with the private sector for the federal network. Firms liked the visibility the project gave them and the prospect of tax savings from laying in infrastructure that would later service more significant markets, like home users.

The existing bureaucracy became a potent ally working toward Hull's blue-sky vision.

By June 1994, Industry Canada had far surpassed its initial goals for SchoolNet. The operation had linked not three hundred but three *thousand* schools across Canada. It was a national triumph, thanks to strong provincial backing and local support. The federal government budgeted $13 million annually for the succeeding four years, and set as its target bringing all of Canada's 16,500 schools online by March 1999.

Once again, Hull's vision grew bolder. He became convinced that schools could become Internet access points for entire communities. After all, many Canadians had neither computers nor access to one.

"The idea," Hull said, "was that all of this computer equipment was being put in the schools, but they were closed in the evenings. We had more capacity than we were using, and we could easily allow the general public in at night."

So Hull went back to his network again: would they be interested in piggybacking wider access onto existing SchoolNet sites—perhaps as a new Community Access Program (CAP)?

They would. The province of New Brunswick took the lead with a rural pilot. Its premier, Frank McKenna, had already invested heavily in moving from an agricultural economy to the information age. New Brunswick's schools were flush with computers; it was attracting call centers and related industries.

"I realized that this was just exactly what we needed to fill in one of the blanks in our province," McKenna said. "And that was the large number of people who were illiterate on computers and who we needed in the labor force."

Others besides Doug Hull were beginning to have blue-sky visions. On a site visit, the mayor of Gagetown, New Brunswick, shared *his* vision with Hull: "When trade was by river, we used to be right on the main route. Then came the real highway, which bypassed this town, and we've been languishing for the last hundred years. Now, with this program, the information highway is here and we don't mean to be left behind. We're tired of our kids leaving town. We want them to stay here. Until now, there has been no prospect for development, because the only highway has been far away. The Internet is changing all that."

What had started as a vision of greater efficiency was leading to a more equitable system for rural Canadians, who would no longer be cut off from the increasingly connected world.

Blue-sky visions don't always start big. Sometimes, a vision starts just by *noticing*. Doug Hull noticed the Internet while he was looking for a cheaper way to distribute his educational materials; he noticed the twelve scrap computers in the ministry's basement; he noticed that the campuses in SchoolNet were empty at night.

Great innovators do a lot of "noticing." General Electric, for example, looks for inventions designed for one market that can work in a new one. They look for "game changers"—what authors like Clayton Christensen have called "disruptive innovations." They look for serendipities—"fortunate accidents" that repurpose existing inventions. They look for "compounds"—solutions that offer innovations across multiple domains.*

Hull, in addition, operated in a world steeped in tradition and politics. He was quite aware of the bureaucracy lumbering along toward the Internet. He could have been stumped here; instead, he took advantage of it. On a smaller scale he could make progress better, faster, and cheaper. He knew his country's history—it had always been up to the federal government to "lay the rails" and connect Canadians. Economic development inevitably followed. Hull was on track with that, too. And he noticed the digital divide separating urban from rural Canada—and made sure to ride Canada's deep commitment toward reducing it.

Doug Hull's vision, simple as it was at first, *aligned* with others' visions large and small. He couldn't see them all at the start. But as his own vision became clear and matured, it aligned with corporate supporters who saw

*See Vinnie Mirchandani, *The New Polymath: Profiles in Compound-Technology Innovations* (New York: John Wiley & Sons, 2010), Chapter 3, "Polymath Profile #1: General Electric," pp. 31–39.

investments now they would make money from later. Provincial leaders like Frank McKenna discovered that Hull's vision aligned with theirs for economic development. And with the network reaching rural Canada, it brought forth the vision of local citizens who wanted to be part of this coming wave—and keep young people home with new-economy jobs rather than lose them to the big cities.

Collaboration requires individuals, networks, and believers working together toward a vision. As new challenges and opportunities arise, visions inevitably evolve.

After the New Brunswick pilot, Doug Hull added forty more CAP sites, stoking the flames of provincial support, gaining more resources. By December 1994, the federal government approved $22.5 million in funding for one thousand CAP sites.

Hull invited remote rural communities and Canada's underserved urban areas to compete for those first CAP programs and design the details themselves. "We are giving them money to accomplish a local project, rather than shoving some preconceived program into their face that was dreamed up in Ottawa," Hull explained. (Years later Barack Obama used this same network-building approach for his Internet campaign!)

The applications poured in. Industry Canada received fifty-nine proposals from the villages and towns of Quebec alone. The executive reviewing them recalled one in particular, from the village of St. Clement. The community had been hard hit when its post office was closed. "Instead of living in a state of sorrow," the villagers wrote, "we will simply energize our community into finding a new avenue . . . a tool that will allow us to see into the future." They would replace their post office with a CAP Internet site. The communities had begun to blue-sky the vision of a connected world for themselves.

Hull made sure the first CAP site opened in Picton, Ontario, within easy distance of the nation's capital, making it practical for his boss, Industry Canada minister John Manley, to cut the ribbon himself—and draw further national press attention to the CAP program. That worked.

"The information highway has a new off ramp into this rural Ontario town," wire service reports ran, "the first municipality in Canada to open a public center with Internet computers."

Soon CAP pilots were opening not just in schools but in banks, libraries, and post offices. Collaboration proliferated. Retired telephone workers volunteered to rebuild computers for the schools. Railroads and air-freight services agreed to ship the repaired machines out to the provinces. Area technical schools provided repairs and training for the new grads. Young workers digitized Canadian artifacts from the nation's archives, museums, and libraries, creating uniquely Canadian content. The collections' owners happily donated space, equipment, and supervision.

Starting with a vision of twelve computers distributing educational materials over the Internet, Doug Hull led Canada onto the World Wide Web. During the 1990s, Canada became the first country to connect all of its public schools and libraries to the Internet—nearly twenty thousand individual facilities. Over 125,000 computers had been delivered to schools and four thousand rural communities had gained Internet access, with a goal in view of one thousand more, and a new goal set to link five thousand urban communities.

How's that for a blue-sky vision?

WELCOMING THE VISION OF THE CROWD

You're someplace today, and you want to be in a better place tomorrow. You may have a modest vision of doing something better, faster, cheaper; you may have a grand picture of a safer, healthier, and happier world. But you can't get there alone.

To make your vision a reality, you have to beckon and call forth the vision of others. That's a potent brew: now two of you see possibilities the same way. Your reasons could differ. How do you get there? The path is yet to be determined. But now you share a passion for moving forward and a basis to do it together.

Your vision needs to be broad enough to appeal to a variety of people and organizations. You can't be all things to all people. But you need to be something to enough people to come together and make their aspirations a reality.

The vision the NYPD's new commissioner offered New York in 1994, for example, was about more than just crime statistics. It was about safer citizens, a healthier tourism trade, reenergized police officers. Chances are, hotel owners didn't give a lot of thought to how much the cops liked their jobs, but they cared intensely about whether tourists were afraid to visit New York. Most citizens didn't care much about hotel owners' profits, but they certainly worried about getting back to their homes safely at night.

For different reasons, all of them shared a vision of a safer city. That was enough to rally New Yorkers from all walks of life. It's where collaboration for a safe New York led by the shared vision of the mayor and the NYPD started.

Think back to how Doug Hull's vision broadened as his need for collaboration increased, drawing in many disparate groups. Teachers saw opportunities to better educate their students. Parents in rural communities imagined providing children with new opportunities for local jobs. Businesses looked forward to a new tech-savvy pool of employees. All shared a vision for a better day. There was something in it for everyone, if only they could connect the Internet to their towns and villages.

Let's take a closer look at how Doug Hull blue-skyed his vision. At the outset his vision was simple: do the same work distributing educational material for less. In his search for an answer, Hull at first became Doug Better-Faster-Cheaper. There's nothing radical about the vision here. Hull's product stays the same. It was just getting delivered *cheaper*.

But Hull needed help. He couldn't very well ship material over the Internet if there was no one on the other end to receive it. So, Hull went outside the Industry Canada ministry to a cluster of potential partisans. He crossed boundaries and founded his first network of users. Collaborating right from the start, Hull became Doug the Network Builder.

A network needs a platform, and a platform takes infrastructure.

Those twelve boxes sitting in the ministry's basement? The office that junked those computers thought their days were finished. To Hull they were a godsend. Doug the Asset Maximizer saw those boxes as essential equipment for a better-faster-cheaper distribution chain over his network. There was plenty of value left in those old boxes. His new network would take great advantage of them.

That's what the *new* vision was all about. By grabbing those computers, hitching them to the Internet, and pushing his educational materials down the pipe, Doug Hull lit up the network. Soon, all were collaborating at the limits of their new technology.

Hull's network added the Newfoundland schools to Ottawa's school system. All of a sudden, he had created *a multinode network*—and with it, new capability. He now had two school jurisdictions on the net, as well as Industry Canada. They were *networked*. Being networked, they could *collaborate* faster, better, and cheaper, yes. But the network was kind of small.

So let's expand, Hull realized. Twelve computers and two schools open the doors to a new kind of collaboration. Think how much more interesting it would be if he got others into the network. He was looking to achieve what economists call *network effects*—the more people on the network, the greater the benefit for everyone. There would be lots of invention, lots of visions coming forward.

Enter Doug the Community Builder. His new vision? Let's add even more value by adding people and locations to our small network. So Hull negotiated more corporate support for bandwidth and equipment, gained federal backing, and engaged senior provincial officials. His networks leveraged local support, which generated more ideas, more users and uses, and more benefit for everyone.

As school organizations mobilized, and school networks engaged, students, parents, and teachers and administrators became jazzed. Then Hull leveraged the schools into the Community Access Program, taking the innovation deeper, into entire communities, capitalizing on the assets already in place but unused at night.

Hull had noticed yet another unexpended asset: those schools had great facilities, good machines; they were in every village and town ready to get connected—yet they were sitting unused at night. All dark for twelve hours, dusk to dawn.

Wait—those are not just schools; they are Internet Access Centers. Let's light them up! Fully wired now, the network created new opportunities—jobs for young people, training facilities, senior citizen engagement, and digitized Canadian-unique content.

Visions started to meld. The DNA of the networks involved was stranding together, becoming one. There was something in it for everyone, from industry to government, from the schoolchildren in a one-room schoolhouse on Pictou Island, Nova Scotia, to the inner-city job training centers of Canada's great cities. Networks spawned networks, soon engaging millions of people, collaborating, delivering steady value, innovating new products, pushing out services and pulling in support, and transforming the nation.

The network was building the network, with Doug Hull as its ringmaster. He'd started out with a simple vision of how to do something more efficiently. He obtained some cheap asssets, reached across boundaries, engaged a small cluster of partisans, laid down some connectivity, created a network, and began collaborating with others right from the start.

Doug Hull did not have a national vision when he started. He did not set out to build the Canadian Internet. Needing only to be better, faster, cheaper at first, Hull found a vision simple enough to execute, enough to energize a few, take the next step together, deliver on the value, find more partners—and eventually millions of others who, sharing that passion, collaborated around a simple vision: we want the Internet.

Throughout, Hull's blue sky was constantly morphing, embracing the visions of others, becoming enriched by them, amplifying the sum of all the value it was creating.

All born from one public servant's ability to blue-sky the vision.

A BLUE-SKY VISION OF PROSPERITY

Remember "Recovery Summer, 2010"? That was supposed to be the summer that the US stimulus package of 2009 finally shook the US economy out of its doldrums.

It never happened. Unemployment stayed high; consumer credit shrank; small companies found credit tight; housing activity fell; home values declined, foreclosures increased. The US trade balance was moving in the wrong direction: exports were steady, but imports were surging.

Nothing was really working right. Even so, the main debate in Washington was whether a little bit more of the same would do the trick—another round of stimulus cash, for example, and credit easing by the Federal Reserve.

Mohamed A. El-Erian, the financial guru who led Harvard University's endowment to record growth over a generation, warned this funk was more than just cyclical doldrums. There's a structural problem here, he said. We're broken in a way the old fixes can't solve.

We need a structural vision, he said, not just chasing after crises.

Here's what El-Erian might have meant—it's Intel founder and former CEO Andy Grove's vision. Grove built Intel with a $3 million investment in 1968 to the multibillion-dollar chip power it is today. Since then, Grove says, the United States has shipped too many jobs overseas. When we ship jobs out, he says, we do more than strip Americans of their livelihoods. "We break the chain of experience that is so important in technological evolution."

Take the battery industry, for example. After many years and false starts, the world is about to see the first mass-produced electric cars and trucks. They all need batteries. But the United States lost its lead in batteries thirty years ago when it shipped all its consumer electronic manufacturing overseas. *Those* firms learned to make batteries. They were ready for battery-powered personal computers. And now *they're* ready to put batteries into every battery-powered electric car. The United States is not and now likely will be locked out of that industry.

"That's a problem," Grove says. "A new industry needs an effective ecosystem in which technology know-how accumulates, experience builds on experience, and close relationships develop between supplier and customer."

What would a vision that provided that ecosystem here in the United States look like?

It would mean building a collaboration between suppliers and customers that continued learning *after* you finished the innovative knowledge work. Patents are great, but that's just a start. There's plenty left to do after you've had a brilliant idea—learning from doing, from *manufacturing*. Yet between 2000 and 2010 the United States lost one-third of its manufacturing jobs—six million positions.

Grove may or may not be right on the diagnosis. After all, the United States still makes 19 percent of the world's goods, about the same as thirty years ago. But he offers a vision. One thing is clear: without a vision, it's hard to move ahead; you'll muddle through.

A vision always leads the way. When there is no one to blue-sky the possibilities, few can mobilize around a shared future. Sometimes leaders like Doug Hull rise to the vision as it evolves. Other times, leaders come to a vision fully formed—and others have to play catch-up if they plan to play ball at all.

IT: THE FIRST PLAY YOU RUN

In the 1980s, Brooklyn district attorney Elizabeth Holtzman grew incensed at the criminal justice system's poor treatment of crime victims and with waste within the NYPD.

Brooklyn prosecutors staffed a twenty-four-hour Complaint Room at the NYPD's Central Booking facility in downtown Brooklyn. After any arrest, cops from each of Brooklyn's twenty-three precincts would bring their prisoners down to Central Booking for processing. Once the "perp" was fingerprinted and checked for criminal history, the cop would bring the paperwork over to the DA's side of the building, where assistant district attorneys would decide how to charge the case, based on the evidence, the cop's statement, and the defendant's history. Then off to jail went the perp, and back to the precinct went the cop. The case was now the DA's.

That handoff from the NYPD to the DA to Corrections repeated itself one hundred thousand times each year in Brooklyn alone.

What about the victims whose information was vital to prosecutors? Victims had to make their way downtown to the Complaint Room on their own nickel—sometimes in the middle of the night, come rain or shine, hobbled, injured, or poor—just to tell the DA the same story they'd already told the cops in the precinct.

Cops, it turned out, could not transport both prisoner *and* victim. With one hundred thousand criminal cases in Brooklyn every year, the NYPD wasn't about to send two cops downtown for every arrest.

If victims made it to the DA's Complaint Room after the arrest—and that was a big if—prosecutors were in a great position to figure out what had really happened. Prosecutors loved cops but always preferred to hear the victim's story firsthand so they could decide for themselves whether the case had enough merit to bring to trial. How bad is this crime? How strong is the case? How good a witness is the victim?

Keep in mind, all of this occurred downtown, in the dead of night, or in the middle of a workday, in the cold of winter or heat of summer—after the victim had been brutalized by a crime, which for many people is one of life's most traumatic experiences.

This is ridiculous, Liz Holtzman thought. Many victims never make it down to the Complaint Room. Prosecutors were working blind. Without a victim present, to be on the safe side prosecutors often tracked cases forward full bore, treating each as the strongest case, involving the worst crime, against the most dangerous offender—at least until an assistant district attorney a few days later could get a better read on it. Meanwhile, the case ate up lawyers, courtrooms, and cops.

At the Complaint Room, for example, cops were working the system hard for overtime, and the system obliged. It might take an hour to take fingerprints, run records checks, and write up the paperwork. But it took seven hours on average in waiting time for interviews.

The bottleneck was fearsome. On a busy night forty or fifty officers might line the stairwells or sit asleep at desks in the Complaint Room, waiting for hours for a fifteen-minute interview with the assistant district attorney. Cops were earning $34 an hour in overtime, waiting.

"Collars for dollars" was a sad spectacle. It was no surprise that the vast majority of arrests occurred in the last hours of police shifts, guaranteeing at least some overtime. There were big bucks to be had—except on weekends, when, as Jack Maple discovered, most cops were "off." Reported crime was high on weekends, but with most cops on their days off, arrests were low, and the waits short.

The system appalled Holtzman. So she came up with a blue-sky vision to give victims fairer treatment, save scads of overtime, and improve the way cases were handled. She was determined to address the inequity, inefficiency, and ineffectiveness she saw.

Her vision: why not just run some video links between the precincts and prosecutors downtown and let the cops and victims stay where they were?

Holtzman already had a long track record of innovating on behalf of victims. She had established a Victims Services Unit to support crime victims while their cases were being prosecuted. She added new units to focus her four hundred prosecutors on crimes that targeted the elderly, or were racially motivated, or affected children—or were committed by police officers.

The DA was intensely interested in using the latest information technology to improve crime fighting. She had introduced the routine use of videotaping confessions and built computer systems to track the Brooklyn DA's yearly caseload. She championed legislation that permitted the child victims of crime to testify via video rather than appear in courtrooms. She led the charge to bring automated fingerprint systems to New York State to solve crimes by matching up crime scene prints with prints already in the state systems.

Holtzman's vision anticipated the digital age: why move bodies and paper when you can move images and data faster, better, cheaper? You can change the world by writing laws, she knew. You can change it with budgets (and becoming the comptroller of the city of New York was the next step in Liz Holtzman's career). But the first play you run, she thought, should always be IT. What could technology do?

To tackle this new challenge, Holtzman turned to Special Assistant for Policy and Planning Zach Tumin.

ZACH TUMIN

Why don't we use some state-of-the-art video-teleconferencing? Liz asked. Link it from the precinct of arrest to the downtown Complaint Room, and let victims talk to DAs right then and there? We can interview the cops then, too. That way victims can stay close to home and arresting officers can return to duty from the precinct. The precinct can use some bulk transport to move prisoners as a group for booking downtown so cops don't have to waste time in transit or waiting. Overtime falls, and DAs get to speak with victims on every case.

It would be faster, cheaper, and more compassionate for victims.

What was not to like?

Well, actually . . . a lot, as it turned out. The promise of saving overtime was a labor relations nightmare for the police commissioner. The police loved their overtime pay. For the NYPD it was a small price to pay for labor peace. As for easing the experiences of the victims, or improving the ability of prosecutors to make their cases, those were the DA's problems, not the NYPD's.

So Holtzman began to blue-sky her vision to potential supporters outside the NYPD. She convinced a philanthropist friend to donate the money to buy the necessary equipment and build the telephone lines that could handle video. NYNEX, the phone company, and PictureTel, the video-teleconferencing firm, pitched in. Holtzman soon had the resources in place to build the new platform and give the idea a pilot run.

Even so, One Police Plaza, or "1PP" as the NYPD headquarters was known, dragged its feet. Holtzman was not part of the old boys' network that ran New York criminal justice. She was the city's first woman DA, and early on in her administration established the first police brutality squad in any New York City DA's office. That both grated on cops and made it difficult for the assistant district attorneys who had to work shoulder to shoulder with cops "in the trenches."

Liz was quick to flog the NYPD—even if her senior staff and line attorneys winced each time. When Police Commissioner Ben Ward dug in his heels on the video links, the DA would have none of his delays. With zeal and talent, Liz litigated the issue in an exchange of letters with Mayor Ed Koch, with whom she had served in Congress. She'd taken on bigger game there: as a congresswoman she had pressured Watergate investigators to take their probe to the White House, into the Oval Office, and to focus on Richard Nixon.

This battle was child's play for Liz. With her famous pen poised for yet another Letter to the Editor of the *New York Times*, and under pressure from city hall, 1PP sent word to Holtzman's office: "We're in, but you're sending Tumin out to the precinct roll calls to explain that it's the DA who's taking money out of cops' pockets, not the police commissioner."

The NYPD assigned as my liaison Bruce Kennedy, a cop and a top aide to Chief of Department Robert Johnston (one of the few senior NYPD officials who enjoyed a cordial relationship with Liz). Bruce Kennedy was a cop's cop: ex–Tactical Patrol Force, he was a skilled "wire man" with a passion for technology who understood wiretapping as well as anyone in New York. He became famous for being called back from a Boy Scout jamboree when a dangerous fugitive was cornered in the Bronx; in full scoutmaster regalia Bruce scampered up phone poles to hang wiretaps on the cornered cop killer.

Bruce reported directly to Johnston. That gave him heft at One Police Plaza. Bruce Kennedy had no love for Liz Holtzman. But her vision of a more efficient police force aligned well with his own vision about how the NYPD could be run better. He was always pitching the use of new technology to the brass and running into the same head-winds Holtzman had encountered. With the DA breaking the bow wave on this one, Kennedy was going to surf her wake. He saw lots of applications where the DA's acceptance of video could improve police operations and performance. Besides, many cops hated wasting time at Central Booking. The travel downtown, the endless waiting, and all the damned paperwork were demoralizing.

For his own reasons, Bruce Kennedy was aligned and on board. Holtzman's vision would be good for New York, good for the NYPD, and would help cops be cops. Her vision had room for Kennedy's. So he kept moving the plan forward in the NYPD.

Back at the Brooklyn DA's office, it was up to me to promote Holtzman's vision. Many experienced prosecutors were reluctant to give up what few face-to-face interviews with victims they had. That was when prosecutors thought they could best evaluate who was exaggerating more—the perp, the victim, or maybe the cop. They worried about taking the delay out of the system that was built into transporting perps from the precinct to downtown. That bottleneck was useful. Would uncorking it flood the network with demand for video interviews? They worried it would bring too many cases into the system too fast. They'd lose control.

Even stressed out, at least the system was in equilibrium; prosecutors knew how to make the system work. How would this new technology change that? Prosecutors came down with a bad case of what I later came to know as "Aadya's Law": every system prefers to stay in a grounded state with low noise levels. Equilibrium, good. Change, bad. Whatever the gain promised, the loss of certainty and the move to a new equilibrium were a concern. A big concern.

Despite that, I kept the plan on track in the DA's office. Having a clear vision is especially important when you are facing skeptics. So, too, is the DA's strong backing. I made sure I worked closely with the chief assistant district attorney so that Liz's vision translated into plans that aligned with the reality assistant district attorneys faced handling cops, cases, and victims at the Complaint Room at two o'clock in the morning in Brooklyn and the next day in court.

Holtzman's vision made her by turns asset maximizer for her own troops and those of the New York Police Department; problem solver for the complaining witnesses straggling to the DA's Complaint Room; and strategic investor in her community as she built the system's capability. In the face of widespread resistance, Holtzman, Kennedy, and I formed our own network: she brought in the financing and visibility; Bruce made sure the technology worked for the NYPD; I made sure it worked for the system of moving cases to court with the best information available to everyone. We collaborated across boundaries to change a system that was functioning well enough for everyone except the victims and the taxpayers—and the cops who wanted to be cops.

Fortunately, the video-link system tested brilliantly. Rates of victims interviewed soared. The NYPD saved overtime by the bushel. More cops became available at the precinct for return to patrol faster. With more cases being handled by video, even the line at Central Booking seemed to shrink. Did video from the precincts strengthen cases? With all that information it certainly made prosecutors' assessment of them more accurate.

The Manhattan DA's office, based on our success, soon began experimenting with video from the precincts themselves. Today, of course, video permeates American criminal justice operations, as it should.

REFERENCE PROJECTIONS

Sometimes, before you can blue-sky a vision, you have to imagine a tomorrow that's markedly worse than today.

Russell Ackoff was a professor at the University of Pennsylvania's Wharton School of Business. He is credited as a founder of operations research and "systems thinking"—solving problems by coming at them with the whole picture in mind.

Ackoff often dealt with corporate and government executives who couldn't figure a way forward from what he irreverently called "the mess," and others like MIT's Donald Schön called "the swamp"—a chaotic place of bad information, little time, and shortened tempers where, unfortunately, most hard choices resided.

Leaders have to change. The times demand it. But how? In which direction? Often, Ackoff found, they had no sense, no compass, no *vision*. It's exactly when the world is moving fast around you, and you're pushed and pulled this way and that, that a vision keeps you on track.

One of Ackoff's clients was the Federal Reserve Bank of Cleveland. One year, Ackoff took bank data and showed the executives that the square footage the bank would need for its projected workload would soon exceed all the available commercial space in Cleveland. In other words, the entire operation would break down.

Fortunately, there was still time to head off the crisis. Ackoff suggested that the bank use its paper-intensive payment systems to create an *electronic* funds transfer system. That's exactly what the bank did. The innovation not only saved the Cleveland bank but soon spread throughout the US financial services industry.

Ackoff called this way of attacking problems *making a reference projection*. Think of a reference projection as a scare scenario. You take a trend that concerns you today, because it threatens your mission, and project where you'll be at some date in the future if no one intervenes to stop or reverse the trend.

How does that future look? Not so good? This realization helps define the vision you prefer *as the opposite*: Not slow, but fast. Not heavy, but light. Not for a few, but for the many. Not costly, but cheap. Now you have the makings of a new vision that will help avoid that bleak future.

A BLUE-SKY VISION FOR REFORM

Harry Spence shook his head. He'd just reviewed hundreds of screens, all part of the Massachusetts child welfare computer system: "We do work with children who suffer neglect and abuse. Yet we use a system whose sole purpose is to ensure the proper care and upbringing of children which never once uses the word 'love.' "

Tomy Abraham and his CIO had just spent the better part of the morning demonstrating the Massachusetts Department of Social Services (DSS) systems to Spence, its new commissioner.

"Most of the time when you show an enterprise application to a C-level executive, they pick up on graphical user interface issues; that is quite natural," Abraham said. "They do look at the end of the system. But they are more interested in changing the labels and things like that."

Spence's reaction to the social services systems was not what Abraham was expecting.

"This was a completely weird sort of thing—'I do not see the word "love."' It's an enterprise application," Abraham said. "You cannot tell how much 'love' there is. Are there adoptions? Are there goals for the children? That is what we are recording here.

"It's not that any of us would *omit* love. It's just that love doesn't have a natural place in the system."

As Spence recalled later, "It was a classic case of absolutely dry, emotionally arid, endless descriptions of the care of children as though emotion were not there and did not exist in this work. It is fundamental to the failings of child welfare."

Built on an old accounting mainframe, every case had lots of drop-down yes/no check boxes, but not much text. Great for compliance, but bad for creating a clinical practice narrative, like a doctor's file did.

Not much room for "love."

Spence worried.

"I can issue all the policy statements, values, and promulgations that I want," he would say. "But in the end, the social workers spend an hour and a half to two hours a day in front of the screen that organizes how they do their practice.

"I might have thought that I was shaping the practice of my subordinates. In fact, the IT system may be much more powerful than I in doing that."

Spence had a blue-sky vision that involved nothing less than overhauling the institution. "Someday," he said, "we are going to redesign this whole system."

In the world of child welfare, a battle over two opposing strategies waged for years. One camp—the "compliance" model—focused on what was missing in the family, and what the parents had to do to keep the child. Child welfare workers in that camp issued families an ultimatum: "Fix this or we'll take your kids."

Workers in the other camp—the "strength-based" model—tried to keep the child with the family if at all possible. They looked for the good things in a family to build on, bolster a family where it was weak and the child most at risk, and call upon a broad network of support from neighbors, extended family, churches, and elsewhere.

When Spence set out to transform his organization, that debate was still raging. But it was far from the only problem. Social workers' caseloads were overwhelming; staff burned out at a frantic pace. Budget cuts decimated even the most senior ranks. The department was spending a fortune on a few truly troubled kids in residential treatment and had little staff or energy left over for the vast majority of families unless they were in full-blown crisis, or the kids were in imminent peril. Sometimes, troubled families eluded notice until it was too late; horrifying stories of children injured or killed in their own homes devastated social workers and infuriated the community.

With reduced staff, little money, and enormous responsibility, there was no way the DSS could continue going it alone. The agency needed to find ways to keep kids in their homes longer or get them back *into* their homes and make sure they were safe—throw a safety net around them much larger than the one it could provide alone with its investigators knocking on doors in a housing project at 2:00 a.m. on an emergency referral.

The compliance strategy had failure written all over it. It was killing everyone—twenty or thirty kids were dying each year. Social workers were demoralized.

"They're all loaded up with the trauma of the kids," Tim Callahan said. Callahan ran a residential treatment center for deeply troubled youth. "If you spend time in these cultures, the state of health of the adults jumps out at you. You don't often see people in this bad shape in other businesses."

"I woke up in a hospital with a heart attack," Robert Maker said. Starting in 1982, coming out of Boston College with a master's in clinical social work, Maker rose fast through the ranks of DSS investigators: "A social worker was interviewing me, asking me all these questions about lifestyle and family history. Then we get to the point. 'What do you do for a living?' I said I work at DSS. She said, 'What do you do for DSS?' I start explaining what my function was. She said, 'Well, maybe you ought to think about getting a new job.' Years and years and years of secondary trauma had stacked up. I had not realized it. I was fifty-three."

Projecting forward, it was just a matter of time till the next disaster struck. Time: something no one had—not children in peril, not overwhelmed caseworkers, and not Spence. No child welfare commissioner ever did. Caseworkers and commissioners together lived on a roller coaster of blame. When something or someone screwed up, the papers hammered the commissioner, the commissioner hammered caseworkers, and caseworkers hammered parents.

"How you treat your workers," Spence said, "is how they will treat the families."

What a cycle.

More mistakes were inevitable, and Spence knew it. "Nobody does well for a sustained period of time what they do not believe in," he said. "So, you do not actually change parental behavior by punishing; you do not improve parenting in any sustained way. You get compliance just long enough to get the hell out of the system."

Then, it happens again.

Spence had great credibility as a reformer in the Boston area. From his first day on the job he cultivated the press. The day would come when a child died in the custody of caregivers who were under DSS supervision. He would need some cushion—take a hit, come back up, keep on with reforms.

Spence's goal for DSS: alter its trajectory and change its future. Get off the roller coaster. And fast.

"I'm a big believer that you can't do a kind of careful sequential one, two, three in an organization like this. You have to move on multiple fronts," Spence said. "If people only hear it from one particular activity, they just don't take it in. If you change just one little piece, eventually the old structure will recapture that area.

"If you're not breaking up the system in multiple places and creating a new message in multiple places, nothing sticks, and nothing changes."

Spence was well aware that in the 1970s one of his predecessors, Jerome Miller, had famously *bulldozed* a Massachusetts facility for youth to make dead certain that it would never return to operation.

Harry Spence was no less determined to see this reform through.

COLLABORATING FOR FAMILIES

With Spence's leadership, change toward a new practice model would soon take hold, and collaboration would begin.

Spence had a vision of parents as partners, not adversaries, and kids raised in families made strong rather than extracted to foster care or group homes. That meant fostering a new collaboration among DSS staffs, parents, and families, few of whom were comfortable with it. The most important work was going to have to start right at home plate—with the DSS social workers.

Many DSS staff found the notion of collaborating with parents heresy. Parents were the problems; the DSS folks saw themselves as "saviors." To them, the proper business of the department was rescuing kids in peril *from* parents.

If Spence was going to change the system, it meant building a new practice model: getting to the families "right from the start," as he put it, before a full-blown crisis hit, throwing a safety net around them of church, neighbors, family, social workers, and law enforcement.

Hard work for Spence and the DSS lay ahead. In a statewide "listening tour," Spence challenged his staff—as well as parents, advocates and providers—to formulate their own blue-sky visions.

"If we could go back to who we were when we started doing this work, without all of the pain and failure that we have had, if we could go back to what we really dreamt of doing—what would that look like?" he asked them.

Spence knew social workers did not embark on their careers to snatch children from the jaws of death. They came to help families before it ever came to that.

Some DSS veterans like Robert Maker bought in. Others did not. Maker understood that.

"A lot of the old-timers say this is a mistake," Maker said. "We are going to miss so much in these cases. We will not be protecting kids the way they should be.

"Others say it is about time that we get back to the roots of social work. Positive people within DSS doing humane social work, drawn to the field because they have a powerful reason to be here—looking to involve more people, earlier.

"Harry wanted both. A combination of safety for families and children, as well as a more respectful approach, proactive—this whole process of working with families right from the start. That was his vision."

Words or no, Spence needed to translate vision into deeds—to show what was in it for everyone, and bring all along with him.

He had a head start. Vestiges of past reform regimes persisted throughout the DSS—small pockets of reformers running essentially rogue or companion operations, sometimes funded by outside groups like the Annie E. Casey Foundation.

Spence, where he could, blew on the embers and fanned the flames. He began to replace old go-it-alone work styles with new platforms for collaboration. *Teams* took over caseloads from individual social workers. More hands on deck meant more chances to search out relatives, set up services, get help to families faster and before they fell into irreparable crisis. Teams helped reduce the caseworker's isolation and expose cases to more eyeballs. Problems surfaced sooner that once might have lingered hidden in a file swept into a drawer. Peers shared the burden, expertise, and emotional toll the work inflicted.

DSS introduced teaming pilots in 2003, telling all: "Figure it out, tell us what works, let us learn from you." Two years later the results were in: reports showed, among other results, that cases closed faster. That was good news.

The old belief that social workers, overwhelmed by impossible caseloads, had to "go it alone" was cracking.

DSS began to change the way families became part of the system. Spence instituted a new screening process, assessing at-risk families, making earlier and different interventions. Where a family was in trouble, for example, Spence expanded the network to find more levers of change and pull them sooner. He looked for ways that religious and neighborhood resources might contribute, for example. He created the practice of Family Group Conferencing (FGC), engaging extended family members, bringing them close, designing collaborative safety plans for the at-risk children. By 2006, every office in the state had a full-time FGC coordinator for such efforts.

Social workers no longer waited for abuse to take place. They moved into position to collaborate. The mind-set that parents were adversaries and children should be taken away at the first sign of danger gave way to a process that built from family strengths.

Spence began to change the culture from one of blame and punishment to one of continuous learning. Spence's message was simple. "You know bad things are going to happen despite our best effort. When those bad things happen, let us learn from them."

"The punishment culture was embedded heavily in DSS," Tim Callahan said. "If something happens to the kid on your watch and you did something wrong, you're responsible, and we're going to come after you.

"Harry really tried to change DSS into a place where you were learning," Callahan said. "And from a place where the family was going to be punished."

If central to the family practice model was the idea of building strengths, teaching parents to be better parents, the same held true for caseworkers.

"These were the values that Harry brought into the system," Robert Maker said. "He expected all social workers to treat people the way we expected to be treated."

"Yes," Callahan said, "the parents were often responsible for that abuse and neglect. But ultimately you have to work with the families to get the kids back in the home and make things right.

"Harry did not throw his own social workers under the bus. He relieved the social workers of feeling that if they made a mistake they were going to get punished, run up the pole, and fired."

Spence expected the same approach with the families. Make a

mistake? Learn from it. Break the cycle of punishment from corporate DSS to social worker to parent.

Spence expedited moving children out of residential centers back into communities and their homes Third-party providers were a critical part of the DSS care network. They had a huge financial stake in maintaining campus-based, residential treatment programs, if at all possible. Spence needed to get these kids back into communities, and get third-party providers to start up community-based care. It was controversial, but the DSS saw grudging progress.

With a change in administrations, Spence left the department in 2007, his work unfinished. His legacy has not resulted in a perfect department, nor one that has all the problems solved. Saving at-risk kids will always be tough, complicated, and exhausting work. But Spence turned strangers and adversaries into collaborators, and got a hidebound organization to collaborate around the goal of safer children and stronger families.

At his farewell party, Tomy Abraham presented Harry Spence with a gift from his staff: a replica of the Taj Mahal.

"The emperor built the Taj Mahal as a symbol of his love toward his wife. I thought it would be more appropriate, rather than a standard gift."

It shows what you can achieve with the power of a vision.

RIGHT-SIZE
THE PROBLEM

3

COLLABORATION ON THE SEAS

At 2:30 a.m. on February 7, 2003, a Cuban gunboat quietly docked at the Hyatt Marina in Key West, Florida. It had entered US waters, Key West's harbor, and finally the marina adjacent to the US Coast Guard station, undetected by the Coast Guard and the Navy.

The four men on the boat—Cuban border guards, all in full military uniform and carrying sidearms—strode up to the Hyatt front desk. The desk clerk, discovering that the men had neither room keys nor reservations, promptly turned them away.

Through the dead of night they wandered Key West—still armed and in full uniform—before finally coming upon a police officer to whom they surrendered.

Fortunately, the Cubans only wanted to defect.

The event has been recounted with some laughter. But as the Coast Guard commander who related this to us said, "It was no laughing matter that they were on American soil for four hours free to move a weapon inland and be gone."

It's not surprising that the Cuban gunboat went unnoticed; neither the Coast Guard nor the Navy had any detection measures in place where it docked.

If the 2001 World Trade Center attacks revealed security problems with airplanes, the Key West incident reminded everyone that the situation was even worse with ships. "We never knew what was going on in the oceans," explained Mike Krieger, director of Information Policy for the Department of Defense's chief information officer. "Hence we never knew what was coming to shore."

Port security had never been a Coast Guard priority. Safety on America's waterways and fighting the drug war on the seas? Yes. Port security?

"Prior to 9/11, I don't know that you could find anybody who knew what port security *was*," a shipping industry executive said. "I'm pretty sure it was just maybe three guys and a dog."

Even after 2001, some officials downplayed the threat of a ship's being weaponized and used as a bomb like the 9/11 jetliners. "I'm just saying it's more complicated," a Coast Guard executive explained. "There are a lot more folks involved in moving ships. Ships stay in channels. Use a ship as a weapon to bring a major bridge down? There are easier things to do."

Others perceived a serious danger. In the late fall of 2005, at President Bush's direction, US Navy and Coast Guard admirals convened in Colorado Springs to map out a formal Concept of Operations (ConOps) to achieve global "maritime domain awareness."

That was the vision. Collaborate with each other, share data, and understand the status of every ship, crew, and cargo afloat anywhere in the world. With good maritime domain awareness the world's navies, ports, and shippers could collaborate to assure commerce and protect shipping, harbors, and cities from attack.

But maritime domain awareness was so big a challenge, planners told the admirals that it would take eighteen months just to map out a plan to achieve it.

That's right—*eighteen months* to create a plan. In the meantime, new investments for maritime security would freeze. It made no sense for ports, companies, or agencies to spend money now on systems that might end up getting junked once the ConOps was finally agreed upon—not when you were fighting two wars and every nickel counted. While individual firms, ports, and agencies tightened security, the real move forward would have to wait for a ConOps.

Meanwhile, the ships and ports of the United States and its allies would remain vulnerable. Overseas, US warships and commercial vessels entering foreign harbors were blind to hidden perils, even though information about a dangerous ship, cargo, or crew could well be in another agency's or company's database. Whether from the bridge of an American aircraft carrier or the desk of a port director, everyone in the maritime domain, on land or sea, saw their small piece of the picture. But no ship driver, analyst, or port director saw any data but his own—or could connect the dots from all the different sources and tell friend from foe.

Here's an example. While the admirals were meeting in Colorado Springs, two thousand miles away a Coast Guard captain was inspecting the newly formed US Department of Homeland Security's New York Harbor Watch Center. Plasma displays showed every dock, warehouse, and pier in the harbor. If there was an incident, every watch center in harbors around the country could pick up the New York data feed and instantly see what was going on in New York. They could size up the threat to their own ports and take action.

Yet the Coast Guard captain was mystified. Despite all this high-tech wizardry the harbor's waterways appeared spotless in the displays. The docks, wharves, and buildings of the port were all there, but not a single vessel was visible in one of the world's busiest ports. Where were the *ships*?

The watch center, the captain learned, did not yet have that feed. So for now the guardians of the port had an accurate, live image of New York Harbor—except for the missing ships.

It was a sad statement on the security of all US ports at the time: no one who needed the whole picture had it. The Coast Guard had data on ships, Customs on cargoes, and the US Department of Transportation on crews. Shipping companies had some awareness of all those elements for their fleets. But no one could put it all together into a common operating picture that screamed to all, "Stop this ship *now*." The 9/11 Commission had warned about just such a problem. Those gaps left ports and harbors open to attack—or at least to a predawn landing by a Cuban gunboat!*

Back in Colorado Springs, as the three-day meeting was wrapping up,

---

*The "small boat" problem is one of the most difficult for US agencies to solve on land *or* sea. In 2002, the US Navy war-gamed Iranian speedboats attacking the US Persian Gulf fleet. American admirals were astonished to see the total destruction of the fleet by the more nimble craft. They reran the game. They lost the fleet *again*. "The whole thing was over in 5, maybe 10 minutes," said the general who led the simulated attack.

everyone seemed resigned to the eighteen-month timeline for developing a plan. Mike Krieger was the last to address the admirals. His charter from the Defense Department's chief information officer was to find and support small clusters of organizations willing to collaborate on tough information-sharing problems.

"I can have you sharing information in nine months," Krieger told the gathering. "You won't have all the answers, but you'll have a solid approach you can build on from there."

What Mike Krieger knew—and what perhaps had eluded the others—was that they could start collaborating faster by right-sizing the problem.

SUCCESS MEANS MOVING TOGETHER

In moving from a blue-sky vision to the first steps of collaboration, success depends on making sure everyone is ready to move together. Inevitably, someone will want to go right and someone will want to go left. Someone else won't know how to move at all. Conflict and confusion are common at the start of collaborations and occur frequently along the way. Folks are pushing and pulling in opposite directions. Folks are stalled by confusion.

To collaborate successfully, you need to right-size the problem—find common ground everyone can agree on now, figure out what can be done, and get started.

When you are first handed a problem, it's often the wrong size and shape. It's too big to take on by yourself, or too small to make a difference. Think of right-sizing the problem as prepping it—in the same way you would prep a room for painting. With a well-prepped problem, you can get everyone heading in the same direction and making a difference fast.

As the admirals and planners gathered in Colorado Springs realized all too well, establishing maritime domain awareness would inevitably lead to conflict over what should be done and confusion about how to do it.

"Achieve maritime domain awareness" was simply too large. But that's what the Navy and Coast Guard were used to: Big Problems that would take Big Time to fix with Big Solutions—building a new class of ship, for example, to handle a new mission or adversary. Those were the drills they knew how to run: first thing you do is build a ConOps. Never mind that all the while the risk to ports and ships remained, or that by the time the ConOps was finished the problem might have changed and the proposed solutions might already be out of date. Or that there was no agreement yet between the services on what a ConOps even *was*.

"Trying to get agreement on what the ConOps would entail was itself going to be an awful lot of work," Rear Admiral Joe Nimmich of the US Coast Guard said. Nimmich, with his Navy counterparts, was in charge of the Maritime Domain Awareness ConOps. Nimmich had seen these cross-agency ConOps get bogged down before. There was conflict ahead over *what* should be done, and even if that got settled, confusion about *how* to do it. "Every agency," Nimmich said, "had a different approach."

Mike Krieger proposed an immediate next move that could be implemented quickly: form a small cross-agency group of topflight talent that could take up a piece of the challenge and deliver a solution within nine to twelve months. The point was to get everyone moving in the same direction—to actually *do* something—without waiting a year and a half for a comprehensive plan.

"Mike Krieger said, 'I can help you start sharing information fast,'" Rear Admiral Joe Nimmich recalled. "This resonated with me."

Continue to develop the ConOps, Krieger urged, but give him a small team of Navy and Coast Guard technicians, operators, and contractors— a Community of Interest (COI)—and let him push ahead as well. The COI could complete a smaller piece of the challenge without waiting for a ConOps.

Nimmich backed Krieger's idea and recruited US Navy Rear Admiral

Nancy E. Brown to cosponsor the effort. This was good news for Mike Krieger. Nancy Brown carried the prestige and credibility of a combatant commander: she was the senior-most officer responsible for all systems for the US North American Command (NORTHCOM). Two admirals, one Navy and one Coast Guard, cosponsored both the ConOps and Krieger's Community of Interest.

While members of the group began to work on the ConOps, Krieger's team worked to right-size "achieve maritime domain awareness" down to a next-best move that would offer the admirals a meaningful solution, however partial, fast.

Nine months later, Krieger delivered.

CONFLICT AND CONFUSION

Before getting into the details of *how* Krieger made good on his promise, let's look at the two enemies of collaboration—conflict and confusion. We want to look at how others sidestepped them by right-sizing the problem.

Conflict occurs when people disagree about *what* to do. Elizabeth Holtzman and Ben Ward were in conflict about whether to move forward at *all* to ease the logjams in Brooklyn. There was no mystery about *how* to do it; but where Ward thought the delays were a small price to pay for labor peace, Holtzman saw them as intolerable for everyone.

Confusion occurs when people are unclear about *how* to do something. Think back to the story of Doug Hull. Canada's leaders knew what they wanted: to connect all Canadians to the Internet. But they fretted about the *how* and the *who*: How fast could a national Internet infrastructure be built? How should Canada balance competition and regulation? How could Canadians be assured of universal access at reasonable cost? Who should pay for it?

Sidestepping the "Big Solutions" confusion, Hull right-sized the problem down to a smaller goal everyone knew how to solve: get a few computers into the schools now. Network them. Get some value into the hands of a few users right away. And see what happens.

Hull didn't need extensive analysis. He didn't have to negotiate grand goals. Here's the promise, he said, and the deal; let's try this out. The answer from Ottawa was "Sure."

The two-by-two table below, adapted from a table originally developed by Harvard professor Jerry Mechling, can help to show where you stand in terms of conflict and confusion—and what you need to do to get your partners ready to collaborate.

Each quadrant has its own degree of conflict and confusion.

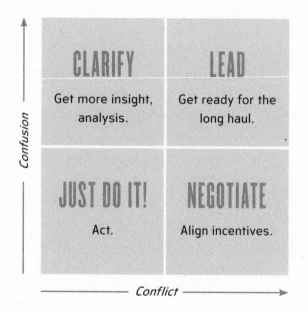

CLARIFY: Conflict is low, but confusion is high. You will need to clarify how to proceed before collaboration can begin. That could involve more analysis; tests, proofs, and pilots; and perhaps training.

LEAD: Conflict *and* confusion are high. Right-sizing is extremely important. If you can't right-size your way out of this quadrant, be prepared for a long haul.

JUST DO IT!: Here, everyone agrees on where to go and they know what to do to get there. You are good to go.

NEGOTIATE: Confusion is low, but conflict is high. You have fundamental disagreements about *what* to do next. Right-sizing may not resolve all disagreements, but it will get you to a next step everyone can agree on.

SCOPE AND DELIVER

When Krieger's COI first met in 2006, he told its members, "When you've got a problem like this"—a problem that stretches across organizational boundaries—"the first step is to define why you want to get together, what problem you're solving, and say it in one sentence."

The group settled on the statement: "Let's get some worldwide situational awareness of what's on the seas."

After all, the Navy, Coast Guard, and, joining a bit later, the Department of Transportation each had some of that data, so the problem seemed addressable. Collaborating, they could create that common operating picture all wanted but none had.

The COI had taken its first step toward right-sizing the problem. But it was still huge. No one knew what to do next. There was still a great deal of confusion and potential conflict.

Mike Krieger told the COI, "The second step is to scope a capability you can deliver in six, nine, or twelve months. The goal is to get some capability into the hands of users fast—even if it delivers a fifty percent solution," he said.

"It took us awhile to stumble on that," Krieger said. "The COI settled on this as a partial solution: 'Why don't we share the data from each of our databases and see if everybody in the community can see everyone else's data in their own native software systems?'" Sharing it would help bring the picture of what was on the water clearly into focus.

Right-sizing was beginning to have its effect: consensus was emerging, confusion falling.

But trying to share *all* information right away and make sense of it still would create a massive challenge. Each database used different names for the same object. There were thousands of different objects. The database owners would have to agree, for example, that the object terms *ship, boat,* and *vessel* would mean the same thing across all systems, and then "wrap" every mention of a ship, boat, and vessel in their databases with a single agreed-upon tag. That way, if you searched on the agreed-upon tag you'd see every ship, boat, or vessel no matter what anyone called it.

With thousands of maritime object terms in their databases, getting agreements on tags and then executing could take months and millions of dollars. The COI would have a lot of wrapped terms to show for it—a partial solution, yes, but one that gave no proof that the tagging process would achieve maritime domain awareness.

The group considered. What if we do this for a few important terms like *vessel*? Run a test. Prove that anyone authorized would have to search only for the agreed-upon tag in any of the databases to discover all mentions of everything afloat, regardless of what the different databases called these objects. Make the *ship/boat/vessel* visible in each agency's native viewer so no special software would be required. Prove you could agree on terms, wrap and tag, and search, discover, and display every ship/boat/vessel afloat that anyone had data on, even if you didn't have data yourself. You could see what everyone else saw. Their eyes would become yours, and yours theirs.

Welcome to the Just Do It! quadrant. Step by step, the COI scoped its problem down from "let's build worldwide situational awareness" to "let's share information in our databases," to "let's agree on the shared meaning of a few terms, tag those terms, and see if we can search for, find, and display them—no matter whose database they're in."

That was what the group felt it could deliver in nine to twelve months.

———

t was now a well-defined problem, "simple in the extreme," recalled John Shea, the COI's project manager. "When we search for a tag, can we find it? When we pull the data up into our native viewers, can we see it?"

In his day job Shea was technical director for the US Navy's "C4I" network operations—command, control, computers, and communications. He was already at work on the Navy's own version of maritime domain awareness when he got pulled into the project. The COI collaboration took Shea across boundaries, beyond just Navy systems and into those of the Coast Guard and Department of Transportation. But a successful collaboration would not only save Shea time, money, and work but also give the Navy something it would never have going it alone: the eyes and ears of the other networks added to its own awareness of the maritime domain.

Technically, Shea knew, the COI's goal wasn't hard to achieve. Database administrators knew how to wrap and tag terms. But getting agreements could be tough. Shea was willing to see whether this new collaboration across boundaries would work—whether it made sense to forgo the old habit of going it alone in favor of collaborating.

By November 2006, the COI was ready to show the results of its work to the highest levels of the Navy and Coast Guard. In the boardroom of the chief of naval operations, the COI team put up a display of Singapore Harbor taken from a single system on board a US Navy vessel. It showed five hundred ships. At the push of a button, new data were added from the Department of Transportation, the Coast Guard, and the Office of Naval Intelligence. Now fifteen hundred vessels appeared on the display, many far out of view, over the horizon.

"Remember what a ship driver wants," Shea said. "The ship driver is definitely afraid of the things that he doesn't know. He wants information. What surrounds me? What kinds of ships? 'Oh, there's a liquefied natural gas ship coming by,' or 'there's a ship loaded with sulfites,' or a ship that's on the 'bad ship' list. All that information wasn't available to them on a timely basis before.

"Now, if I'm a ship a hundred miles away, I can see what's going on. We showed them a way of not only enhancing the information for a particular ship, but how to share that situational awareness with the world."

The COI didn't solve the entire problem of maritime security. But it addressed a small piece fast—delivering a new and vital capability that could be scaled and repeated. Where before all the players saw only their own piece of the picture, now they could access and understand others'. That capability was huge. It gave mariners of all stripes—ship captains, admirals, fleet owners, intelligence analysts—a common operating picture of the maritime domain.

"That is what we've been looking for," the Navy and Coast Guard brass agreed. "Let's expand it."

Again, you don't need to tackle the entire problem all at once. Mike Krieger's mantra was "scope and deliver." Scope the problem down to something that "goes against the problem"—chips away at it—and get a partial solution into users' hands fast. Set a deadline and establish benchmarks to keep on schedule. Cut the conflict and the confusion. Get everyone moving in the same direction through collaboration. Get some early wins. Then repeat.

That's the heart of right-sizing.

BILL BRATTON in Los Angeles

The LAPD had been in conflict with itself and with Los Angeles for fifty years. Little had changed by the time I arrived in 2002—except by then the "thin blue line"—a term coined by LAPD chief William Parker in the 1960s—had worn desperately thin.

LA had always starved its police department of resources, and the city—its communities, businesses, and government—was paying for it.

After forty years of "my way or the highway, we'll go it alone, no one does it better" policing, the LAPD had cost itself support, equipment, facilities, and officers. Through scandal, corruption, and violence, it had been failing for years, with rising crime rates and citizen dissatisfaction and anger, particularly in the poor minority communities. Now the LAPD was under a federal court's supervision and consent decree, its every move under a microscope, every shred of resources devoted to compliance.

Meanwhile, crime was growing, community fears were rising, and terror in the wake of 9/11 was a new and pressing demand.

In LA, "the thin blue line" had never been about a few police trying to keep the forces of anarchy at bay as much as it was a line to keep whites separate from blacks, the poor separate from the rich. "If the community and the political leadership leave me alone," Parker seemed to say, "I'll take care of business."

The affluent would stay safe in their walled gardens. How many more police did LA need for that mission?

In the '70s and '80s, as drugs, crime, and gangs soared, the LAPD adapted by becoming more aggressive, more controlling, more commanding, and, from the perspective of the community's minorities, more abusive.

The LAPD—much like the NYPD—was built in silos. The patrol bureau, detective bureau, narcotics bureau, administrative bureau, and tactical special operations bureau were each under independent commands. These tall vertical units had very little interaction; each bureau was separate, coming together at only one place: the chief at the top of the department.

With resources strapped, each department clawed for its share of a shrinking pie. Collaboration? Forget about it. Sharing? Only when ordered. Coordination? Very difficult.

During this era, Chief Daryl Gates took perverse pride in this hardening of the police line, wearing his poor relations with city hall like a badge of honor even as the LAPD ran on fumes. Who paid? Communities suffering crime and disorder; the rank and file driving around in ten-year-old cruisers and working out of police stations that were dumps. On Gates's watch the growth in the number of cops didn't keep pace with the city's surging population and growing problems—a disaster that the city and its police department would pay for dearly in years to come.

Two chiefs later, in 2002, not much had changed. That's where I came in.

The city in many respects was where New York City was in the 1990s. Things had been bad and they seemed to be getting worse. Nothing was working.

I was going to need support for a number of goals, including growing the size of the LAPD. The NYPD had thirty-eight thousand cops; LAPD had nine thousand. Getting money to hire more cops would not be easy in a city that so deeply distrusted its police force. The city council would sooner cut cops than libraries. I understood that—but it was a false choice.

My job was to help make that choice easier—actually, to change the choice. To make them understand that with more cops more people would feel safe to walk the streets, more people would use the libraries. The libraries would be empty if people were terrified to leave their houses and apartments.

In New York I had a large police force and was able to initiate changes in all precincts at the same time. In LA I would not have the resources to make an impact everywhere at once. Instead of tackling the whole city at once, I decided to right-size the problem by concentrating on five key areas of Los Angeles. We chose them for what they represented, as well as for their potential for success. We'd use these as miniature laboratories for a number of strategies and tactics. We called the initiative Safer City.

Through success in the Safer City initiative, the LAPD would learn for itself what it could do. It would build support at the grass roots. We would trust that everyone working together could make progress and that would make it hard for politicians to say "no" to our budget requests for more staff, equipment, and facilities.

All five of the targeted areas were in significant crisis when we started. Some had been given up for lost.

MacArthur Park was overrun by gangs. It was a beautiful park, similar to New York's Bryant Park—and in need of the same turnaround. Businesses, restaurants, Loyola University, and the Mexican Consulate all sat on its periphery. The potential was there. The idea was to reclaim this famous park that has been featured in just about every movie that's been made about Los Angeles. It would serve as a symbol to show that even in the midst of a gang-controlled area, the police—in collaboration with the community—could dramatically improve the quality of life.

A second area was Baldwin Village. It abutted a well-to-do African American neighborhood, Baldwin Hills. And it was almost adjacent to the University of Southern California, as USC was starting to expand from downtown. But the area was deeply affected by gang problems exacerbated by the movement of Latino gangs into a neighborhood once dominated by blacks. It had been the scene of a number of high-profile incidents.

Hollywood was the third area. Hollywood and Los Angeles are inseparable in the public's imagination. It's where people go when they come to Los Angeles as tourists. But the Hollywood visitors experienced in the 1980s was sordid; it had a lot of crime, and it was barely hanging on.

By the late '90s Hollywood was experiencing a bit of a building boom and renaissance. Sunset Strip and Hollywood Boulevard had been improved, and the billion-dollar Kodak Theatre was the new home for the Academy Awards. The area had begun to tip in a positive way, but the recovery was fragile.

The fourth area we would target was the San Fernando Valley.

Politically, I had to do something in the Valley, home to much of the city's middle class. It had about a third of the city's population. Five of the city's fifteen council members represented it. It's more suburban than other parts of Los Angeles, but it also had a growing gang problem. In certain parts of the Valley business areas were trying to come back. Some housing developments showed promise. But like the rest of Los Angeles, it was really struggling. The Valley felt alienated from the city proper to such an extent that it had recently attempted to secede from Los Angeles and form its own city.

Last was the area known as Skid Row, in the heart of downtown Los Angeles. It reminded me of how parts of New York City looked in the late 1980s. This, though, was the worst skid row in America—block after block of blight, decay, homeless shelters, tent cities, and tens of thousands of people living on the street twenty-four hours a day.

All of this existed literally next to police headquarters and city hall, adjacent to the downtown area and the business financial district. The *Los Angeles Times* sat on the edge of Skid Row. Reporters could look out their windows to see it. It was an example of government out of control, of a city that didn't care. Hundreds of thousands of people saw it every day as they passed through to get to work, school, or the Staples Center or L.A. Live sports and entertainment complex.

It was also an area that showed the first signs of the gentrification that had gone on in New York City in TriBeCa and SoHo. Along Main Street, which was one of the border areas, pioneers had opened restaurants. It was becoming a destination location. Apartments were becoming available as developers bought up buildings and renovated them. Professional people, singles and couples, were moving into the area. The "dog factor"—people out walking their pets in the morning and the evening—went up.

So it was an area in transition. Of all our efforts, this was probably going to be the one area that would attract the most attention in terms of advocates, media coverage, and political leadership.

Focusing on Skid Row, we once again right-sized the problem. The people who lived in those tent cities that clogged the sidewalks and created an atmosphere of lawlessness and despair suffered from a number of problems—drug addiction, alcoholism, joblessness. There was a huge mentally challenged population.

We dealt with professionals who had very different ideas and theories about what to do—what caused homelessness, how the city should respond, how to treat the illnesses involved, what the role of the police should be. The Business Improvement Districts (BIDS, as they are commonly known), for example, had been fighting the health care professionals who were running the missions. Some factions even viewed efforts to clean up the area with suspicion—seeing it as a way to push vulnerable people out of sight without addressing any of their needs.

Rather than engage in the debate, we broke the problem down into parts that everyone, at least for the time being, could agree on: high levels of violent crime, hospitals dumping indigent patients still in their wheelchairs and hospital gowns onto the streets; frequent traffic fatalities involving intoxicated people; gangs dealing drugs; kindhearted charities donating clothing and food that simply became more garbage and filth. By coordinating all our efforts, we would reduce the overall chaos of the tent city culture and the harm it was causing everyone—especially the residents themselves. After everyone saw positive results, we could decide what to do next, while they continued the debate about homelessness and its causes.

I was fortunate that I had capable police leaders down on Skid Row. One of those police commanders was Charlie Beck, who is now the chief of police of Los Angeles. Charlie "got" community policing. He had a lot of specialized units down there, including a homeless outreach team—officers who'd volunteered to spend their time

BRATTON

working with the most troubled people on the street. They were highly committed, highly focused, highly engaged, highly motivated. There just weren't enough of them. To take this challenge on, they would need a surge of their own.

We faced plenty of opposition. A radical group made up largely of homeless and student activists, LA CAN, criticized the gentrification efforts. Throughout, the ACLU was critical of department policies, though never of our leadership. The fights were over our methods, not the people involved. It was understood that we were all taking different paths to get to a similar goal—that we were all interested in the well-being of these people.

We ended up with a number of court suits that defined what we could or could not do in policing that area. We had to work out some agreed-upon protocols, new ordinances relative to the ability of people to occupy public space. So Skid Row had lots of conflict, but it was also about a new collaboration.

The court orders delayed us for almost a year. During that time, Skid Row grew much worse. Once we had these clarifications and tools, we took the seemingly negative news of court orders and turned them into a positive against the worsening crisis. The original crisis of Skid Row was now exacerbated to the point that people were ready for change. We were able to get in there and tip it much more quickly than we would have been able to a year earlier.

I assigned an additional fifty officers to the area. Their role was to enforce quality-of-life initiatives, to give us a sizable police presence to break up the street drug dealing and all the other stuff that gets people off the sidewalks. The city attorney assigned additional resources to help us with the increased numbers of arrests and citations. The mayor was critical in getting coordination of the other city agencies. We got an additional 150 streetlights installed. The Business Improvement Districts collaborated on garbage pickup— thousands of people living on the streets can generate incredible amounts of trash.

And the city attorney was able to make some very strong cases against some of the largest hospitals in Los Angeles for dumping patients onto the street. That helped engage the *Los Angeles Times* and brought additional attention to how bad things were down here.

There was something in this for everybody. And that is what collaboration often is about—what's in it for me?

For the business improvement districts, it was a better environment in which to operate; for the new residents, a safer home. For the homeless, it was safer, too: the number of assaults and deaths and the number of hospital runs and admissions went down. The homeless were, in many respects, physically better off.

People who had been fighting each other or working at odds were standing together on common ground. We showed that we could bring the city attorney, the mayor, the county government, and other municipal leaders into the mix and create the critical mass that could then take on the critics, when necessary, and prove them wrong.

There are still people living on the streets of Skid Row, but the number's way down from the five thousand to seven thousand a night that used to be there—now on average there are fifteen hundred per night, an 80 percent reduction. When you drive to Skid Row in the daytime now you're not going to see tent cities blocking the sidewalk. You're not going to see open-air drug dealing; that's not to say you won't see any drug dealing, but you won't see it in the great amounts you did in the past. It is cleaner and safer for everybody.

As we moved into those other areas targeted in the Safer City program, we continued the process of right-sizing the problems, breaking them down into smaller problems. LAPD continued to be the principal catalyst for change. But the police could not have dealt with these situations alone. Each involved collaboration among police, community, city, and business resources.

BRATTON

BRATTON

Once we tipped an area, we wouldn't take those resources out. We were there to stay—to show that with collaboration we could succeed against these intractable problems.

With our successes, finally, we were able to get political, business, and community support to grow the department by one thousand officers. Most people felt I had good budgets. I think I had okay budgets. But I had to work like hell to get them. While the increased number of cops helped, ultimately it was how they were focused and used that made the difference all could see.

FOUR TESTS OF READINESS FOR COLLABORATION

As you look at a challenge, how can you tell if it's shaped and sized right for collaboration, and ready to move on together?

Here are four tests that can help you figure out whether you need to clarify because confusion is high; or negotiate to deal with conflict; or both, because everyone is conflicted *and* confused—or, if you are ready for action, to "Just Do It!"

THE CRUSH TEST: In his book *The Character of Harms,* Harvard professor Malcolm Sparrow writes, "The Crush Test says, basically, 'How would I feel if I were made responsible for solving this problem? Would it feel overwhelming and hopeless? Or would it feel challenging, but possible?' "

When you right-size the problem to a goal you can achieve—creating a *vision* of getting to the top and a *plan* to take the next step—you move from "overwhelming and hopeless" to "challenging, but possible." That's what Mike Krieger did with the Maritime Domain Awareness COI. They right-sized this Big Problem down to something John Shea called "simple in the extreme."

THE RESULTS TEST: The Crush test addresses the *emotional* side of right-sizing a problem, but a problem can't be so small that moving it makes no difference.

Food Lion and Kimberly-Clark right-sized their stock-out problem down to a clear plan of action with defined metrics: get more up-to-date in-store data to sales; keep the shelves filled; avoid stock-outs; increase sales.

You can make a difference based on that and fix something. The problem is right-sized, and the Results test will prove it.

THE "AMEN!" TEST: Have you charged people up to get them supporting you? Is the team excited about solving the problem? When your partners are enthusiastic about being involved, they will put their shoulders against the shared obstacle and push, big time.

Mike Krieger's proposal earned the support of Admirals Nimmich and Brown. It promised results faster than the ConOps, while keeping the ConOps moving, too. The prospect of a win that saved time, staff, and money jazzed up John Shea. The display showing fifteen hundred ships rather than the original five hundred energized the admirals in the boardroom of the chief of naval operations. At each step, the COI passed the "Amen!" test.

You improve your chances of passing the "Amen!" test if you get results in the hands of users fast. As Krieger showed, you don't have to solve the whole problem, just "go against it"—that gets a partial solution into users' hands. The faster you do that, the faster the "Amens!" will come.

If you can leave that partial solution behind for folks to continue using while you move forward—so much the better. Maybe they'll customize it, and you can add those improvements to your next version. Users will become advocates, and add their "Amens!" to the chorus.

Doug Hull built networks of advocates doing exactly that.

THE SANDBOX TEXT: Last, there's the *political* side of right-sizing. That means making sure you have the right partners collaborating with you.

Sometimes, especially in a networked world, you right-size the problem by making it bigger—by up-sizing—to bring in partners who can make the difference.

"Problems that resist solution can often have their backs broken by enlarging the system we consider changing," said Russell Ackoff. Broaden a narrow problem and often you will find more levers for change.

NYPD CompStat did exactly that. CompStat *expanded* the sandbox to include the courts, corrections, probation, and the DA's offices—the entities that controlled the system that set the price of crime in New York. Until CompStat convinced them to play in its sandbox, the NYPD had pretty much given up altogether on enforcement against "minor" crimes. The streets of New York showed it.

The US Secret Service did something similar a few years back. The Secret Service's twenty-five hundred special agents had always collaborated with local law enforcement agencies. There is no way the Feds can go it alone when protecting the president. Theirs is a risky business, requiring every resource available. Since Lincoln, one-third of US presidents have been physically attacked—and four of twenty-nine assassinated.

In the post-9/11 world, where threats emerge faster than ever, the Secret Service had to adapt. But its computer systems were dilapidated and its technology staff inadequate. There wasn't enough money in the budget for the needed upgrades, and competing for its slice of a too-small pie would still leave the Secret Service starved for needed funding. So the Secret Service turned to collaboration and right-sizing.

Rob Zitz was on loan to the Secret Service from the National Geospatial-Intelligence Agency to help the Service rebuild its computing platform. An experienced technologist, adept at budgets and bureaucracies, and well-connected in the intelligence community, Zitz turned first to his colleagues in the agencies—would they lend the Secret Service staff to help develop its systems? Of course.

Next, Zitz helped colleagues throughout the intelligence community join forces to deal with a problem they all shared: *everyone's* IT systems were too antiquated to address the threats all faced.

Instead of fighting over pieces of a too-small budget that would make little difference even if successful, Zitz upsized his problem to make it a shared one and bring in more partners. Collaborating, the Secret Service and its partners successfully pushed for—and got—more IT money for everyone.

Managing a collaboration sometimes involves right-sizing a problem in *both* directions—up *and* down—to build support and achieve the results you need.

Right-sizing is dynamic. Some days you right-size up, and the next, as new problems arise, down. In LA, for example, Safer City right-sized the problem *down* to five priority areas. With its small patrol force, the LAPD couldn't make a difference everywhere. Whenever they tried to, they would fail. Once the LAPD right-sized the problem down, it took on issues that mattered, achieved results that showed, and gained a chorus of "Amens!" from cops and community leaders to newspapers and politicians.

But the LAPD also right-sized the problem *up* in a way that passed the Sandbox test—by bringing allies into play who were crucial for success. Partners such as the city attorney, the mayor, and business and civic interests brought authorities and resources; they funded new streetlights and sanitation and changed hospital routines and practices. Collaborating, they burnished the Safer City effort with political support and economic development.

In both LA's Safer City and New York's CompStat, problems that could have been framed as "the police department needs more funding" or "there's too much crime" were right-sized down to "scope and deliver" and right-sized up to bring more collaborators into the game, gaining their tactical help and political support.

TOMATOES, TRACEBACKS, AND SALMONELLA

ZACH TUMIN

Four months into 2008's raging salmonella *Saintpaul* outbreak, fourteen hundred Americans lay sickened in twenty states. In May the US Centers for Disease Control (CDC) blamed tomatoes. By June the CDC said it wasn't so sure. By July the CDC still hadn't decided what had caused the outbreak, but it was now pretty sure that it wasn't tomatoes.

The "all clear" for tomatoes came too late for hundreds of growers, packers, shippers, and seasonal workers. By then US restaurants, wholesalers, and stores had canceled tomato orders totaling $100 million.

Tomato businesses in California, Florida, and Mexico were staggered. And the US Food and Drug Administration (FDA) reeled, running down dead-end leads to the wrong farms searching for the wrong produce, all in the national spotlight.

The traceback investigation, as it was called, had become a nightmare—for food safety, the FDA, and industry. It was August, four months in, and the FDA was back at square one. Tempers were short, and fortunes were at stake.

There was no shortage of questions. Why didn't the FDA use the agricultural industry's own data to do a faster traceback from store to farm—and sound the "all clear" sooner? The information needed was right there in the invoices for every transaction along the supply chain.

For that matter, many wondered why the FDA was slogging through invoices at all while big retailers like Walmart could just "flip a switch" and see their entire distribution chain on computer displays in minutes?

The FDA and industry were at each other's throats just when they most needed to collaborate.

The FDA food safety czar, Dr. David Acheson, and I decided to create a temporary collaboration platform—a safe, trusted place away from the fray of Washington where all could have frank dialogue and together find a path forward. We invited FDA chieftains, state food safety executives, tomato industry leaders, and technologists to a one-day roundtable in Cambridge.

The discussion was candid and charged.

"You're looking in the wrong place and hosing us with information requests. We have everything you need. Just ask the right question!" Ed Beckman, a tomato industry executive, exclaimed.

"You don't understand *what* we need," Jeff Farrar fired back. Farrar at the time was head of food safety for the state of California. "We have done tracebacks where we have been presented with shoe boxes and written notes: 'Here're my invoices, my traceback information, here's the keys to the attic, you guys figure it out.' Boxes upon boxes of meaningless printouts."

"You do not know our systems," charged Martin Ley, a major Mexican tomato producer. "You only knock on the door or ring the phone when there's a problem. 'Death shows up with a plate'— that's what we say when you walk in with a uniform and tell us, 'Hey, we need information.' "

It was a rough crowd—angry, with some good work together in the past, but once again riven with distrust. Between them they shared a food safety system that kept America's food supply astonishingly safe most days, but failed in crisis.

There was hope, though, in a shared vision. It was in all parties' interest to keep America's food as safe as possible. What both sides needed was a process for collaborating in advance of a crisis so that when a crisis hit, everyone was already connected, communicating and collaborating, and they could end the crisis fast.

Where to start?

David Acheson began to bring the problem down out of the clouds, making a first pass at right-sizing the problem. "The key here is speed," Acheson said. "We've got to be able to run these tracebacks not as an indictment of an industry but to test our hypothesis about what's happening in the field. Even before all the facts are in, continuously narrow it down, and throw resources against the emerging culprits."

Speed was important to everyone: the sooner the FDA could help the CDC clear certain produce and regions, the faster commerce could resume, and the smaller the industry's loss. At the moment it was taking months.

The FDA moved in painfully slow motion, starting only after the CDC identified the culprit fruit or vegetable. That could be weeks after the first reports of infection. Once in the game, the FDA would have to hunt down the farm source by slogging through paper invoices. They'd try to rule out some fields and focus on others based on evidence that might have long since vanished, or on memories stretched to the limit trying to recall what someone had for breakfast three weeks earlier.

What if the FDA could begin its process of elimination lightning fast, when the first clusters of infected folks showed up in hospital reports? What if the FDA could know, even before the CDC did, what foods could and could not be the source of the outbreak? That would help the CDC, growers, and shippers everywhere, and the FDA. There was something in it for everyone.

The Cambridge parties agreed that faster tracebacks would be awesome.

"The fact is," Acheson said, "we are never going to get the 'last mile' figured out without FDA investigators pounding the pavement." He was referring to the very end of the food distribution system, which was crowded with tens of thousands of mom-and-pop restaurants and stores that bought their produce from thousands of wholesalers, often using paper invoices. "That last leg from the store or the restaurant back to the wholesaler is just a hard slog. So be it."

Everyone had been stuck trying to figure this out. In a traceback, the "last mile" of sale became the "first mile" of the FDA's hunt. With thousands of mom-and-pop shop retailers and restaurateurs, how could any initiative that promised faster tracebacks deliver so long as it was stuck wading through all those "last mile" points of sale?

But Acheson had his eye on the entire supply chain. He saw a lot of promise in the early and middle sections—from the farms to the distributors to the wholesalers.

The wholesalers, he knew, bought their produce from relatively few distributors, who in turn bought from well-known farms. This part of the supply chain was all electronically invoiced. That meant there should be data that would be easy to get ahold of—from wholesalers back through distributors to farms. In other words, the middle part of the food supply chain could be illuminated easily and quickly all the way back to the farms.

Eventually, all roads from a mom-and-pop shop, store, or restaurant would lead to their wholesaler. Once we know there's an outbreak, Acheson was saying, let's illuminate all the supply chains we can from the farms forward to the wholesalers electronically.

And there, we'll wait for the front end investigation to reach us. Once it reaches us, we'll trace the suspect supply chains back to the source in minutes.

That, all agreed, could speed up the traceback by days or even weeks.

It would be transformative. Even before the hard slog finished, the FDA could look at the farm-to-wholesaler chains and the

hospital clusters of infection, and rule out certain regions or vegetables as the source of the infection. No tomato from California
ever got shipped to a wholesaler supplying Milwaukee, for example,
where hospital cases clustered.

Acheson's insight into right-sizing a problem gave the group
permission to forget about the unsolvable for now. "Let's go for the
win we can get here first," he was saying. Get a partial solution into
users' hands fast.

Did industry have the farm-to-distributor-to-wholesaler data that
the FDA required? Discord surfaced again. Industry said the data it
collected on invoices was just what the FDA needed, but the FDA was
skeptical.

Two weeks later, industry executives showed us they did have
data captured electronically on invoices. The FDA agreed it was
exactly what it needed for its investigations. Beckman's group
showed they could stitch the data together so that a spreadsheet
tracked a single tomato as it was boxed, reboxed, packed, and
shipped to its wholesaler. Two weeks after that our team of technologists from TIBCO/Spotfire and Microsoft had converted the
spreadsheet data to visualizations—pictures of the network—that
made it easy to watch hundreds of thousands of tomatoes move
from farm to distribution center to wholesaler.

Gradually, with a feasible target in site, conflict and confusion
were falling away. A picture of an American wholesale distribution
network for tomatoes was literally emerging for the first time. FDA
officials responsible for the tracebacks were amazed. "We are seeing the light at the mouth of the cave," one said.

Could FDA investigators use this data and the visualizations to
run a simulated traceback? Speed was good, everyone agreed. But
the proof would be in the execution.

In the summer of 2009, we ran a test with FDA investigators
using the data and the visualization displays. With seasoned indus-

try experts as guides making sense of arcane produce-industry business processes and data, the FDA investigators completed the simulated traceback from wholesaler to distributor to farm . . . in thirty minutes.

Acheson's insight helped this group start right-sizing a problem away from something too big to solve down to the "Amen!" corner, where everyone agreed on a way to slice days, weeks, and even months off the traceback.

MAKE A CLEARING

4

A platform is where people come together to collaborate. If you have no platform, there can be no collaboration.

What do we mean by a platform? Most people associate the term *platform* with technology. The Microsoft Windows operating system, for example, is a well-known platform for integrating your computer programs.

But our concept of *platform* is much bigger than that. The military thinks of its planes and ships as combat platforms, for example. Citibank might think of its branches as platforms where people manage their money. A hospital's surgical rooms are high-performance platforms—in fact, the entire hospital is a platform where doctors and sick people easily find each other and engage.

While platforms are about more than technology, increasingly today collaboration takes place on digital platforms. Google is a platform that links advertisers with searchers; Twitter is a platform where people exchange brief, anywhere-anytime messages.

All platforms are *clearings*, spaces that make it easy for folks to find each other, engage, and, if all goes well, collaborate to achieve something together they can't accomplish alone. A platform should be the WD-40—the lubricating oil—of collaboration. Some platforms are exclusive by design; others are intended to attract new partners, growing the network and increasing the power of the collaboration.

A platform, ultimately, is where you meet up to work together on solving right-sized problems to achieve a blue-sky vision.

BUILDING A PLATFORM TO EDUCATE A CITY

Signing on as secretary of education for the municipality of Rio de Janeiro, Claudia Costin inherited a platform for the schooling of children that was broken: inefficient, ineffective, and tragically inequitable.

A longtime public servant, World Bank official, and policy wonk, Costin was shocked upon entering office in 2008 to discover how badly the system was serving its one million elementary, middle school, and high school students. Forty percent tested below grade level in math; twenty-eight thousand students from the fourth, fifth, and sixth grades were completely illiterate. "Social promotion"—passing students on to the next grade no matter how ill prepared—was rampant. Even so, many students were much older than grade level. Having started school late, they sat in classrooms with children two and three years younger.

Unequipped to pursue or even imagine a better future, children were easy to exploit. "It is my strong belief that it's not acceptable that a ten-year-old kid will be working for narco-traffickers," Costin told a gathering of industry and government executives. "Twelve-year-old girls are being prostituted because they want to have kids from those guys because they will be respected if they are mothers. So, I want to change the lives of those kids."

These were complex problems, but Costin held to a simple vision: "You have to have the teachers with you. You have to build trust in the teachers. Otherwise, you won't change education."

Costin breathed life into platforms for communication and engagement that have encouraged teachers to collaborate with her on school reform efforts. While her efforts were anything but haphazard, she discovered one of the most powerful aspects of her platform by accident

"Let me be frank. I entered Twitter because I have five kids," Costin said. "One of them was in Italy. And I wanted to connect. One of the kids—they are my teachers in technology—said, 'Let's write what you're doing.' And then I noticed that teachers were following.

"I said, 'Why are they following? Why do they want to know what

I'm saying to my daughter in Italy?' Very quickly I discovered that Twitter is the key for success in mobilizing teachers."

In today's digital world, serendipity can be a potent force for finding and making new "friends" fast. But converting "friends" and "followers" into collaborators takes work. Since stumbling onto the power of Twitter, Costin has zealously taken advantage of it. She spends two hours each day communicating with her more than sixteen thousand followers, many of them teachers. Those exchanges are the cornerstone of a complex platform for collaboration that also includes e-mail, a private online channel called "Fala, Professor!" ("Speak, Teacher!"), and intensive in-person engagement.

Rio de Janeiro's teachers had for a long time felt abandoned. First the middle class fled Rio's schools, leaving only the children of the desperately poor behind. Then the state let the schools physically crumble—plumbing, electrical systems, and air-conditioning were in disrepair. Some teachers, frustrated and dejected, developed chronic absenteeism; administrators turned on many teachers for the sins of a few. Finally civil authorities fled narco-trafficker-controlled areas until the schools were the state's last outpost standing—surrounded by gunfire and armed gangs, a traverse of filth and danger that teachers and students had to cross simply to reach the school grounds.

The municipality of Rio de Janeiro was failing its schools, and as a platform for education, the schools were failing Rio's children. Costin sought a clearing—a safe zone—where teachers could find her, catch their breath, and together begin the arduous process of healing themselves, recommitting to their profession, and restoring Rio's schools.

Twitter helped her engage lightly, broadcasting answers to all. The "Fala, Professor!" platform was where more serious work on online collaboration took place. To get everyone moving quickly in the same direction, she right-sized the problem. "We decided to first offer a task to start with, 'What should the teachers teach, the kids learn?'" Costin said.

"Here is the current existing guideline for curriculum," she offered. "Propose your changes." Using the "Fala, Professor!" platform, teachers did exactly that. It was a much-needed icebreaker. "They didn't trust us," Costin said. "In the beginning my Twitter had some huge offenses. I kept on responding nicely in the sense that, as a leader, you too are a teacher."

As Harry Spence did with his social workers, Costin was teaching teachers how to teach by treating them as she wished for them to treat all others—especially their students.

Within six months, Costin had in hand a standardized curriculum for each grade and for each discipline, courtesy of the collaboration over "Fala, Professor!," Twitter, and other channels. From there, Costin right-sized again, asking, "How do we effectively use this curriculum to improve learning?"

She hoped to ensure that every teacher had a laptop—that would make collaborating on the platform easy and uniform for all thirty-eight thousand teachers. She would also ensure there was one laptop for every three children, and perhaps that every classroom would have a projector. There would be a portal with blogs for teachers to share insights and best practices, and stronger tools for curriculum design and development, including a new Wiki-based platform—Educapedia—importing video, best practices, and digital classroom materials. With Ministry of Education funding, Costin selected ninety teachers to develop platform content and agreed that it would be shared throughout Brazil.

The Rio schools' collaboration platform energized supporters and brought in new ones. Telecoms provided connectivity, the British consulate supported free English classes, firms contributed educational videos. The network effect was working. As the platform attracted more and more supporters, the collaboration became even stronger.

Meanwhile, Costin also attended to the little stuff. Teachers tweeted her attention to school events and conditions without having to go through hierarchical channels. She now had a direct link to everything from complaints about bathrooms that didn't work, crumbling stairwells, and impossibly littered playgrounds to the roar of anguish when in October 2010 a child of eleven was shot sitting in a classroom, killed by narco-gang cross fire.

Costin used the platform to track and reveal results—were children learning what they should be? She started rewarding outstanding performance, giving teachers long-overdue recognition.

"We give visibility to those unknown heroes," Costin said. The same was true for kids; every month, each of the twenty students making the greatest gains received a bicycle. Their teachers also received rewards. Schools that met goals for improvement gave bonuses to each teacher and administrator.

The collaborations have been paying off. Student performance has improved across the younger grades, though by 2010 not yet in the older ones. Teachers are more engaged. As we write this, eighteen months into her tenure, the teachers haven't staged a single strike since Costin became secretary.

Costin recalled her boss, Mayor Eduardo Paes, taking her aside one afternoon and telling her, "I don't know what's going on. I'm in the streets and people are saying, 'Wow! Thank you for the way you're changing the schools.'"

"Sometimes," Costin said, "we have the illusion that we in social policy are changing things. But a teacher, once he closes the door of his classroom, he does what he wants because he is alone with his classroom. So, either we succeed in convincing them that learning matters—that we can do a wonderful job changing the lives of those kids—or we will be selling illusions to the citizens."

"I will continue using Twitter every day," Costin said. "It is the only way to know if what we are proposing is really happening or not, and if there are problems on the street and in the schools that have to be addressed."

The work isn't finished. But having built a platform—a clearing where formerly disenfranchised teachers become valued collaborators—Costin has the entire system moving toward that blue-sky vision of schools with the power to change children's lives.

PLATFORMS: THE ARCHITECTURE
OF COLLABORATION

The success of a platform, and therefore the collaboration it supports, begins with getting the architecture right. Harvard Business School's Thomas Eisenmann has written extensively about platforms; each, he says, has *infrastructure* that enables people to collaborate and a *set of rules* that governs their collaborations.

Digital platforms make the "search-find-and-engage" precursors of collaboration easier than ever. If everything else is aligned, they speed collaboration. JetBlue was one of the earliest firms to monitor Twitter, for example, jumping all over negative tweets to fix what was wrong for dissatisfied passengers even as they still stood fuming on line. Senior executives in industry and government have internal company blogs where they communicate new directions and take comments from employees—right over the heads of managers. Former vice chairman of the US Joint Chiefs of Staff James Cartwright, a Marine Corps four-star general, was famous for his blog. Many cities use digital platforms to let constituents weigh in on budget priorities. Should we add streetlights, pave the street, or (as hundreds preferred in Seattle) add a nude beach?

Claudia Costin stumbled on Twitter and found it a pretty good way to start. It doesn't always work that way. Sometimes, you can't just stumble on first steps. The world *demands* change—collaboration to do together *now* what no one can achieve alone. That may mean you have to forge a new platform that quickly bridges the gulf between groups where someone has the iron, someone the carbon, someone the smelter—and they all need to come together to make steel. When you stitch together that archipelago, each island has its own rules, ruler, and infrastructure. Who's in charge of the overall platform? Trying to agree on the infrastructure, rules, and governance can create conflict and confusion. It can take strong leadership to resolve the issues.

LA-JRIC: BUILDING AN
ANTITERRORISM PLATFORM

In the aftermath of 9/11, the city of Los Angeles felt especially vulnerable to attack. Its seaport, its airport, its vast entertainment industry, and its large Jewish population all put a big red bull's-eye on the city.

The region's law enforcement agencies raced to spot terrorist plots. Every whisper of a plot was investigated, every lead pursued. Already there were huge new expenses, massive increases in security, and daily distractions at even the hint of a threat from al-Qaeda.

Under all the commotion, though, little had changed in how the FBI, the LA County Sheriff, and the LAPD dealt with the threat of terrorism. The habits and culture that over the years resisted collaboration and information sharing were as strong as ever.

"Everybody was in their own little basket," Gary Williams, head of the LAPD's Antiterrorism Division, said. "They weren't talking to one another. I include us in that. LAPD wasn't taking in information from our *own* department."

It was as if the LAPD, FBI, sheriff, and dozens of local chiefs in the LA region were each working multiple jigsaw puzzles at once. None knew how many puzzles, or what any one overall picture looked like. Yet the leads kept pouring in. Workloads were staggering. Yet there was no cushion, no room for error.

The agencies badly needed a clearing where everyone could find each other and exchange insights—a platform that took the friction out of information sharing. Without that shift to a new platform, information sharing would be left to the same "who ya know" basis that led agencies to miss the warning signs of 9/11 in the first place. In the press of doing business, data, information, and suspects could easily get stuck at the boundaries of units and agencies—and suspects fall through the cracks.

There were plenty of joint task forces around. The LA County Sheriff had organized the region's "first responders" into its Terrorist Early Warning Group. The LAPD's Terrorist Threat Assessment Center focused on threats and analyses. The FBI had established a Field Intelligence Group in each of its fifty-six field offices, including in LA. So LA didn't lack for platforms.

But each agency had its own limited view of the problem. What the LA région needed was a *regional* platform of platforms—a clearing where anyone with pieces of the puzzle could spread them on the table and see how they fit together, and how others' pieces fit.

Gary Williams envisioned an intelligence center bringing together data and staff from around the region, the nation, and the world to make sense of it all for LA's decision makers. And not just data vetted by law enforcement agencies, but intelligence gathered from building inspectors, fire department investigators, and cops on the beat who noticed suspicious activities. The center would also collect information from the owners of potential targets like the port, power plants, gas lines, and financial institutions.

Right after 9/11 Williams and some of his colleagues from the sheriff's department traveled widely through the region and the nation, seeking support and resources to build this center. They gained some attention and a few commitments, but not enough. By the end of 2002, there was little money or wherewithal to do more than the ad hoc information sharing that left threat detection to chance. That left LA's citizens vulnerable to a 9/11-style attack.

When the LAPD needed it most, Williams's plea to pitch in and collaborate was met with empty hands and deaf ears. Was Williams paying the price for decades of LAPD go-it-aloneness? Perhaps. Tip O'Neill, the great Speaker of the US House of Representatives in the 1980s, once said, "Make friends before you need them." The LAPD had not been paying attention.

Its culture could be summed up in one word: *isolation.*

Williams's boss, John Miller, was a former investigative reporter from New York and in the CompStat era the NYPD's deputy commissioner for public information. Upon his arrival at the LAPD in

2003, Miller quickly came to understand LA's fractured law enforcement landscape; it reminded him of home. When Williams proposed a Joint Regional Information Center, Miller's first instinct was to let his New York stripes show. Suspicious as ever, Miller asked, "Why do we want *that*?"

Williams argued to right-size the problem by making it bigger and more expansive—go beyond terrorism to include ordinary crime. That's where terrorism might show its face first, and the LAPD had the eyes and ears on the street to see it. The Madrid railway bombers, for example, had financed their attacks with local hashish dealing, counterfeit CDs, and credit card fraud.

"All terrorism is at some point local," Williams said. "The formation of attack is always local, so eyes and ears on the street are critical. The response is always local because the target is cities." That argument won Miller's support.

To make the center effective, they needed reports from the county's sheriff, chiefs of police, and LAPD patrol officers. They also needed the FBI's classified system. The FBI saw things globally that might give new meaning to the LAPD's local data. Information collected locally might give new meaning to the FBI's global data. Together, if shared, the information from all platforms could create a much-needed common operating picture of threats to the region.

Even if the need for a regional platform for collaboration had become obvious, that didn't make financing the platform, setting its infrastructure, and making its rules easy.

Miller and Williams, who had secured $1 million in funding for the center—good enough for some early work, but not enough to sustain it past a start-up—considered locating at the Los Angeles County Regional Criminal Intelligence Center ("LA Clear"), a "deconfliction" facility run by the county chiefs in partnership with the sheriff. LA Clear tracked the region's narcotics cases to avoid "blue on blue" incidents, where cops might inadvertently come upon each other's cases. The LA Clear facility had

computers and a room to operate multiple wiretaps and surveillances—
infrastructure the Joint Regional Intelligence Center, or JRIC, could use.

"They had a high interest in getting us in their space, seeing our million and perhaps hoping to get into the counter-terror funding stream
that was just opening as counter-narcotics was drying up," Miller recalled.
"We had a high interest in their space. It was high quality and free."

The FBI offered to contribute some analysts to JRIC if it went into
LA Clear. But when Miller asked the bureau, "And what about FBI systems?" the answer came back, "No." The bureau didn't consider LA Clear
secure enough to house top-secret information.

Without FBI systems bringing in classified data and intelligence from
overseas, Williams and Miller were convinced, the JRIC effort would
be pointless. "A Mickey Mouse Club," Williams cautioned. "Secret de-
coder rings but no access to the tree house."

Ron Iden, the FBI's LA bureau chief, was willing to work with Miller
and Williams. But if JRIC wanted to use FBI systems, the FBI would
have to lead or at least house JRIC in an FBI space. There was room adjacent to the FBI's Joint Drug Intelligence Group facility just southeast
of LA. With FBI systems, the LAPD staff could get clearances, clean up
the data, and boil it down for local law enforcement. Moreover, the FBI
would add $2.5 million to help fund the center.

Williams urged caution. "The FBI meant well but didn't quite have
the same vision," he told Miller. "They're very headquarters-centric, and
they march to the headquarters beat. At the time," Williams said, "headquarters did not have a clue about what was needed from state and local
governments in terms of dealing with terrorism."

Ultimately, Miller acquiesced to the FBI's demands, figuring that he
could negotiate a shared governance arrangement to keep the bureau in
check.

LA's Joint Regional Intelligence Center would be made secure to FBI
specifications and use FBI systems. The agencies would share governance,
with each partner contributing staff and finances. With the FBI and

LAPD involved, Miller had no doubt that others would soon join the platform and add their data.

The arrangement was acceptable to the LAPD, but it infuriated the LA Clear chiefs and the county sheriff, who felt snubbed and frozen out.

"Bratton worked overtime to persuade them that a federal link to JRIC was essential," Miller said. "It was his political savvy, his investment, and his contributions to their Association that made this a wrinkle instead of a disaster."

The "new" LAPD's efforts to "make friends before you need them" seemed to be paying off. As negotiations and clarification took hold, conflict and confusion receded. LA JRIC moved from the Lead quadrant of high conflict and confusion to the Just Do It! quadrant of "good to go."

Now on a roll, LA JRIC found financing easier and easier. In addition to the FBI's $2.5 million, the Sheriff's Department ponied up $450,000, $1.5 million came in from the state of California, and the LAPD kicked in its $1 million.

But who was going to run what? That's when the serious wrangling began. What were the details of governance? What records would be kept? How long would they be retained? How would the names of sources from one agency be safeguarded as the information flowed to others? Who would have access to whose system, and which data?

Agencies that were used to collaborating with each other only on an ad hoc, "who ya know" basis now had to make collaboration formal. Agencies exchanged draft agreements, with each agency or department using a different color font for its corrections, turning the document into a Christmas tree of multihued inks.

"Iteration by iteration the color started to disappear in the drafts," Miller said. "A little bit at a time, as we reached agreement after agreement, the document came back to being black and white."

The partners finally agreed that the FBI would act as administrator of JRIC, and that governance would be shared but rotated among agency leads. They created both classified and unclassified areas—"high" and "low" sides—where law enforcement and intelligence could operate alone, or together with fire, health, and other agencies, as needed.

The Los Angeles Joint Regional Intelligence Center finally opened July 27, 2006. Even after it commenced operations, questions remained about how to scale it up, how to sustain it, how it would be staffed, and what the next technological steps should be.

"What we did accomplish," Miller said, "was to get all the systems running into one place—narcotics, organized crime, street crime, terrorism—and we got the people sitting next to each other."

With that clearing operational, the LA JRIC platform started pulling in new network partners.

Las Vegas was among the first, Miller recalled. "They said, 'Our criminals are your criminals. Our gangs are your gangs. They just go back and forth. Why,' they asked, 'should we set up a fusion center in Vegas when JRIC has the same crooks, same cases, and same information? We'll add some, take some.'"

A PLATFORM NEEDS A STEWARD

Having established LA JRIC, the LAPD, the FBI, and their partners became the stewards of the platform. It was up to them to ensure that it ran smoothly and operated as agreed; that people could search for, find, and engage each other and share information; and that it produced the promised results that drew the network partners to it in the first place.

That's the nature of a platform. You can't just build it, forget it, and assume it will always be there for you. A platform needs constant tending. Architecture that once made sense can become outdated, and your platform obsolete. Securing data, for example, is an investment that's never finished. Something can come along—a heightened challenge, a stronger competitor, a more capable adversary—to reveal weaknesses the platform had kept hidden.

It's not likely that LA JRIC, of course, will have to fend off competitors. After all, the FBI and the LAPD have monopolies on the information they gather, whether classified and from overseas or confidential and local. One day, though, one or more of the partners could walk away from LA JRIC, or just stop paying attention to it.

As a platform steward you will need to tend to its infrastructure and rules, and ensure that it does its job: to create a trusted clearing where people can search for, find, and meet like-minded souls, share assets, and collaborate to achieve together what they can't alone.

Without vigilance and leadership, you may find the sands under your feet shifting until you no longer have a platform to stand on.

A BAND OF EQUALS:
HOW A COLLABORATION PLATFORM
TRANSFORMED THE CREDIT CARD INDUSTRY

Back in the mid-1960s, while rummaging through the bank's trash bins looking for a missing transaction slip, Dee Ward Hock wondered whether he could stoop any lower. After sixteen years in the business, he was now a trainee again, this time at Seattle's National Bank of Commerce (NBC). Hock had been dispatched to a branch to learn the teller's business. Hired at NBC as a promising young executive with a track record in consumer finance, he had been treading water ever since.

Two hours and eleven trash bins into his search, the missing slip he needed to balance the day's books was nowhere to be found. Hock had gone nose to nose with the head teller and all he could think was "I'm outta here."

Summoned to the bank president's office the next day, Hock expected the chat to be brief and his employment to be over. He was wrong.

The president told him NBC wanted a new bank card operation up and running in ninety days. Bank of America ("BofA") had licensed its BankAmericard product to NBC and dozens of other out-of-state banks. BofA's plan: break out of its home state beachhead in California, where regulators had it pinned down and where BofA had already supersaturated the market with two million unsolicited blue, white, and gold BankAmericards. BofA looked to build a national market using partner banks like Seattle's National Bank of Commerce.

Hock's ninety-day mission: qualify 120,000 NBC customers, get a BankAmericard with their name embossed on it in the mail, and get them spending. His partner was to be Bob Cumming, a top bank branch manager.

Hock could not have known then that he was about to create a platform for electronic payments that would prove irresistible to billions of consumers and businesses worldwide—or that it would spark one of the great collaborations in the history of modern finance.

Pause for a moment to reflect. In 1965, there was no such thing as MasterCard or Visa. There were plenty of specialized cards around: American Express for travel and entertainment, Diners Club and Carte Blanche for restaurants, Sunoco or Esso for gas. There were regional bank cards, like MasterCharge in the eastern United States, and BankAmericard in the West. But those cards were tethered to their home base. BankAmericard was for Californians to use *in* California, for example, not for trips to Aspen, New York, or Vegas, let alone for jetting to Paris, dining in Rome, or getting massages in Tokyo—all of which consumers were beginning to do.

There was no all-purpose charge-anything-anywhere-anytime bank card. Institutions like Bank of America noticed that. They also realized that unlike Sunoco or American Express or Diners Club, banks didn't have to go in search of consumers or merchants—they already had millions of them as account holders. If Bank of America could figure out how to put a piece of plastic in a customer's wallet and guarantee payment to a merchant when he accepted the card as payment—even when one bank owned the merchant account and another owned the customer account—there might be millions of dollars in fees to be had on both sides of the transaction.

Actually, it turned out to be *trillions* of dollars.

Fast-forward to the year 2009: 1.7 *billion* Visa-branded cards were in use globally; Visa handled 57 *billion* transactions, valued at $4.3 *trillion*.

Talk about a platform.

Visa is what BankAmericard became, after Dee Hock got his hands on it.

To Dee Hock and Bob Cumming, BofA's so-called "strategy" for new card partners, including National Bank of Commerce, sounded desperate, like a Hail Mary pass by the quarterback on the losing end of a football game. Send millions of cards out. Sign up every merchant in sight. The rest will take care of itself.

Except this was no end-of-the-game miracle play. It was BofA's opening play in taking its card national. It quickly became obvious that the BofA licensing crew knew little about consumer lending or card operations.

But there was no turning back. BofA and NBC had a forty-year business relationship and the chairmen were pals. Hock and Cumming realized they would have to home-grow a fix at the level of day-to-day bank operations. They'd have to scope vision, right-size, and deliver. And they had seventy days to do it.

First things first: NBC ordered the gear it would need no matter what Hock and Cumming came up with—embossers, thousands of imprinters, two hundred thousand plastic cards. Hock and Cumming knew the price of failure: someone would melt all that plastic down for guitar picks. Hock and Cumming would be strumming tunes for spare change on a San Francisco street corner.

Hock and Cumming baked some bankers' common sense into NBC's upcoming rollout. In their plan, NBC's frontline lending officers would prequalify their branch's customers before the cards went out. None of the managers liked these new card products much. Unsecured credit? "Worse than financing cars," they grumbled. Stand by for fraud and losses.

But like Hock, the managers all held a dozen niche credit cards in their own wallets—gas, merchandise, airlines, entertainment. They understood the vision: a single bank card would replace them all. The bank would claim all those fees. With that came the much-needed frontline support. Thirty days later, NBC had sent 120,000 prequalified customers invitations; 100,000 accepted. Hock's team embossed and mailed a card for each. One hundred thousand prequalified NBC bank card customers were now armed with shiny new blue-and-gold plastic, ready to spend. All in ninety days.

Meanwhile, Bank of America continued to push the Hail Mary play, with predicable consequences. By 1968, other licensees had sent out millions of cards, often without prequalification or other safeguards. As a result, fraud was rampant, hitting banks with losses and dragging down consumer confidence. Banks' reputations were being sullied (yes, there was a time when that was still possible!). Congress was calling for hearings.

Bank of America turned out to be a poor steward of its platform. It branded the card—and that was about it. It was as if it owned a campground with a scenic overlook, but never emptied the garbage or groomed the trails. It just did some advertising and went around collecting fees.

Problems started at the point of sale when merchants made authorizations by telephone and voice with a customer waiting. This was the era before the advent of magnetic stripes and swipe machines, or even touchtone phones. Voice authorizations were painfully slow—five to twenty-five minutes on average. Customers waiting to sign the slips balked and left or opted to pay cash instead. Rather than lose sales, merchants completed purchases without authorization, with predictable consequences for fraud.

In the back office operations, payments were backlogged and error ridden. With no standard way for member banks to clear payments, every bank was on its own to square away its transactions with every other bank. Interchange fees—the "vig" that merchants' banks paid customers' banks for the convenience of accepting the card—varied widely. Each bank and merchant seemed to be making it up as it went along.

Glitch after glitch slowed payments between banks; customers weren't billed; banks couldn't balance their books at night; millions of dollars were being held in suspense ledgers. It became an accounting nightmare.

By 1968, BankAmericard's licensee banks were in revolt. Bank of America Service Corporation (BASC)—the corporation that BofA had formed to front its card operation—called a meeting of its restive licensees for October, in Columbus, Ohio.

Senior Bank of America executives didn't even bother to show up. Instead, BoA sent a pair of mid-level managers, adding insult to the licensees' grievances.

Dee Hock, who by then was running NBC's bank card business, attended the meeting. Accusations flew: licensees took aim at each other and BASC. Hock was about to give up when he drew a committee assignment: recommend some fixes. Hock was reluctant. The problems were huge; incremental fixes wouldn't work. "How about we step back," he told the others on the committee. "Instead of BASC convening us small banks, *we* will convene us and take a look at what needs fixing top to bottom."

In other words, they shouldn't count on the organization responsible for this hopelessly flawed platform to build a better one.

BASC agreed. It would be off the hook; Dee Hock would be *on* it to fix the platform. Why not? the other licensees figured. The worst that could happen is that BofA would ignore their recommendations and the licensees would be back where they started.

On the flight home Hock carved up a map of the United States torn from an airline magazine into seven regions. Each region, he decided, would convene four committees organized around operations, marketing, credit, and systems. The committee leaders would make up the region's executive team and sit on national committees.

A band of equals. None was more equal than another. In essence, he'd form a collaboration platform to work on building a new platform.

The Visa card as we know it today was born on the torn-out page of a seat-back pocket airline magazine.

REBUILDING THE PLATFORM TO A VISION

In Hock's call to look not just at bits and pieces of the problem but at its entirety, you may hear echoes of Harry Spence from our discussion of vision in chapter 2. Like the platform Spence came on in 2001, this platform, too, was not delivering on its promise. The potential of the network to create value for all was barely touched. The current vision had no blue skies for anyone but Bank of America (and those skies were by now cloudy, too). The steward could not be trusted to reinvent the future. It was time to get back to basics—to what the licensees like Hock had signed up for in the first place.

Dee Hock started by taking a hard look at the existing platform. He'd need to listen to the data.

Region after region, Hock and his committee discovered the true extent of the licensees' problems. Fraud losses were in the *hundreds of millions* of dollars and accelerating (in 1968 dollars—real money!). There would be no quick fix.

As long as there was no quick fix, Hock argued, let's fix this right. What assets are we actually dealing with here? Let's deconstruct and revision this thing: how do we use our assets to greatest advantage?

A bank, all knew, was made up of brick-and-mortar branches, teller windows, deposits, and currency. Banks brought them all together; customers experienced them as trust and security. A great asset.

The card was a halfway physical thing, a piece of plastic in your pocket from which a merchant read numbers into a telephone. The merchant's voice linked the brick-and-mortar bank by telephone to the point of sale.

Dee Hock's vision began to take shape. That voice authorizing the card transaction was made up of nothing but electronic impulses. If you could get rid of the voice and just move the impulses machine to machine, with a transaction started by a card at point of sale and completed by computers in the back-office operation, you could buy and sell stuff 24/7, around the globe, all in seconds. You didn't even need a card physically present. You could shop from a catalog in the comfort of your home!

Why, for that matter, did you even need a brick-and-mortar bank? Answer: you didn't. A bank was in the business of the exchange of monetary value. Start there, and invent the best organization to accomplish that exchange. But Hock, like Spence and many others, was seeing a vision of blue skies when reality was anchored to earth, in old-time systems and processes.

Hock needed many eyeballs and brains on this problem. He retreated with his committee for a week's getaway at a hotel in Sausalito. "Let's go back to first principles and build from there," Hock urged. He gave them a blue-sky challenge and a one-sentence problem statement: "If anything imaginable was possible," he said, "if there were no constraints whatever, what would be the nature of an ideal organization to create the world's premier system for the exchange of value?"

His thinking: just as you could reduce money to electronic impulses, you could deconstruct an organization to its minimum principles. From there, you could reinvent the minimum platform necessary to provide for the anywhere/anytime transmission of electronic impulses and the exchange of value.

In fact no one, Hock later wrote, could imagine the complexity of this organization. The rate of change coming in the new digital world would be so fast and furious that nothing anyone could plan today would make sense tomorrow. It was beyond the "power of reason" to design even if all the variables could be known—which they couldn't.

The ideal organization would therefore be one that thrived on emergence, on continual change, not top-down "my way or the highway" thinking. A hierarchical organization like a bank would simply re-create itself. It would take a network to invent a network capable of continuous change.

What principles should govern this network? Simplicity itself: the Golden Rule. The organization should be equitably owned by all participants. Rights and obligations should be tiered but uniform within tiers. It should be open to all qualified participants. No cartels, blackballs, or club rules. Revenues should flow to the owners, with the organization retaining only as much as it needed to continue growing. Governance should be of the governed, by the governed, for the governed.

Coming back down to earth, Hock had to deal with the eight-hundred-pound gorilla in the room: the Bank of America. Was there any way BofA would cede control to a band of upstart licensees?

Bank of America, Hock later told its vice chairman in a face-to-face session in San Francisco, "should be the leader of a movement, not the commander of a structure." Bank of America, Hock argued, would benefit as the size of the pie grew; its share would grow beyond anything it could achieve if it ruled this world alone.

The vice chairman bought it. Perhaps he saw MasterCard, Bank of America's credit card competition, in his rearview mirror; maybe he saw a well-organized band of banks attempting to do something together *without* Bank of America. In any event, Dee Hock's argument carried the day.

Next, the member banks would have to make the change as well. Hock needed two-thirds of the licensees to vote yes. He got 100 percent. And with that, he moved quickly to establish National BankAmericard Incorporated (NBI).

Hock brought on a small senior staff—the best in the business in bank operations, technology, and law. Aram Tootelian, for example, came over from TRW to work with Hock as technical lead on the new platform. Tootelian was an expert in bank technology, airline reservation systems, and credit-checking platforms. As a TRW guy, he understood that the bank card platform required high reliability—not far from the fail-safe methods used in top-secret military projects.

Hock's team first addressed the problems members felt most pained by: the interchange fees. Making them transparent and consistent, Hock quieted a persistent grievance, gave his team credibility, and increased the licensees' conviction that this could work.

Setting the interchange fees accurately came at a cost: member banks had to report their key performance indicators to NBI each quarter so NBI could fix the interchange rates accurately. Hock converted that pain into gain: those numbers helped NBI understand the members' card business as never before, and proved that banks were beginning to profit from their card operations. That built confidence. It also showed Hock which banks were stumbling, and let him send in fix-it teams to pull up those struggling operations. There would be no weak links on this platform.

Next up: authorization delays. Hock couldn't take it all on at once so he right-sized the problem down to the point-of-sale authorization issue. Hock didn't like any of the commercially available options, so he turned to his technology team. They were to design a credit card authorization system for members that not only reduced wait times from minutes to seconds but was fail-safe and infinitely scalable.

On April 1, 1973, the team delivered: a real-time system and switch for authorization requests coming directly from large merchants' cash registers, as well as from card centers handling the smaller merchants. NBI required each bank to build its interface to the switch so every system, diverse as they were, "looked" the same to the switch and data could flow easily.

The platform reduced point-of-sale authorization time to under sixty seconds. It was reliable, with safeguards against everything from power failure to people failure. It was able to grow as the business grew. Hock accomplished all this while letting the local card centers run their businesses as usual, with the NBI switch performing only the community functions no one could take on alone.

With business soaring—first quarter sales in 1973 were up 43 percent over 1972—upgrades were constant, and pressure to keep the projects small, scoped, and delivered on time was critical. These were tough schedules tightly managed by Hock's in-house team.

"One was given latitude and support to do what had to be done often with unrealistic deadlines," a developer recalled of Hock. "But he made sure—and nobody questioned—who was really in charge."

Lax management and governance would not be an issue. There was a new sheriff in town now as platform steward. The community had been called to order: a platform governed by a guiding principle of "no one more equal than another" had been built. Democracy notwithstanding, Hock led his members forward with a firm grip.

The results proved the platform and Hock's leadership. More banks joined, giving customers and merchants assurance that the card was in fact "everywhere you want to be." More people went traveling with their cards, generating more fees, making members richer. Hock kept proving the platform, the collaboration, his team, and his leadership.

The NBI name soon changed to Visa, USA, signaling the final break with the past and a forward march to a future of global membership growth, massive expansion of the cardholder base, near-universal merchant acceptance, staggering sales volume and—even after forty-four years in business—dominance in the global bank card system.

Hock had the advantage of building upon a platform that already existed but was floundering and unfinished in terms of infrastructure or rules. The wildly underperforming BankAmericard was underserving the collaboration, putting the entire network at risk of collapse. Having convinced Bank of America that together they could make the pie bigger for everyone, Dee Hock convened his members, and together re-visioned the future, right-sized the problems, rebuilt the platform, and delivered unsurpassed value for all.

Sometimes the platform steward resists such a radical restructuring. When that happens, you can have a fight on your hands.

CAN YOU HEAR ME NOW? RESTORING THE US NAVY'S UNDERSEA ADVANTAGE

On November 2, 2004, on a target range off Kauai, the US Pacific Fleet sank one of its own, the USS *Valley Forge*. A Ticonderoga-class guided missile cruiser armed with Lockheed Martin's famed Aegis combat control system, the *Valley Forge* had been commissioned eighteen years earlier. But halfway through its expected thirty-five-year service life, the ship was too expensive to upgrade or modernize. Stripped of its sensitive electronics, the *Valley Forge* was tethered like some goat to a stake and sent to the ocean bottom in a hail of gunfire. All for practice.

"The US Navy is sinking its ships," a US Navy captain said, "making them reefs. We lost 50 percent of what we intended when we invested in that ship. We cannot afford to keep doing this."

By November 2010, Ashton Carter, on leave from Harvard and then US Under Secretary of Defense, had had enough. In a sternly worded directive to the Secretaries of the Army, Air Force, and Navy, Carter ordered them to move to "open architecture" using easily swappable components, commercially available and well-priced, and to make sure it all worked together.

The idea was simple: Stop using "closed" systems from vendors that required ripping everything out to fix one broken component. Deal with a fast-changing world—and fast-changing technology—by shopping commercially for gear; measuring, testing, and proving best in class; refreshing it constantly; and assuring that everything afloat could "interoperate"—work together coordinated by computers.

If they needed inspiration, Carter said, they should look to the submarine service. The Navy's newest *Virginia*-class submarines had proven the benefits of the approach, as had every back-fit class of submarines afloat. Now, Carter said, "You do it."

Bill Johnson could only feel satisfaction. Fifteen years earlier, Johnson had brought the submarine service back from the brink of destruction by Russian submarines running superior sonar systems—using commercially available off-the-shelf systems, just as Carter was now demanding. He knew Carter would have a fight on his hands.

Throughout the Cold War, finding, stalking, and exposing the Soviet nuclear submarine fleet had been a top priority of US forces.

The Soviets ran noisy subs but they were good. One day in the midst of 1962's Cuban Missile Crisis, four Soviet Northern Fleet subs surfaced inside the US quarantine line around Cuba. Even with the US Atlantic Fleet on a wartime footing, with 85 percent of its assets at sea, the Soviet boats had somehow made it through the northern seas to their stations off Cuba without detection.

The US fleet hit the panic button. Over the next thirty years the United States developed and deployed an amazing array of sonars: surveillance sonar sitting passively on buoys or ocean bottoms, or sonar towed in arrays tethered thousands of feet behind surface ships and submarines, or active pinging sonar in the subs themselves. The Soviets may not have known it, but through the 1970s and '80s the United States Navy enjoyed a decisive acoustic superiority.

Then in the 1990s, the oceans suddenly became very quiet. Unbeknownst to the United States, for twenty years naval-officer-turned-spy John Walker and his gang had been supplying the Soviets with the Navy's secrets. The Soviets came to understand just how thoroughly trumped they had been and adapted. Using Walker's data and Toshiba's manufacturing prowess, the Soviets quieted their "boomer" missile subs and, keeping them closer to home, defeated US efforts to find them.

"This is the first time since we put *Nautilus* to sea," Admiral Jeremy Boorda, US chief of naval operations, told the House Armed Services Committee, "that the Russians have had submarines at sea quieter than ours."

Deep at sea, Russian subs stalked US subs mere yards away without being detected. In one incident, the American attack sub *Augusta* had been trailing a Russian ballistic missile sub off Bermuda. Unseen by the *Augusta*, another Russian sub was close behind, stalking the American.

The two collided, forcing the *Augusta* to return to the sub yards at Groton, Connecticut, for a $3 million repair.

Meanwhile, with the Cold War "over," Presidents Ronald Reagan and George H. W. Bush slashed US strategic nuclear forces. That included reducing the number of nuclear missile-launching subs from thirty-six to eighteen.

Alarm bells were ringing all over Washington. Not only was the US Navy down missile subs, it was clear that the Navy had lost its long-dominant undersea acoustic advantage.

In 1997, for example, Norman Polmar, a long-time observer of US submarine strategy, testified before Congress. "Last month," Polmar said, "the Director of Naval Intelligence wrote that the Russian submarine force, despite its reduced numbers and manning problems, 'still remains the technological pacing challenge by which the US submarine force measures itself.' Is there another area of naval warfare in which Russia— or any other nation—is the 'technological pacing challenge' for American forces?"

Bill Johnson's mission was to restore that advantage. Navy admirals figured it would take six years; that was the yardstick they'd always used for major overhauls.

Johnson figured eighteen months, and he was right.

By 1999, Admiral Malcolm Fages, director of the Submarine Warfare Division, testified in the US Senate to a much-changed state of affairs:

The Submarine Force is making significant, rapid improvements in acoustic sensors and processing. In real-world exercises and operations, towed array and sonar systems are ensuring our submarines retain the acoustic advantage. Use of commercial off the shelf equipment has resulted in substantially reduced costs with significantly improved processing capability. Each ship-set costs only a small fraction of the price of its predecessor, yet improves processing power by an order of magnitude. Improvements in processing

**power allow the use of powerful new algorithms that result in much
improved detection ranges in testing to date.**

What had happened in the two years between Polmar's and Fages's
testimony? Johnson had been at work, and by 1997 had quietly delivered
on the promise. By 1999 the US submarine fleet was well along a program of renewal, restoration, and recapture of its acoustic superiority.

How did Johnson effect such a dramatic turnaround so quickly?
With a new platform that unleashed the power of collaboration.

Johnson's vision was (as John Shea might say) "simple in the extreme." US submarines will hit and hold new levels of acoustic superiority without coming out of service for time-consuming rebuilds.

Johnson's plan was decisive and right-sized: we will rip the guts out
of the compromised sonars now in subs and replace them with commercially available, easy-to-upgrade, off-the-shelf gear. The sonar systems will
refresh constantly to match latest technology against new fleet challenges.
The US Navy will no longer wait to build entire new classes of boats to
bring its combat platforms current.

Johnson's method: he would collaborate in ways that would soon
shock contractors, acquisition bureaucrats, fleet commanders, and scientists alike, using collaboration methods that became the essence of the
transformed combat platform itself.

And Johnson delivered unprecedented performance. Fast.

But Johnson faced powerful opposition from groups that had benefited from the old, broken platform. Like Dee Hock, Johnson knew he
needed to go beyond the tight circle of insiders who stewarded the old
platform. Figuring out what needed to be done from a technical perspective was easy compared to dealing with the politics of changing the platform. Getting beyond the conflict and confusion would test Johnson's
mettle and his leadership.

Step back to 1995. America's "acoustic superiority crisis" had become critical. "We're getting way too close to the bad guys. We can't hear them. The danger of collision is high. We need to get that standoff range back," said Bruce DeMars, a four-star admiral and director of Naval Nuclear Propulsion.

Fear of collision was half the Navy's concern. But the greater concern was having a hot Russian torpedo coming at US subs out of the blue. For US submarine captains, not knowing where the Russian subs were was a disaster waiting to happen.

Crystal City, Virginia, was ground zero for the crisis. It was there that the Navy convened the first meeting of the Submarine Superiority Technology Advisory Working Group (SSTP), a distinguished group of ten outsiders led by the esteemed Johns Hopkins University researcher John Schuster and chaired by MITRE Corporation's Ken Hawker.

Their mission: figure out what's wrong with the US sonars, prescribe a fix, and do it fast.

At the time, Bill Johnson was the lead civilian for submarine sonar in the Navy's Submarine Combat System Program Office. That made him the top acquisition expert for new submarine sonar. Even so, Johnson recognized only a few faces at the SSTP session—those of his counterpart from the surveillance sonar community, who ran the passive seafloor listening systems, and his surface group counterpart, who ran towed arrays behind cruisers and destroyers.

Strange as many faces in the room were, Johnson was even more in the dark about what had caused all the fuss. The US Navy was so compartmentalized that he had little direct contact with the fleet. Everything Johnson knew about the performance of his sonar systems at sea—in navyspeak, "forward deployments"—came filtered down through the Office of Naval Intelligence or the Naval Undersea Warfare Center (NUWC) at Newport, Rhode Island.

Six months down the road, as expert as he was, Johnson had received quite an education from the SSTP briefings. By his own account, Johnson had had his eyes wide shut, head in the sand.

First, the SSTP discovered staggering waste. For each new class of boat the Navy developed, for example, it had vast, duplicative organizations and infrastructure—sonar platforms, labs, and test facilities.

Second, Johnson learned that although the Walker spy ring had given the Soviets all sorts of quieting advantage, the United States could still hear Russian subs. The Americans' ocean-floor sonar, for example, was effective.

Sitting in the Panel meetings, Johnson saw the data for the first time. The Office of Naval Intelligence (ONI) had processed a recording of a Russian sub using the ocean-floor surveillance systems, and then put the same signal through the submarine-based systems.

The difference was astounding. Like a heart-rate monitor, the ocean-floor system showed a healthy straight line across a chart: it had maintained nearly continuous contact with the Russian sub. The submarine-based system was on life support: nothing but dits, dashes, dots, and gaps—mostly gaps, mostly noncontact.

Pictures—"lofargrams" in sonarspeak—were worth a thousand words. The data spoke: ocean-floor signal processing was superb. Submarine signal processing was broke.

The difference was in the gear and the algorithms. The ocean-floor listening devices had been constantly improved with the latest off-the-shelf technology and dazzling new software. They'd been able to reap the dividend of plummeting costs of signal processing and microchips, and skyrocketing performance in both.

In contrast, NUWC's sub-based sonar was refreshed at best every five or six years. Not surprisingly, sub-based sonar had fallen well behind. Once compromised, it would stay compromised until the next major rebuild.

Only now, sitting with the other Panel members, did Johnson realize how far the United States had fallen behind.

Bill Johnson didn't wait around for orders to fix it. As he gained insights over the months, he'd put his plan together. By September 1995, when the Panel reported its results, Johnson was ready to move.

Johnson's vision lined up perfectly with the Panel's recommendations: Quickly adapt and use the ocean-floor systems on US subs. Over time, standardize 80 percent of the infrastructure for all sonar platforms, and then highly customize the last 20 percent. Buy commercially available off-the-shelf (COTS) hardware and software, saving money and time. Plan for system refreshes every couple of years. Don't waste money stock-piling soon-to-be-out-of-date spare parts. Engage the fleet and expert peer groups of academics, operators, and vendors for design and evaluations of the fleet's sonar.

Johnson disagreed with only one Panel conclusion. "There is no quick fix to the sonar problem," it reported. Johnson thought he could get the first fix on the subs and out to sea within eighteen months of authorization.

It would be a complete overhaul of the platform—not just the technology, but the way it was conceived, designed, developed, and deployed. It was imperative that this new platform for acquisition and procurement support a new broad-based collaboration, from the fleet itself to scientists, engineers, and vendors.

And Johnson vowed to make the process transparent. He would rely on peer group evaluations and data-driven analysis collected directly from his labs or subs at sea.

Johnson had the latitude to do it: he ran a post-Panel working group tasked to incorporate the best features of all signal-processing techniques into the Navy's new sonars.

The key to platform overhaul: performance, budget, and cover.

Johnson wasn't looking for more. He already had $80 million allocated, which he would redirect to the crash program. His promise: retarget funds I already have; boost performance without new money.

Better than that, Johnson's new strategy promised a *steady* spend. Rather than refresh systems by total system overhaul, or buying a new boat class with huge upfront expenditure, sub sonars could refresh every year with low-cost processing upgrades. Where the Navy stockpiled $600 million in spare sonar processors for the the 23 oldest *Los Angeles* class attack subs alone, Johnson's strategy relied on constant refresh and commercial, off-the-shelf (COTS) gear: it would end stockpiling. The performance of sub sonar would be stellar; its costs steady and low.

With his captain, John P. "Jack" Jarabak, Johnson coined the term for the initiative: the Acoustic Rapid COTS Insertion Program—ARCI, for short (pronounced AR-kee). Behind that awkward acronym was an idea that audaciously challenged the old ways of doing business and threatened long-entrenched forces for the status quo. Johnson's world would soon feature combat of the bureaucratic, not nautical, sort.

Johnson and Jarabak soon got their first green light: put the ocean-floor software onto a submarine and see if they could replicate the performance ONI had demonstrated in Crystal City, but this time at sea.

Resistance began to mount. A blue-ribbon panel had warned Congress in 1989 to expect bureaucratic warfare from any major submarine overhaul. "The Navy establishment," it said, "is burdened with internal vested and sometimes conflicting interests that encumber innovation and execution on the scale required here."

Top NUWC executives were having none of Johnson's ways. NUWC was the sub's signal-processing experts—"design, develop submarine sonar" was their "house." From the moment the ONI demo in Crystal City tore the veil off NUWC's poorly performing sub-based signal processing, NUWC executives felt their franchise was under threat. Johnson's plan to put some other shop's software onto actual submarines and take it to sea infuriated them. Johnson's plan to test other sonar designs against NUWC's was practically sedition.

NUWC executives fought back, even as NUWC managers began quietly supporting Johnson and ARCI. One afternoon Jarabak grabbed Johnson at his desk. "Come on," he said. "We're going up to the admiral's office. He's being briefed by NUWC." It turned out NUWC was wrapping its own sonar in the same COTS "flag" Johnson was waving. "Hey," NUWC's executive was saying, "NUWC already has a commercial off-the-shelf system out there in the fleet. Let's use that and take our time with ARCI and do it right." Johnson went up to the front of the room, took the pointer from the briefer's hand, and critiqued the NUWC claim.

"It was a hard pill for NUWC to swallow," Johnson said. "They had a lot of good ideas. They just didn't have *all* the good ideas. And some were incapable of being objective when it came to comparing their own ideas with somebody else's."

By June 1996, Vice Admiral George R. Sterner, commander of the Naval Sea Systems Command, approved the ARCI plan. Eighteen months later—in November 1997—Johnson's group had developed, tested, and certified the new ARCI system and readied it for sea trials on the first ARCI-equipped sub, the *Augusta*, the same boat that had collided with the Russians and started the whole sonar saga.

The *Augusta* set sail in January 1998; it was the first submarine equipped with the ARCI system sonar running the new algorithms from the ocean-floor community on commercially available software militarized for the purpose.

The engineers' reports from a predeployment workup at sea had been raves: the new sonar algorithms let the sonar operators see things they'd never seen before. But when the *Augusta* returned from its ninety-day deployment, the report was "Nice job on the new sonar—but 'no change.' We don't see anything different."

Johnson didn't get it. The *data* from the *Augusta* confirmed the pretrial engineers' reports: huge gains. Why was the crew reporting no improvement in performance?

Johnson turned to a user-group of active duty master chiefs. He'd convened these savvy operational sonar guys from the fleet to help configure the new sonar displays. "What gives?" he asked.

"We have a training issue here" was the reply. "And we're still working with the old legacy system displays. We need to put the new signal through new displays that can handle it."

"When I developed this system I was thinking of it in terms of hardware and software," Johnson said. "The people part of the equation was really somebody else's to deal with."

Which led Johnson to ask of the fleet, "Do you guys really know what you're looking at?"

A test devised by the chiefs soon answered his question. Among two hundred sonar operators, expert-level personnel correctly answered the question "What is this thing I am looking at?" 76 percent of the time. (These were the "Jonesys" we all saw in the movie *The Hunt for Red October*.) But the average operator got it right only 25 percent of the time.

No wonder the fleet reported that the subs were not seeing much difference. Its glasses were fogged up; no one was seeing much of anything.

"Here we were pouring hundreds of millions of dollars into these sonar systems that extracted the last decibel of information out of the ocean," Johnson said, "and it's all falling on the floor because these guys don't recognize what they're seeing."

Johnson didn't run training—he had no budget for it, no say in it. The people who did pushed back. "We know what we're doing. Look at these testimonials!" But the data were clear. Nothing on Johnson's platform would deliver the performance expected without training.

Nevertheless, no amount of logic would move the trainers. So Johnson went to the admirals, showed them the tests, and embarrassed the trainers into compliance.

Together with new flat-screen displays that made signals easier to read, a four-hour training session for the operators did the trick. The flat screens were the master chiefs' handiwork, ARCI's first user-configured component. Once trained on the new screens, younger, less-experienced operators actually did *better* than the experienced crew used to working the old screens.

By March 1998, Johnson's team in Manassas, Virginia, was at work retooling the "baseline" ARCI platform from the *Augusta* for a first wave of fleet-wide installations. Johnson would run sea trials in the fall of

1998; the fleet wanted the ARCI build operational on the USS *Memphis* by the spring of 1999. That worked for Johnson: he wanted his master chiefs to see their idea in the fleet in months, not years, to keep them jazzed up and engaged.

If the chiefs were thrilled, Lockheed Martin, which owned the Aegis-class system displays and was looking to lock up the submarine franchise, too, was less so. ARCI was like some new trophy wife. Its slick flat screens displaced twenty years of custom monitors. And what was with this "fleet-sourced design" of the master chiefs? "Operators will be running around changing their minds with every deployment!"

For Johnson, that was exactly the idea. Fleet operators—"customers" like his master chiefs—collaborating with designers was the ARCI platform's " new normal." A new Advanced Processing Build ("APB") would be done each year for the next four—an exhausting pace. The technology permitted it, and Johnson fixed the business process to accommodate it.

There was a "war" on; Johnson was point man in the race to restore American acoustic superiority. Johnson took the display work away from Lockheed Martin and gave it to DRS Technologies, which would build the display hardware, and Digital Systems Resources, which would write the display software. These smaller firms "got" the concept of fleet consultation and were more than willing to follow the sailors' lead on this. And Johnson got better prices: DRS Technologies charged $180,000 for displays that performed better than the old $1 million monochrome Lockheed sets.

True, a small firm like DRS Technologies lacked Lockheed's lifetime stockpile of already out-of-date spare parts. But DRS's displays were built with off-the-shelf parts, which meant they could be refreshed faster, better, and cheaper anyway. And for good measure, DRS Technologies was good politics. Located in Johnstown, Pennsylvania, the company was smack in the middle of the Twelfth Congressional District. That was "Murtha Country," home base for Representative John Murtha, the chairman of the US House Appropriations Subcommittee on Defense.

Johnson's initial Advance Processing Build would be ARCI's first peer-reviewed system choice, involving world-class signal processing experts like MITRE Corporation's Gary Jacyna. Until then, NUWC had almost always had final say on what went into the boats. And NUWC, with Lockheed Martin, had already developed a new high-frequency sonar for the Navy's next generation submarine, the *Virginia* class.

Using newer technology, another Navy group working with the University of Texas claimed to have NUWC's approach beaten.

"I saw that none of us had the market cornered on sonar brains," Johnson said. "These guys came from university labs, Johns Hopkins, Penn State, University of Texas. My idea was we're going to get the best idea from wherever they are, including NUWC—and it's to my benefit to collaborate with these other domains," Johnson said.

In the fall, Johnson sent the two systems to sea, and convened a peer panel of Penn State and Johns Hopkins experts to review performance. Johnson roiled NUWC managers further by using submarine funds to pay nonsubmarine sonar experts to peer-review NUWC plans.

The data spoke, proving the superiority of the University of Texas system. With some tweaking, Johnson's group added in the best features of the NUWC system. Johnson made the call: the *Memphis* goes to sea in the spring with the University of Texas system.

It was a bizarre situation: Johnson was backfitting his older subs with technology that had already leapfrogged the *Virginia* class systems *before the Virginia subs were even built*. Wherever the *Memphis* went on that highly classified mission in the spring of 1999, the admirals rated it one of the most successful deployments ever. "Spectacular, actually," Johnson said.

Johnson, too, was satisfied. The first APB used peer-reviewed beamforming and passive sonar processing improvements, many of which originated from the University of Texas. It used displays conceived of by the master chiefs.

"This first APB," Johnson said, "proved the value of inclusiveness and transparency in our new process." The ARCI platform had delivered price, performance, and agility.

By the end of 1999, the ARCI backfitting program was well under-way. Fifteen subs were backfitted and ready for sea. The rest of the fleet was to come.

The acquisition and procurement platform Johnson developed—with architecture that invited the collaboration of universities, fleet operators, and private companies that weren't part of the inner circle, that based decisions on peer review and data analysis, and that supported a constant refresh of technology—was nothing short of revolutionary.

As in any revolution, those who saw their power, hegemony, and bottom lines threatened fought back. The fleet took a different perspective. US Navy Admirals Edmund Giambachianni, George Sterner, Frank Bowman, and Bruce DeMars saw the results, backed Johnson, briefed Congress, and won support.

Overall performance gains were astounding. Using ARCI-based so-nars, all operator detection rates—not just experts'—were now 87 percent, a factor of four improvement. False alarms were down 40 percent, to fewer than one per deployment. Time to detection—and once detected, classification—was twenty-seven minutes faster. Mean contact holding time had improved by twenty-five minutes per detection.

By 2007, every submarine hull in the American fleet had been con-verted to ARCI-based sonar. Many boats already had had five or more hardware and software upgrades. For the operators, ARCI meant dra-matically faster, more accurate detection. US undersea acoustic superior-ity was restored, and holds to this day.

After much conflict, Johnson, NUWC executives, and Lockheed made their peace. The ARCI build and major contributors like MITRE Corporation received two of Vice President Al Gore's "Hammer" awards for innovation. At the awards ceremonies, Johnson insisted that every ARCI collaborator's name be announced—all five hundred.

MAKE IT PAY

5

In collaboration folks come together, give something up, and get something back that's even better. They achieve something together that none can alone, and are better off for it.

A good platform makes collaboration easier, but only if people want to collaborate. "The availability of Lotus Notes," Thomas Davenport and Laurence Prusak write in *Working Knowledge,* "does not change a knowledge-hoarding culture into a knowledge-sharing one."

In other words, to be successful, you have to make collaboration pay. There's always an "ask" and a "get."

Sometimes the negotiating is best done machine to machine and takes milliseconds once the infrastructure and rules are set. That's what a credit card authorization swipe is all about. But figuring out the architecture for that platform so that when the time comes the execution is flawless—that's the work of humans collaborating. Everyone on the authorization platform has to want to be part of the deal—the customer, the merchant, and their banks. For agreement to happen, collaboration must pay—and pay better than the status quo.

Sometimes the negotiating is best done face-to-face, such as at Comp-Stat crime reviews, for example, which tracked progress and shared innovations at One Police Plaza in New York. Figuring out how to scale innovation, assure uptake and adoption, and improve performance on the streets is the work of humans, too. For shared discovery to translate from lab to the field, collaboration must pay across the entire platform—not just for commanders at meetings, but for patrol officers on the beat who deliver innovation on the street. Change has to pay better than doing nothing—the status quo.

A blue-sky vision offers others something better. But as deep blue as that sky may appear to you, it's still *your* vision. People will weigh the give and the get of making it *theirs*. They will always ask, "What's in it for me?"

The fact is every collaboration has its own currency. It might be money or job advancement and prestige; it might be the deep satisfaction of a mission accomplished, a job well done, a world made better. Often it can be all of those at once.

Whatever currency matters, collaboration has to make sense *in that currency*. It has to pay. The costs and benefits of collaboration may well *start* with hard dollars and cents—and end there, too. But often the currency of "yes" goes right past the world of reason into the world of emotions. Once there, collaboration has to make sense to the head *and* the heart.

WHEN COLLABORATION FAILS

A few years back hospital administrators in Cambridge, Massachusetts, thought they had a sure winner—a new system that would save lives, money, and reputations. Harvard researchers had just added up the shocking numbers on "medical errors," everything from wrong diagnoses to surgical mistakes to medication missteps. In the United States alone, they found, medical errors injured 900,000 patients and killed nearly 200,000 each year—more than all the people killed by car crashes, breast cancer, and AIDS combined.

If you wanted to change this dynamic fast—and who wouldn't?—one right-sized piece of the problem looked especially ripe for action: *adverse drug events,* or ADEs. It turns out that ADEs from allergic reactions, bad cocktailing of drugs, or overdose caused the most patient injuries. Right-sizing further, one might tackle ADEs that were caused by prescription error, which accounted for half of all ADEs.

Researchers touted a solution: computerized prescription order entry systems, or POEs. POEs, they said, promised to prevent nearly 100 percent of prescription errors. A test at Boston's famed Brigham and Women's Hospital had proved it: a POE had virtually eliminated prescription errors and reduced serious ADEs by half.

Coalitions of employers and health professionals endorsed POEs as "breakthrough" essentials. The economics of POEs suggested that a hospital like Brigham and Women's might reap annual net savings of $5 million to $10 million. Also, there was ample motivation to get this problem fixed; years earlier but still fresh in memory, a prescription error killed the *Boston Globe*'s own health beat reporter when doctors wrote up her four-day course of chemotherapy as a single-day dose.

A POE system could mean fewer injuries and deaths, lower costs, and enhanced reputations. If ever an investment screamed "Just Do It!," this was it.

In 2002, administrators at the hospital in Cambridge moved into action. The vision was clear, the problem right-sized, the platform understood. It seemed to be a perfect storm of collaboration.

Except it failed.

Physicians complained that the POE system that replaced their handwritten prescriptions with online orders was slow. That it was inconvenient. That the built-in error checking didn't work. They resisted mightily, slowed adoption, and limited its rollout to a few departments. Most doctors wanted to keep writing prescriptions by hand and faxing them to the hospital pharmacy.

Habits aren't broken easily.

Presumably, everyone had shared the vision: sound medicine, reduced risk, improved performance, and cost savings. But not everyone experienced the *loss* of the pad-and-fax system, or the *gain* from computerizing, in the same way. Not everyone added up the switch to be an unalloyed good.

It turned out that the collaboration "ask" of the physicians, in particular, was high compared to the physicians' "get." The hospital was taking something away from the doctors they already had and held dearly. Handwritten prescriptions were time honored, steeped in tradition, under doctors' direct control, and called upon their judgment as physicians just as doctors' judgment had been called upon for hundreds of years. The loss of the pad-and-fax method would be painful—signifying, perhaps, all sorts of negative things about the old, familiar, comfortable way of practicing medicine, a changing of the guard, the new digital world.

The ask of physicians—that they give up the pad-and-fax and accept and use the POE—turns out to have had unexpected costs. The doctors' get—in terms of benefits that the hospital promised them—could not begin to match up. None really dropped to the doctors' bottom line—not financially, emotionally, or professionally. With a lot of ask and little get, the prospect for collaboration plummeted from "easy sell" to "sure fail."

By assuming everyone was aligned on a shared rational goal, and not recognizing the hidden but deeply felt costs to doctors, administrators turned physicians from potential supporters into opponents.

How could administrators have made that mistake?

It happens all the time.

THE 10X FACTOR

When we ask others to collaborate, we step into a vortex of potentially powerful headwinds. Too often we underestimate how much change we're asking for, and what that change means emotionally.

Professor John Gourville at Harvard Business School has stranded together research by leading economists and psychologists to give new insight into these headwinds—and why innovations that should be home runs sometimes turn into game-ending strikeouts.

HEADWIND #1: The "status quo bias." People like to do exactly what they did yesterday. Ask for something different and they resist. They'd rather stick with what they have, even if a better alternative exists. People's status quo bias makes them reflexively unhappy about change.

HEADWIND #2: The "endowment effect." People overvalue what they already own—typically, researchers find, by a factor of three. That means for you to give something up that you already own you'd need to get back something that was *three times better*. Even then, it's a draw.

Why? Because psychologically, researchers have found, *losses loom larger than gains*. Psychologists refer to this as loss aversion. Try it for yourself. Would you make an even-money bet on the flip of a coin—heads you win $1,000, but tails you lose $1,000? Most people would refuse. Most people would want to know that they stood to make $2,000 or even $3,000 before they'd risk $1,000 on a coin toss.

That's the endowment effect at work. People endow things they have with all sorts of emotional attachment—three times more value than things are actually worth. Because of the endowment effect, giving up the old for the new is hard, even when it makes "sense."

Companies behave the same way. They are often reluctant to unload a division, for example, even though they would not now create it from scratch, nor buy it from someone else.

They also overlook planning for the endowment effect when introducing new products. Electric cars and satellite radio are just two of many innovations that ran into the endowment effect headwinds. With gas stations everywhere, for example, car owners view unlimited driving range as part of their endowment. Radio listeners view free radio as part of their endowment. Electric cars with limited driving range and XM radio at $10 per month both felt like losses and initially failed.

When the consumers of change overvalue the status quo by about three to one, that's a serious headwind. Whatever you're offering has to be a lot better, from the perspective of the "getters" than what they are giving up.

HEADWIND #3: The developer's curse. Most inventors think of their innovation as a godsend. They know it, they've lived it, they love it.

Developers—like the administrators and the IT staff in the prescription order entry account—can fall too much in love with the promise of new products. Research shows they *over*value the invention by a factor of three.

What does all this mean for collaboration?

It means there are always headwinds to start, as folks who are asked to buy into collaboration exaggerate their losses—and those selling collaboration overestimate the gains. The gap between the two groups may be huge. If your potential partners *underweight* the value of change by a factor of three, and you as a developer *overweight* it by the same amount, there's a potential mismatch of nine to one in your assessments.

That means that if you're selling a better mousetrap, it has to be *ten times better*. It's what Professor Andrew McAfee of MIT has called the "10X" factor.

Now, maybe the degree your better mousetrap has to be better is really 12X or 6X or even just 3X. Every time out, and for every new product, service, or collaboration, that factor will be different. The point is this: answering the question "What's in it for me?" sends you into a stiff headwind where the seller of the benefit might be far ahead of the buyer who, looking at what he is giving up, is just saying or at least thinking, "No way."

COUNTERING THE HEADWINDS

When you run smack into strong headwinds, Gourville and others suggest workaround techniques that can keep you moving forward:

SHRINK THE "ASK": In other words, reduce what you're asking for—in terms of money, time, emotional investment. Make the risks seem lower than the potential gain.

Right-sizing a problem almost inevitably shrinks the ask. The smaller the problem, the smaller the ask, and the less risk. But you may need to reduce it even further.

A modest ask made Vice Admiral Nancy Brown an enthusiastic

sponsor for Mike Krieger's Maritime Domain Awareness initiative. "It would be a huge cost saving to me, plus it was a faster way to get the information; it was a much more effective way to deliver capability to my commander. So there was no risk to me at all: even if it failed we'd just fall back to the way we always did things and bring in a contractor, try to get money, and build it on our own," Admiral Brown said.

"But it didn't fail, because everybody saw the benefit and that they stood to gain much more than it was going to cost them to be a participant."

BACKWARDS COMPATIBILITY. Make collaboration seem less risky by aligning what you're asking for as closely as possible to what exists now, while still achieving the needed change. That's what Toyota did for its Prius hybrid. By using gasoline as well as batteries, the Prius fit into car buyers' habits while delivering all the "green" benefits they were looking for.

Backward compatibility helped bring John Shea into Mike Krieger's collaboration. By using a new system that would fit well into Shea's existing platform, Krieger promised to deliver great value to Shea without making him move too far out of his comfort zone or invest in a whole new infrastructure.

SKIP THE ENDOWED. Court the people who aren't imbued with the endowment bias. Sports equipment manufacturer Burton did this for snowboards. Why bother trying to convert older folks away from skis? Go after younger consumers who've not yet been "endowed" with skis, then position snowboarding as supercool. The result: Burton now has dominant market share, and in the United States there are now more snowboarders than skiers.

As we'll see later in this chapter, that's what the state of Massachusetts did when it launched its experiments using electronic medical records. Just as doctors at the Cambridge hospital did with POE, older physicians pushed back against using electronic medical records—there was too much uncertainty, too little gain. But the younger docs who had no such endowment pressured their colleagues to buy into the digital system—helped along by payments the state made to cover the cash costs of enrolling. The new generation of physicians prevailed.

REFRAME THE STATUS QUO. Redefine the status quo to make it seem like change is giving something back, not taking it away. When gas stations first accepted credit cards, many tacked a surcharge onto card purchases. Consumers and card companies revolted. Why punish the cardholder? Fine. Instead, stations eased prices upward overall and then gave a discount for cash. Oil companies, gas stations, and card companies made more money. Consumers thought they were getting a good deal. All because the status quo at the pump was redefined from gasoline at $0.89 per gallon with a $0.04 surcharge for cards, to gasoline at $0.93 per gallon with a $0.04 discount for cash.

When a crisis hits, the status quo abruptly reframes on its own. The balance of risk and reward shifts. The cost of doing nothing can skyrocket; options that folks might not otherwise consider—including collaboration—look newly attractive. With that shift, a crisis is a good time to move the organization and the issues forward.

That's what Dee Hock did. He made standing still seem expensive for his would-be Visa collaborators, and framed taking first steps together as the lower-cost choice. First he accentuated the negative of the status quo: his collaborators all agreed the current arrangement with Bank of America was bad and needed fixing. Then he created a blue-sky vision that seemed both limitless and within reach: here was a promising way forward. Finally, he lowered the risk of taking that first step together. At worst, Bank of America would turn the insurgents down, and they'd be no worse off than where they started: the status quo.

BETTER THAN GOOD. Press the right buttons and you can have the home team squarely behind you. The collaboration around maritime domain awareness saved John Shea time, attention, and staff—for something he'd have to do anyway. It was like "found money." The Navy's own master chiefs helped design the ARCI displays. They took pride in ownership and felt valued as contributors. The chiefs became ARCI's ardent supporters.

SHOCK AND AWE. Make the benefits so great that people switch despite their bias. MRIs were huge compared to X-rays, for example; calculators were huge compared to slide rules. Mike Krieger's maritime domain awareness gains and Bill Johnson's ARCI-based sonar performance were so astounding that the admirals clamored for them. The support of users like John Shea and the subs' master chiefs only added to the innovations' value.

BRUTE FORCE. Coerce the switch—eliminate the old or legislate the new. For example, laws force car drivers and passengers to wear seat belts and motorcyclists to wear helmets. Plenty of organizations have simply pulled the plug on old systems and switched over to new ones.

Many collaborations that stretch out over time require some combination of all these methods, from "shrink the ask" and backward compatibility, to "shock and awe" and brute force. How and when and where to use which approach is a matter of time and circumstance, judgment and decision making, leadership and courage.

AUTOMATE OR PERISH

In the 1980s, US Customs commissioner William von Raab was driving hard to move shippers and customs brokers onto his agency's new automated system for clearing imports into American markets fast. He was fighting quite a headwind: with the exception of a few big players, the world of customs brokers was still all "green eyeshades and pencils"— hundreds of mom-and-pop shops doing manual entry the same way they'd done it for . . . was it two centuries now? Little had changed in basic customs processing since Customs collected the fledgling nation's first revenues in 1787.

President Ronald Reagan had tasked von Raab with waging the war on drugs, and doing it with less staff. It was an inconvenient moment to declare a new war. Commercial imports were surging, US docks were jammed, and industry was growling. Now von Raab had to siphon his inspectors off to the high seas to fight drug smugglers. Something had to give.

Customs rolled out the Automated Commercial Environment (ACE), a new electronic cargo-processing system that would make all invoicing electronic, reusing the same data at every step from ship to warehouse to truck to store. It would speed clearances, reduce rework, and decrease the amount of staff needed.

To be part of this new system—this global platform for trade processing—shippers and brokers had to buy gear, build programs, cast off the processes they'd used for a hundred or more years, reinvent new ones, and hitch their systems onto the main ACE backbone.

They looked at von Raab's blue-sky vision of a vastly more efficient system and saw little proof, all cost, and nothing in return but heartburn.

The industry balked and hoped to wait out von Raab. Many commissioners had come before, and many had gone; surely he would, too. Employee unions appealed to Congress to fight the job cuts. No firm would move—no one was going to make that initial investment in terminals, servers, training, and new processes, the equivalent of becoming the first fax machine owner ever.

The status quo bias headwind was blowing hard.

But von Raab battled back. His unequivocal message blared across the trade dailies: "Automate or perish."

He backed up his command as only a US Customs commissioner could. US Customs controls whose freight moves off the docks first. That move-to-market gives a huge competitive advantage to brokers waiting to get paid and stores needing to stock up with the latest fashions, appliances, and toys. It doesn't do anyone much good to get a shipment of Christmas tree-toppers from China in January.

More than that, delays cost money: goods sitting on docks slowed payments from merchants to importers, who had to deliver goods before they could send a bill. They often paid hefty penalties for each day of delay.

"The more we get better information about shipments, the more we are prepared to let apparently legitimate shipments go," von Raab told a reporter. "If an importer comes in and he's always clean, his entries will gravitate towards getting a general inspection; if he's always off, he's probably going to be inspected every time."

Von Raab's executives were even more blunt. Customs would process the electronic entries first. "We no longer are promising to treat everybody the same," one Customs official told the trade in 1985. "If you invest in automation, you have the right to expect quicker service than somebody who didn't. And you'll get it."

Von Raab had shifted the status quo. He moved from low-cost cargo clearance where everyone suffered delays (and he had no authority to charge a premium for expedited service) to squeezing all costs higher with the threat of fewer inspectors on the docks and more delays, and *then* promising a discount for those who went the all-electronic route.

Von Raab knew that if he gave competitive advantage to one firm, the holdouts would crumble. Those who broke ranks and adopted ACE would see their cargo move off the docks first. Their competitors would see it, too, and would want to get in line fast.

The trade soon caught on—either comply with the Customs Service's automation initiatives or lose business to competitors who would. The price of not collaborating now seemed much higher than the cost of change. Those who were slow to automate might never recover.

In 1985, 20 percent of entries were filed electronically with Customs. By 1988, 57 percent of American brokers were online with Automated Broker Interface, and 40 percent of all entries were filed electronically.

Customs reported that its cost per entry had fallen from $28 in 1984 to $3.

Over the next five years, brokers spent more than $600 million to automate and keep pace with the Customs Service. By 1990, *American Shipper* reported that 90 percent of all brokers' entries were handled electronically. Imports had increased by 50 percent, and revenues from duties and fees climbed to $20 billion annually.

ACE had become the electronic backbone of global trade, and it remains so today,

PENGUINS ON AN ICEBERG

Who moves first? Economists liken this to the dilemma facing hungry penguins on an iceberg. There are plenty of fish in the dark sea, but also some hungry orcas. All the penguins want to feed, but nobody wants to become a whale's dinner. Who dives, and who waits?

That's what the Customs brokers confronted. Everyone faced steep investments. Who would move first?

Von Raab was pressed for time. Foot-dragging by the trade and by the unions working their connections on Capitol Hill could undermine his strategy. He had a war on drugs to fight, and freight backing up on the docks to clear. Von Raab couldn't wait for natural market forces to work to pull this network together. He needed to get those penguins diving.

Von Raab helped the penguins solve their dilemma by making it safer to dive than to linger on the iceberg. He championed what economists call "penetration pricing" for his first adopters, and "aggressive promotion" to get his network going. The key was shifting the cost of the status quo upward so that the benefit he offered—streamlined processing—looked like an advantage.

Sometimes the steward of a platform has incentives to hand out: he doesn't have to wait for collaboration to come about in due course. He can help those first penguins take the leap, get that innovation going, and forge the collaboration that will return benefits to all.

FREE ISN'T CHEAP ENOUGH

In 2006, the nation's move to electronic health records was under way. Dr. John Halamka, Harvard Medical School's chief information officer, had been working on the effort for years. Starting in 2004, Halamka had helped create the first electronic records in Massachusetts. It took years of innovation, invention, and collaboration, and a staggering sum of money. A $50 million grant from Massachusetts Blue Cross, for example, had paid for installing electronic health records (EHR) systems in the offices of every physician in three Massachusetts communities and networking them together, at a cost of about $35,000 per office. The effort wired three communities, with four hospitals, 597 physicians in 142 practices, and 500,000 patients.

Halamka learned a number of lessons from the Massachusetts experience. "Free is not cheap enough," he said. Just handing the docs the technology wouldn't convince them to adopt it. A private-care physician practice (average size: three doctors) needed hand-holding, training, and equipment installation—about $35,000 worth.

The investment was well worth it. Massachusetts eventually went all-electronic on 90 percent of claims and dropped the per-claim cost from $2.50 to $0.25.

But most of the nation was still back in the last century when it came to medical records. In 2004, President George W. Bush began pushing EHRs from the top down. "On the research side, we're the best," President Bush said. "But when you think about the provider's side, we're kind of still in the buggy era."

Getting physicians, administrators, and the rest of the medical establishment on an EHR platform would reduce some of the billions of dollars the nation was losing every year to error, wasteful practices, and redundant care.

To move out of the "buggy era," labs, offices, and hospitals all had to speak the same data language. Each had to deal with complex legal, operating, and technical issues, such as addressing the privacy and security of patient and corporate data to the others' satisfaction. And moving to the new platform, each would have to reinvent long-established, well-tuned, and quite comfortable business practices.

Those were stiff headwinds. Even though communicating by paper was bad for business, bad for medicine, and bad for patients, hardly anyone outside of a handful of closed systems like Kaiser Permanente had made the move to EHR. Society paid for the waste and errors created by paper records, but individual physicians and hospitals saved money by sticking with paper. None of these penguins was about to jump.

President Bush asked Halamka and a core group of colleagues to help jump start a national move to EHR. In 2006, bringing all these players, their data, and their individual platforms into any kind of collaborative alignment looked impossible. A typical medical record contained on average sixty-five thousand different elements. Some seven hundred different standards, many backed by different vendors, fractured the industry. Meetings on the issue were spectacles involving upward of eight hundred stakeholder organizations.

Yet, by 2009, Halamka was able to claim that both standards and security problems—the rules and infrastructure of the platform—were essentially solved.

Halamka's group began its work with priorities set by a presidential board: "Go find and create standards of harmony around a critical set of use cases"—exemplars of information sharing everyone might agree to.

Halamka began by right-sizing the problem. *Which* use cases? Best would be those that involved data that providers now shared millions of times each year on paper. Common as these were, everyone would see the value of getting them right; everyone knew how to do them; and they might give everyone early wins and prove the whole process. With success, all would have confidence to tackle more complex matters sure to arise down the road.

"Labs? Okay, we all need that," Halamka said, going down the checklist of capabilities. "Radiology images? We need that. Personal health records? That sounds good."

With a list of capabilities in hand, Halamka chaired the process of finding data standards for each. That meant whittling down the chaos of seven hundred standards to a few they'd recommend the industry adopt for each use case.

Some calls were easy. "If somebody has a standard that's a million dollars a copy to use and is only available under a non-disclosure agreement—bad!" Halamka explained. "If someone else has a standard that's a hundred dollars to use, is freely available and the world can consume it, modify it and enhance it—good!"

As steward of this restive collaboration and its emerging EHR platform, Halamka saw that getting to "perfect" would be hugely expensive and time-consuming. He calculated that creating a single uniform data stream for every primary care physician and every hospital would cost on the order of $100,000 per user. Instead his group settled for "good enough"—not a single standard per use case, but two or three. That dropped the cost of standards adoption from $100,000 per user to $1,000.

It was good enough for starters and supported the goal, a standard designed not just for deep-pocketed players but for the little guy—and for mass adoption. Getting down to two or three standards for data exchange over the EHR platform would take much of the friction out of their collaboration.

"Good enough" was good enough for privacy and security, too. There was no way to get to a uniform national policy. Every state controlled the policies within their own boundaries, governing "the final mile" of any national network. Halamka's team decided that some national requirements would ensure "good enough" uniformity; the rest would be left to the states. No sense tangling with fifty state regulators. Was it perfect? No. Was it adequate? Yes.

The same was true for the technology architecture. A general description would suffice to make sure differing computer systems could talk. As long as vendors could then build to the architecture and be compliant, they would support new rules—anything that clarified requirements and ensured the future. With vendors on board, the move to EHR could assure basic interoperability across all users.

"You're not going to not drive a car because you're better off waiting for Scotty's transporter (from *Star Trek*) to beam you aboard some day," Halamka mused in his blog. "The same can be said of EHRs and health information exchange. Why wait?"

Halamka and colleagues hadn't completely solved the challenge of establishing a fully coordinated, national EHR system. But step by step they were taking the vision and right-sizing. Soon, they hoped, they would get a partial—and meaningful—capability into users' hands fast.

But the costly switch from paper to EHRs made sense only if it was done en masse. It made no sense to be the only EHR-ready provider on the network. How to get those penguins jumping?

The Bush administration refused to require that health providers make the move. Instead the government's strategy relied purely on market pull: they would endorse and certify the products and wait for doctors and hospitals to buy them, gradually expanding the network.

Halamka estimated that would happen around the time Scotty's transporter beam was ready for mass production.

He needed a way to make collaboration pay fast.

The Massachusetts experiment was one of several that showed that getting small-practice physicians—about 80 percent of American doctors—to adopt new standards, new gear, and new processes was an uphill slog. Many were already in financial difficulties, and the cost per practicing unaffiliated clinician had by then risen from $35,000 to $50,000. Then as now, there were good public interest reasons for doctors to hop on the bus, but few compelling personal business reasons.

There had to be a "first mover advantage"; someone had to jump first.

Halamka advocated for a new package of incentives and penalties. Given the clear public benefit that would flow from the move that private care physicians would have to make, he argued to the Obama administration that taxpayers should fund that move, in the form of direct payments, low interest loans, tax credits, or pay-for-performance incentives. Those who lagged behind, he argued, should face penalties.

At Halamka's and others' urging, the Department of Health and Human Services secured $27 billion in federal "stimulus funds" to reward EHR first movers. Any doctor's office or hospital that could demonstrate "meaningful use" of electronic health records could claim its payment. Each would have to prove it could handle twenty different EHR exchanges—the best practice "use cases" Halamka and colleagues had identified, comprising standardized records on everything from a patient's smoking history to clinical lab tests.

That $27 billion got providers' attention. On April 18, 2011, the Beth Israel Deaconess Medical Center, Halamka's own hospital, became the first hospital in the country to achieve "meaningful use."

The lead penguin had jumped, proving the waters safe for all. The move to a national system of electronic health records was on.

THE CURRENCIES OF COLLABORATION

Prizes, stature, career advancement . . . helping others, solving problems, saving the world—collaboration can offer many means of payment.

IBM INNOVATIONJAM: What happens when 150,000 people from 104 countries and 67 client companies accept an invitation to a "massively parallel conference" online? Answer: the IBM InnovationJam. In its first

InnovationJam, which lasted more than seventy-two hours, and with a promise of $100 million in funding from IBM's chairman for "best in show" ideas, forty-six thousand suggestions were posted around thirty-one core ideas for bringing IBM's new technologies to market faster, better, cheaper.

The result? Ten big ideas that represented first-of-a-kind new businesses for IBM. Pilot programs offered by the bushel. Ultimately, IBM made a $1 billion investment hoping to change the fundamentals of how IBM and its customers used energy for computing.

What else happens? You get a proven method for bringing the wisdom of the crowd, wherever it might be, on whatever topic, to a platform. You find one another, exchange visions, collaborate on problems, and make plans that translate ideas into actions.

If you're IBM, you market a generic version of the platform to other corporations like Eli Lilly. Their C-level executives connected on "VisionJam" with half their global employees and devised new strategy for the company. NATO used IBM's platform to launch SecurityJam, addressing twenty-first-century security threats. The World Urban Forum created HabitatJam for global brainstorming on urban sustainability.

There seems to be something in the Jam platform for practically everyone. Innovators connect to an audience of peers and with executives whose pocketbooks can turn ideas into reality. Executives, for their part, find thousands of creative minds pushing ideas that range from the outlandish to the complementary to the transformative. The CEO gets new ideas, improved corporate performance, worldwide engagement for his troops, and a high-visibility demonstration of his vision and leadership.

"Nothing coordinates like cash," policy analysts like to say. But collaboration can pay in many currencies.

COMPANYCOMMAND: Collaboration is what happens when US Army captains just coming off deployment have an insight about the latest convoy tactics to share with captains coming into theater.

CompanyCommand started when US Army Captains Nate Allen and

Tony Burgess were preparing for deployment to Iraq, talked with many seasoned officers just back, and compared notes at day's end over beers on their front porch. They'd picked up hard-won knowledge. Invaluable stuff. Unlike the dogma of training manuals, these were the "just in time" insights of men and women fresh from the battlespace, where move-countermove is rapid; where innovation doesn't wait for bureaucrats; and where "asymmetric advantage" is everything. This is innovation at its best: innovation that defeats even the adversary's most potent new capabilities.

In Iraq and Afghanistan, for example, senior commanders estimated a thirty-day innovation cycle for improvised explosive devices. "You figure out how they're doing it, defeat it," said General James Cartwright, vice chairman of the Joint Chiefs of Staff, "and they're quickly going to figure out how to build a new fuse."

These were insights way too important to leave to the chance encounters of a couple of captains in front-porch conversation. If they could share the latest knowledge from the battlefield with army captains everywhere and refresh it continuously with updates from the field, they'd transfer hard-gained knowledge fast, accelerate adaptation and innovation, and make a life-or-death difference.

CompanyCommand.com came to life in 2000. Its aim: create a dynamic repository of living knowledge from the men and women who'd gained it. Source it straight from the battlespace, continuously refresh it, and pass it on to the next waves of commanders.

Within the year, ten thousand captains and peers were logging on for ten or fifteen minutes every day from forward operating bases, command posts, West Point, the beach—wherever there was a connection to the web. Eight thousand lieutenants did the same on Platoonleader.com, trading insights on the latest in weapons and tactics, training and readiness, families and friends.

The websites generated 427 page views in the first month—and 400,000 within a few months. Here are a few of the snippets from this online conversation, recounted by *The New Yorker* in a recent profile:

Never travel in a convoy of less than four vehicles. Do not let a casualty take your focus away from a combat engagement. Give your driver your 9mm, and carry their M16/M4.

Tootsie Rolls are quite nice; Jolly Ranchers will get all nasty and sticky.

Soldiers need reflexive and quick-fire training, using burst fire. If they're shooting five to seven mortar rounds into your forward operating base, whatever you're doing needs to be readjusted. It's not always easy to reach the pistol when in the thigh holster, especially in an up-armored Humvee.

If they accept you into the tent, by custom they are accepting responsibility for your safety and by keeping on the body armor, you are sending a signal that you do not trust them. Do not look at your watch when in the tent.

Supply each soldier with one tourniquet; we use a mini-ratchet strap that is one inch wide and long enough to wrap around the thigh of a soldier.

You're more likely to be injured by not wearing a seatbelt than from enemy activity.

You need to train your soldiers to aim, fire, and kill.

Burgess, Allen, and two other captains who stewarded Company Command.com from a "pickup game" to widespread acceptance risked censure from their higher-ups and conflict with the established training organizations. But the payback was unparalleled, and fast.

"Great leaders tend to journal. This is a low-barrier way to capture thoughts, share them, get validation from others," said Pete Kilner, one of the captains. Together, they witnessed a community of officers explode in conversation—all eager to prepare the next wave.

For the army's trainers at Fort Leavenworth, Kansas, the innovation—now on a military server and called MilSpace—meant cautiously embracing a competitive platform where commanders were gathering not just for vetted talk-at-you one-way delivery, but for spontaneous multiparty posts. That was risky.

For the US Military Academy at West Point, it meant a new way to engage the younger command corps—"a virtual apprenticeship"—so that freshly minted leaders can get advice from seasoned ones.

To preserve the innovation West Point gave the captains safe harbor. They were brought into PhD programs, promoted, and tenured.

CompanyCommand.com's collaboration offered officers the wisdom of the battlefield. There was something in it for everyone. It was paying dividends to all.

INNOCENTIVE. What do you do if you're a commercial R&D lab with a problem you can't solve, but are willing to pay to see if others have the answer—even if they're from another industry, company, or sector?

If you're Procter & Gamble, Eli Lilly, Janssen, or one of eighty other firms that have posted their industrial and research challenges on the InnoCentive.com platform, you'll get a community of 180,000 "solvers" from 175 countries putting eyeballs on your problem. On average you'll get seventeen responses per challenge, and a usable solution 45 percent of the time. One-third of your problem solvers will have doctorates. Many will come from disciplines far distant from your own.

The cost to you? Fifteen thousand dollars to post on InnoCentive, and if you are satisfied with a solution, prize money of $10,000 to $25,000 to the solver.

What's in it for the solvers? A chance to be noticed by professional peers. Opportunities to be seen by other industries, and to have your wisdom pay dividends in unexpected ways across those boundaries. A chance to make a difference—and to pick up some cash.

What's in it for InnoCentive? Making a market: InnoCentive brings together "seekers" and "solvers" who would otherwise never find each other. Making a difference: InnoCentive helps many clients conquer big, intractable problems. Making a living: as the platform steward Inno

Centive provides the infrastructure and makes sure everyone plays by the rules of intellectual property. It has shepherded about a thousand challenges, half leading to solutions.

THE APP STORE. What's in it for you if you run an App Store platform? At Apple, you get customers flocking to your site, downloading about 225,000 apps for the iPhone five billion times over two years, collecting about $1.4 billion in revenue. Apple keeps 30 percent—that was $420 million over the first two years—while the app developers keep 70 percent of the revenue from the sales of their apps.

The App Store drives iPhone sales. That was the idea. Apple practically gives away the apps (about 80 percent of apps are distributed for free), but charges a hefty fee for the iPhones. When Apple opened its App Store in July 2008, there were 6.1 million iPhone 2Gs in use. By June 2010, 100 million Apple iPhones had been sold.

What's in it for the app developer? The exalted few make millions. But half of all Apple developers make less than $700 over the first two years.

It costs, on average, somewhere between $10,000 and $50,000 to develop an iPhone app. That means it will take the average Apple app developer fifty years to break even. But many developers are paid in another way.

Government agencies like Washington, DC's Apps for Democracy, for example, run contests for apps that "mash up" city data, combining old data sets to create new and useful apps. Cities boast huge gains for very little investment. DC, for example, received $2.3 million in software value from forty-seven apps developed by prize seekers and paid out a total of just $50,000 in prizes. First prize in 2009 was $10,000 split across a three-man team.

The Apps for Democracy contest helped DC exploit information in its computers and archives. Best of all, all that data was already gathered and paid for. By opening its data to developers, DC was able to create new value in ways never thought of or tried before. Some developers mashed up the DC crime data with bus stop locations, for example, to show the safest walking routes to and from public transit.

What's in it for the developers? Washington, DC, touts the benefits as "community building efforts," "self-actualization," "feeling valued by city/government/peers," and moving from "obscurity to recognition." These benefits seem to work for the developer and the sponsor.

Only time will tell whether the App Store business model is sustainable—where "what's in it for me" is answered so favorably for the store owner, while the apps developers receive only crumbs and glory. Apple's competitors are already giving developers a bigger piece of the pie, reducing their own take to a competitive 20 percent.

But there are clear lessons to be learned here about collaboration. By making the platform available and encouraging apps development, you can get tens of thousands of solutions faster, better, cheaper than you would by waiting to create the same apps in-house. Instead of a few major developers, you invite an unlimited number of creative minds to solve the problem.

The ask is worth the get.

MAKING CRISIS PAY

BILL BRATTON

Throughout my career, I've found that a crisis often creates the best opportunity for collaboration. It brings the payoff from change into sharp relief.

When I was brought on as chief of the New York City Transit Police Department in 1990, fare evasion was bleeding the system dry; crime and disorder were making people fearful. Both were symptoms of a system in crisis.

The Transit Police force was demoralized and badly equipped. Many cops hated the job. Their station houses and cars were broken down; their weapons and radios worked poorly. There were too few of them standing by barricaded token booths to make much difference. Protecting the transit system's money was not what they signed up for. Turnstile jumpers—170,000 of them every day—ignored their presence. And cops would ignore them: for $1.15 theft in service a single arrest might take a cop out of service for the rest of the tour.

Transit cops were the poor stepchild of a system focused on getting people to and from work that was itself strapped for cash: fare evasion alone cost the system $80 million per year. The cops looked bedraggled in their rumpled uniforms, which was understandable, as subway stations in the summer could easily reach temperatures of one hundred degrees.

There was no pride of appearance—just another sign cops were suffering a crisis in confidence, in morale, and in sense of purpose.

We turned that around by getting the cops reinvolved in policing—doing what they had joined the force to do—creating decoy units, new patrol plans, and new tactics.

Our data showed that one in seven turnstile jumpers was wanted on a warrant or probation or parole violations, and one in twenty-one was carrying an illegal weapon. We persuaded the Transit Authority to outfit a couple of buses as mobile arrest processing centers—we called them "bust buses"—and put them near the stations that had the most turnstile jumping. Now, when cops made collars for fare jumping, those arrests could quickly turn into felony arrests for outstanding warrants or weapons. All of a sudden, transit policing became real policing, not just "protecting the money."

With cops now in the game again, not only did fare beating decline, but so did the number of bad guys on the subways.

There was something in it for everyone: the riding public concerned about safety, the Transit Authority that worried about revenue, and the cops who wanted to be cops.

When it comes to making change happen, a crisis speeds up the process. It allows for the forceful breaking down of barriers; it gets people off the old tried-and-true methods. A crisis means they have less time to get into their bunkers and resist. Instead, you build up momentum that keeps things moving.

One of the things you're looking for is a trigger to get people to question their existing beliefs, the way things have always been done. To weaken the bias toward the status quo.

You also want to loosen the grip of the "endowment effect," as we described it earlier. Even people who are willing to do things differently can be pulled backward by a feeling of loyalty to the organization, to the people they've grown up with in the organization, to the old way of doing things.

To counter that, you have to get as much buy-in as possible for your vision and your change strategy. People need to see "What's in it for me?" That's what people are always asking, whether they express that or not. It's human nature. Most people are not natural risk takers.

A crisis reframes the status quo. It can make standing still seem dicier than moving forward. It can make change seem desirable.

When you want to spark organizational change, sometimes you need a crisis. If you don't have one, create one.

In the New York City Police Department the change that Comp-Stat brought started at the top. Before CompStat, the three police departments in New York—Housing, Transit, and the NYPD—each reported to different chiefs. Residents in public housing—there were six hundred thousand—phoned in complaints about drug dealing to the city's joint 911 line, or to the NYPD precincts. But stove-piped and unaccountable, the precincts often failed to forward them to the Housing Police. I learned from Jack Maple this practice was so standard that these reports were called "kites." They'd just fly away out of sight.

In 1995 the three New York City police departments merged so that all city cops, Housing and Transit included, reported to the NYPD commissioner. The Housing Police, now under my command, continued their practice of regular drug sweeps into the housing projects. They'd come back all pumped up because they'd made a hundred drug arrests. The problem was that these sweeps didn't have any effect. The next week they'd be back making a hundred new arrests at the same location.

CompStat mapping made it very clear that there were two worlds out there: the world where complaints were coming from (inside the public housing high-rises) and the world where the arrests were occurring (outside on the street). The cops were going to the old reliable fishing hole instead of where the real problem was. "That's the outdoor drug markets," the commanders said. "We can get a lot of arrests over there. Isn't that the measure of success?"

Our goal was to change the quality of life—that meant making arrests where the worst problems were, not just where they were easiest.

Well, along comes Jack Maple, my deputy police commissioner at the NYPD and the inventor of CompStat. Maple, an outsider who'd been with me at the Transit Police, wasn't bashful about speaking the truth. He told the New York cops: there are little seventy-five-year-old ladies living in these housing projects. Are you telling me that you're a New York police officer and you're afraid to go into those hallways that are basically controlled by drug dealers? But you expect someone's mother with her shopping bags to walk through them every day on her way home? Is that what the NYPD is about?

Maple created a crisis of embarrassment, a crisis of confidence about the old way of measuring success by the number of arrests rather than by impact on the real problem. He focused on the crisis of confidence in the police culture itself.

That began the process of buy-in from the top of the department. I already had a kitchen cabinet of trusted advisers, many from outside the NYPD. Now it was growing to include insiders—a new collaboration. Chief of Department John Timoney, Chief of Patrol Louis Anemone, and others began to get on board. Timoney went public to the department with a mea culpa: he took responsibility for his part, for what he called twenty-five years of failed policing in New York. "A lot of arrests . . . but I wasn't doing my job. And I'm doing it from now on."

From there it snowballed. The expanded kitchen cabinet helped create the vision and the goals—to save lives as fast as we could in New York. There was no time for academic study. Our goal was to reduce crime, fear, and disorder. Disorder was critical because it was so prevalent in the city. Eight million New Yorkers saw disorder day in and day out, but it had not been targeted by the department for thirty years.

The expanded kitchen cabinet also framed eight strategies that would focus those three goals for maximum impact. From there we created a concept called "re-engineering teams," ultimately with five or six hundred people working on all the elements of what needed to change in the NYPD to reach the vision of a safer New York City.

That's where you get maximum buy-in, just by being very transparent about what you are trying to do. At each level, you attract more people who appreciate the vision, who appreciate how this is going to impact them, individually and as a group. That's very important. The idea is to get as many people as possible into the game, as quickly as possible, and involve them in every aspect. That creates multiple benefits, so that out of every action many groups benefit.

The vision quickly spreads out like a Christmas tree. The overall goals are the trunk. You have people who have been frustrated by the status quo and are now seeing that these goals are going to meet some of their needs. Their efforts become the tree's branches.

As you bring more and more people in, you have more branches and the branches get fuller. Then you push the process down even further as you get down into the rank and file. They contribute the tactics in each case, and that's like the ornaments going onto the tree.

That is where you get buy-in. You don't need to have huge amounts of money if you have other capital to spend. People want to have some degree of creativity. So give everybody their own piece of the Christmas tree. Give them the ability to personalize their part of it, so long as what they add doesn't end up taking away from achieving the overall mission.

For CompStat, we created the vision and goals. A larger group—farther down the Christmas tree—created the strategies and best practices. We left it up to the precinct to create tactics because each was so different. We pushed responsibility as far down in the organization as we could go and demanded accountability in return. We gave discretion to precinct commanders, who passed it down to the cops riding around in radio cars, for what was expected of them in their area. That got more and more people engaged not only in understanding the vision, the goals, and the strategies but in developing the tactics.

In the submarine saga described earlier, Bill Johnson was riding the US Navy's crisis in sonar. The fleet came back with reports of collisions. Johnson was able to make his first moves because the data showed the sub sonar wasn't working; as in CompStat, the data revealed all.

Johnson wanted to open up the design and get more people involved. Sonar design had been closed to a few for many years. So, too, had policing. Innovation and collaboration benefit from inclusion. The more people that you have talking about an issue, the more ideas you're going to generate, the more feedback you're going to get, and the more you will accelerate the process of change.

So start with a crisis. Then empower others to innovate new ways to move beyond the crisis. Make people feel included and comfortable enough to put forward ideas and take risks. My job as the leader was to make it safe to take risks—so the "penguins on the iceberg" will take that first leap with you. Instead of a risk-averse culture, where people are punished because they took a chance and it didn't work, you want to create the experience of people taking initiative and being rewarded.

That's how "What's in it for me?" makes collaboration pay for all. Like a Christmas tree, it's a beautiful thing to behold.

WAITING FOR VERIZON

On Tuesday, September 11, 2001, when the World Trade Center in New York was destroyed by a terrorist attack, the New York Stock Exchange closed. This massive, proven, beautifully architected platform stayed dark for four straight trading days, longer than at any time since the Great Depression.

The attack exposed a hidden risk—not from terrorists, but from beneath the platform itself: telecommunications. Although ready to trade, no traders could buy or sell via the NYSE's platform. Telecom service to and from the platform had been destroyed underneath the collapsing Twin Towers. The crisis made collaborating to fix it not only attractive but imperative.

The 9/11 attacks had decimated lower Manhattan. Even so, by

Wednesday, September 12, most traders were ready to get the financial markets up and running. Like the New York Stock Exchange (NYSE) itself, their primary trading floors were mostly unscathed, even those just blocks away from Ground Zero. Others, more directly affected, had quickly switched to backup sites.

By Thursday, September 13, the Federal Reserve was eager to get trading going, to pump liquidity into the markets and keep the global economy humming.

"If the market can trade," Jill Considine, the head of the Depository Trust & Clearing Corporation (DTCC), told the Fed, "we will clear and settle." Before the attack, DTCC processed more than twelve million trades daily for all the major exchanges—trades valued at $105 trillion each year. In New York and London, DTCC staff had been hard at work through Wednesday night clearing and settling the backlog from Tuesday. By Thursday DTCC, like many in the business, was good to go.

There was only one problem: 90 percent of the lines running from traders to the major exchange floors ran over Verizon. And most of them were down. Telecom was out.

On that clear September morning when the world changed, giant concrete slabs tumbled from the disintegrating Twin Towers of the World Trade Center and slammed into the Verizon Central Office exchange (CO) at 140 West Street, crushing cables running from the CO into and out of Wall Street. Steel girders free-falling dozens of stories sliced five stories deep into Verizon's basement vaults, shattering water mains and flooding the CO's basement. Power was lost. No one could even find the manholes, let alone start repairs: the concrete slabs and steel girders had jammed against the building, creating an impassable set of ruins.

The NYSE lost a thousand lines instantly. Throughout Lower Manhattan, the toll to telecom was huge: two hundred thousand voice lines, one hundred thousand business lines, and 4.5 million data circuits. Ten cellular towers had been destroyed.

Without their telecom, traders from firms like Goldman Sachs, Lehman Brothers, Merrill Lynch, Morgan Stanley, and Salomon Smith

Barney couldn't connect to the NYSE, and via the NYSE, buy and sell securities. Wall Street was disconnected and the global economy was on hold.

The New York Stock Exchange is a giant among platforms, supporting collaborations among its members since 1792. In 2001 (as today), it seamlessly transacted billions of trades and exchanged trillions of dollars with astonishing speed and accuracy.

Until 9/11, calls to make the NYSE's telecom infrastructure more resilient fell on deaf ears. Long before the attack there had been just such a proposal from the Securities Industry Automation Corporation (SIAC), NYSE's engineering arm, for a secure fiber-optic network that would loop around and out of Manhattan.

At the time, SIAC's costly proposal ran straight into the headwinds of the status quo bias. It felt like expensive insurance that NYSE members neither needed nor wanted to buy. Against what risk, they asked? Airplanes flying into the Twin Towers and collapsing them onto the Verizon CO below? We'll take our chances, thanks just the same.

By Monday, September 17, after four dark trading days, Verizon had restored enough telecom that trading could resume. But Wall Street grasped now for the first time the true extent of its reliance on telecom providers, and the risk that created. Good as the NYSE platform was, its global prowess was utterly dependent upon—hostage to—a network literally under its feet, but one it neither controlled, understood well, nor ever again could afford to lose.

Part of the problem lay in the "last mile" with the trading firms themselves. Over the years, firms had continuously upgraded their telecom, buying hundreds of the latest communications services (all of which hooked onto carriers like Verizon and AT&T). As firms accumulated new services, they rarely got rid of the old. They didn't have to: every new system was backward compatible. (That had made the sale easier, of course!) But this "last mile" clutter was loaded up with risk.

And there was a "first mile" problem. Each was wired point-to-point to the NYSE's data centers. Every upgrade required unique customization where it touched the SIAC data center. That made upgrades expensive, cumbersome, and time-consuming.

All this accumulated "crud" in the "last mile" and each firm separately hardwired to the exchanges in the first made getting back to business after the 9/11 outages harder. Some of the telecom service was so old that the only people who knew how to restore it were dead or retired. For the future, that crud was going to have to go, as would point-to-point connections to the exchanges.

That still left the problems with Verizon.

Verizon's practices, such as concentrating its switches and services at the 140 West Street CO and other downtown Manhattan locations, created massive unseen risk for the trading platforms. On September 11, 2011, that risk finally revealed itself, hit Wall Street hard, and occasioned a new look at Wall Street's telecom provider. Wall Street didn't like what it saw.

Verizon, Wall Street learned, had had the securities industry's circuits running underground through PVC piping. The piping was easy to handle and cheap, but it proved poor at withstanding the impact of steel girders raining down like scalpels from one hundred stories up.

Carriers guarantee their customers a certain level of "diversity assurance." "Diversity" in this case means that carriers run identical traffic via different routes so that if one circuit goes down, the duplicate survives, and business goes on.

In the aftermath of 9/11, Wall Street discovered that it was practically impossible to determine whether it had true diversity—although its telecom outages that day indicated strongly it had little.

Such obscurity worked to the carriers' business advantage: they made a lot of money off of it. Carriers are always looking for opportunities to move traffic to more efficient pathways—and make higher profits. Key to that was a practice called "groom and fill": as new contracts came in, perhaps with better prices, or as carriers bought and leased communications and fiber from each other, carriers switched older customers' paths around—doubling up circuits and reducing diversity below what was required in the older contracts.

Carriers' "groom and fill" practices created so much risk of a telecommunications failure that at the time the Federal Aviation Administration required an audit of its circuit diversity once a month. As the guardian of the nation's skies—the steward of the civil aviation platform—FAA had to discover anywhere that a carrier's groom and fill operations reduced that platform's operational resilience. If a telecom carrier somehow "erred" and reduced FAA circuit diversity, a thirty-day audit meant it wouldn't last longer than thirty days.

For Wall Street, after 9/11, thirty days wasn't good enough. The exchange platforms supported trades whizzing by in milliseconds. Wall Street wanted real-time diversity audits. And as proof, it wanted to see its carrier's network maps.

But no carrier, Verizon or anyone elese, was about to give out maps of its network architecture to NYSE or anyone else. Carriers held these close, treating them as highly competitive industrial secrets. Furious, Wall Street was now pretty sure that its telecom providers were putting its trading platform at grave risk. Someone was going to have to pour money into the telecom infrastructure to ensure the trading platform's resilience—ground zero for America's global financial prowess and the heartbeat of the world's economy.

To which the carriers, in a joint-industry report to the president of the United States on improving financial services resiliency, basically said "Tough."

"The demand for such services," the report read, "is insufficient to allow the marketplace to support the specialized requirements of national security and emergency preparedness functions on a wide-scale basis."

To carriers, it just wasn't worth spending their money to make Wall Street's platform more resilient.

The crisis brought home just how shaky the stewards of the NYSE's platform had allowed its infrastructure to become. They resolved to break from Verizon, achieve communications independence, strengthen the platform, and control their own destiny.

R ight after Labor Day 2002, SIAC announced it would provide a new telecom network for NYSE members called the Secure Financial Transaction Infrastructure, or SFTI. SIAC would lay fiber-optic cable in rings around New York. Members would hook onto the cable and connect to SIAC's exchange servers that way—no more direct point-to-point connections to the data centers. There would be real-time diversity assurance. The network would be owned and operated by SIAC.

SIAC would switch conduit providers from Verizon, which owned the telecom conduit franchise in New York City, to ConEd, which had conduit rights for the city's electrical grid. ConEd ran its high-voltage lines all around New York, wrapped in long concrete boxes. ConEd assured SIAC it would run its fiber at the lowest rung in the box—meaning if a missile, girder, or backhoe broke through several layers of concrete it would cut through ConEd's high-voltage lines before it even touched SIAC's fiber.

NYSE members would connect to SFTI at a few SIAC-controlled points in Manhattan, eliminating their dependency on the downtown Verizon facilities. The fiber would help standardize the ways members hooked onto the ring, helping to clear out all the legacy telecom crud. And only SIAC's fiber would touch SIAC's servers: good for control, safety, and security.

There were huge upfront costs to making the change. Even major players like Merrill Lynch couldn't afford to build a network that was truly independent of the carrier infrastructure. Only by pooling resources could the industry make the move to SFTI.

Prior to 9/11, SIAC's proposal for SFTI had gained no traction. It all made good tech sense, good continuity sense. But it never made bottom-line sense. It was like buying insurance. No one really thinks the risk is real until the tree comes down on the roof or the hurricane floods the basement. Or concrete slabs and steel girders slice and dice telecom and leave Wall Street dark.

After 9/11, SFTI didn't make just business sense, it made emotional sense. NYSE owned the infrastructure and made the rules: anyone who wanted to trade on NYSE had to be on SFTI. No outliers or weak links. Everyone on the platform. Costs would be shared equitably throughout the industry—and with everyone participating, costs would be kept down.

Wall Street swallowed hard and reached deep. The first NYSE members came online in 2003. By 2004, eighty-five percent of the securities industry was on the network.

The collaboration's biggest potential payoff is something no one ever hopes to collect on: a global trading platform that rights itself quickly after a devastating attack by nature or man. One day, we now know, it might have to, and it can.

FROM PLATFORMS TO PAY TO PEOPLE

Collaboration trades in many currencies. But collaboration must make sense to the head and the heart. For Claudia Costin and her teachers in Rio de Janeiro, the payoff is knowing they are changing kids' lives. For Bill Johnson and the submarine fleet's master chiefs, it was the urgency of moving to reclaim underwater superiority for the nation. For Dee Hock, it was the satisfaction of freeing the bankcard from the shackles of its old forms and letting it soar unconstrained into the future.

A platform makes it possible. People make it happen.

ADD PEOPLE; STIR

6

A vision sets the goal. Right-sized plans show the way. A good platform takes the friction out of collaboration, making it easy for folks to find each other, get together, and collaborate. With friction low costs fall, benefits rise, and collaboration pays, with something in it for everyone.

But ultimately people drive great collaborations. The right people engaged at the right time will help you start fast, build networks and support, and deliver promised value.

BRING YOUR A-TEAM

Start by assembling a strong team—people in your organization whose very presence signals the seriousness of your mission, confers status to your group, and gives you the capability to deliver.

When you begin a collaboration, you are in a marketplace competing for others' time, attention, and investment. You're asking people to take a chance and bet on you. You have the blue-sky developer's view, but others are still deciding whether or not they are on board.

In any marketplace, no one has perfect information. Potential customers and partners look for signals that you're a good bet, that you'll deliver on your promise, that you'll make it pay in whatever currency they need.

In every marketplace well-established brands can charge premiums. For example, buyers are willing to pay a few thousand dollars more for a "preowned" sedan from a Mercedes dealer instead of a "used car" on Craigslist. The dealer has a reputation and is known; on Craigslist, buyer beware.

When you're "selling" collaboration, potential team members are making the same judgments; they're looking for clues that the collaboration will be successful. Having a strong team helps sell your collaboration: it's shorthand for "We will deliver on your trust." The nature of your team helps assure all—including the team itself—that your chances of success are strong.

Trust is especially important when reaching across boundaries. You'll encounter different organizational cultures—some *very* different. Outside partners can be even more cautious than insiders. They know less about you; they're looking for every signal they can find that you're a safe bet and a good fit. Having on your team experienced people with strong track records of success puts fuel in your collaboration tank: it buys you enough trust to take the next step, deliver, and build.

Beyond reputation, a strong team brings to the collaboration skills, knowledge, and experience to deliver. Some on the team may be great communicators who are able to translate results into meaning and sell the thinking back into their native organizations. Others may be technically proficient. Still others may have expertise in a specialized subject area.

In any team, you'll need a mix of people with different strengths and characteristics. Here are a few kinds of people who might be part of a collaboration:

AN EXECUTIVE SPONSOR: Since Admiral Nancy Brown was a combatant commander, her support conferred immediate legitimacy and status on Mike Krieger's Community of Interest initiative. That carried over when soon after Brown received a promotion to vice admiral and became the Joint Chiefs of Staff's ranking officer responsible for computing and communications. Her continued support for the Maritime Domain Awareness initiative made a difference throughout the armed services.

ONGOING TEAM SUPPORT: Chief John Timoney's backing of CompStat signaled that respected "old-school" members of the NYPD believed in the initiative. Timoney had risen through the ranks and served at the NYPD's highest uniformed levels. His endorsement convinced NYPD traditionalists that CompStat was safe and worthy of their support.

USER-DESIGNERS: Bill Johnson used the US Navy's own highly respected master chiefs to help select the new monitors and design the ARCI displays. That signaled a product design "owned" by the fleet's most experienced and trusted users. It reduced the "10X" factor of resistance and encouraged widespread acceptance of the new gear.

SPECIALISTS: A successful collaboration depends on execution. Dee Hock brought Aram Tootelian over from TRW, for example, where Tootelian had built high-reliability systems for industry and government. Tootelian's credentials helped to reassure banks about the reliability and sophistication of the new Visa platform.

OUTSIDE SUPPORTERS: In the FDA salmonella investigation, Ed Beckman, representing California's tomato growers; Reggie Brown, representing Florida's tomato growers; Martin Ley, representing Mexico's; and Ana Hooper, representing a major restaurant chain, all became convinced of the power of collaboration with the FDA in tracebacks. But they had to sell that collaboration back to their boards. Reputations were at stake: working with the FDA on a salmonella matter could imply a "problem" to a marketplace looking for any and all signals of a problem at a company or produce line. Sharing confidential industry data was risky, too. Beckman, Brown, and Hooper all convinced their organizations that collaboration with the FDA made sense. Microsoft and TIBCO/Spotfire, which would handle the data, made that "sale" easier: they each brought strong reputations for managing sensitive industrial and government information.

RESPECTED CONSULTANTS: George Kelling provided the academic bona fides behind the "broken windows" theories rolled out to the street by the NYPD and the LAPD. Kelling connected the daily policing tactics to a body of research. His unimpeachable credentials helped to ground potentially controversial policing strategies in reputable scholarship.

A "COOL" FACTOR: George Hotz's promise to create an untethered iPhone jailbreak if he won DARPA's red balloons Network Challenge signaled true coolness for anyone pitching in. As a renowned hacker of Apple's precious iPhone code, Hotz's pitch resonated with thousands around the world who saw themselves as kindred hacker spirits, always stunting and proving their chops to one another. Many of them mobilized for Hotz in the Network Challenge just to be part of his crew.

GREAT COMMUNICATORS: David Plouffe, Barack Obama's presidential campaign manager, kept collaboration on track among rank-and-file backers, volunteer staff, and high-end supporters with a constant flow of updates on campaign efforts and results. That reassured and energized everyone. Early on he fashioned "state of the race" memos supplying real-world facts against a tide of doubting reporters who'd all but conceded the Democratic nomination to Hillary Clinton. Plouffe showed backers proof of Obama's on-the-ground strength in Iowa—the first and critical state caucus. That kept wealthy backers happy and giving. Plouffe's "selling" never stopped: even after eleven consecutive Obama wins the New York newspapers were still calling the nomination for Hillary. In a face-to-face sit-down, Plouffe ran the numbers by the *New York Times'* election team, showing them how a technical misunderstanding had given them an incorrect count of delegates. That week, the *Times* ran a column headlined "Obama's *Lead* [our emphasis] in Delegates Shifts Focus of Campaign."

IMPOSING TRANSPARENCY

In 1996, New York City schools chancellor Rudy Crew made a deal with the state legislature. He had won new powers to hire and fire school district superintendents. In exchange, Crew agreed to give the districts much more budget authority to spend money as they saw fit on education—while incorporating values, strategies, and controls Crew would articulate.

Crew had negotiated a monster task for himself—getting a $9 billion New York City schools budget with controls and accountability into the hands of thirty-eight school districts and one thousand principals—all on a promise of improved instruction. Ultimately at stake was the performance of seventy thousand teachers and the education of one million public school students.

Enter Beverly Donohue, the school system's new chief financial officer.

Years earlier, Donohue had come out of Radcliffe and the Harvard Graduate School of Education to New York City ready to teach. That was 1975, and bad timing: New York's umpteenth fiscal crisis was unfolding. Ten thousand teachers were cut. It was a difficult time to find work in education.

Donohue rebooted her career, rising through New York City's government as a financial analyst first under Mayor Ed Koch; then as Office of Management and Budget deputy director under Mayor David Dinkins; then commanding OMB's Board of Education portfolio as its chief budget examiner under Mayor Rudy Giuliani.

At the time, conflict between city hall and the schools chancellor at 110 Livingston Street in Brooklyn filled the front pages and sold a lot of newspapers. The city paid a third of the school system budget, but the chancellor reported to the Board of Education, not to the mayor. The Board of Education reported to five borough presidents and the mayor—in effect, the Board reported to everyone and therefore to no one.

City hall was exasperated. "No one knows where the money goes!" And no one did. Nevertheless, mayors and chancellors had to work together, especially on budget. With the new schools chancellor, Rudy Crew, replacing the embattled chancellor, Ramon Cortines, Donohue accepted Crew's offer to become the New York City public schools' first CFO. She had the "chops": education reform credentials, proven financial system prowess, and the battle scars of past city budget wars. She was tough and smart. "Twice as smart as anyone over at City Hall," Crew's then deputy chancellor for operations, Harry Spence, said. "She ran rings around them."

First things first for Donohue: fix the Board of Education's budget platform, put an end to the board's financial shenanigans, and quiet the racket from city hall.

And shenanigans they were. Traditionally, the Board of Ed's central budget office allocated money in time-frozen categories that had long made sense to central budget administrators but reflected little understanding of how superintendents and principals actually needed to spend money to keep classrooms open, teachers teaching, and kids learning.

And so, every year like clockwork, once the money hit the schools superintendents and principals quietly worked to undo central's decisions. They spent as the real world required, sometimes skipping formalities. Good people having to get it done, but putting themselves and systems at risk. "Most of the good things I do in my school are illegal," a principal once told Donohue.

As Donohue knew, the handoff from central to the districts was a giant sieve, an unaccountable fiscal mess.

Step one in Crew's reform plan was better reporting. Six months in, Donohue delivered a new budget platform that cleared up major reporting issues. It lined up the allocation categories of the central budget office with the real-world spending categories of superintendents and principals. Central budget bureaucrats still made all the decisions about *how* to spend at the school level. But with the new reporting system, everyone could at least see *where* the money went as it moved from central down to the districts. The mayor, the chancellor, and the board all had new transparency into pens and pencils, desks and lunches, books and teachers.

With Crew having gained hire-fire authority over superintendents, and with new transparency into spending, he could now hold schools-based personnel to account for performance as never before. But first, he'd have to give them the power.

"Performance-driven budgeting" became the catchphrase. That was the theory, the vision, and the deal Crew made: those closest to the classroom should be making decisions about how to spend money on instruction. The proof should be in results: gains in student performance.

It was safe now, and necessary, to launch step two: give superintendents and principals authority over how to spend the money at the school level.

That was Donohue's job: deliver the financial systems that would help make it happen. "From that point forward," she said, "our mantra was, 'This has got to be a system you do not have to lie to.'"

D onohue assembled an A-Team: six top operations executives she recruited from the districts. Each director Donohue recruited was a master of marrying budgets to operations and performance at the district and school levels. Each had homegrown solutions, as well as workarounds from years of translating central's allocations into schools-based results.

Not unlike George Hotz and his backers, each had the respect of their district-level peers and the schools for years of "hacking" school budgets and making them work in the real world. And like the tomato industry executives working with FDA executives in Cambridge, each had doubts about this new relationship. "Can we trust you with our secrets?" they asked. "Is this real?"

"These were high-capacity operations and finance people who really were intrigued by being taken seriously," Donohue said. "They were among the most looked up to, the most capable of the directors. Having them vouch for the authenticity of the process and the quality of the product was very important." The signal they sent by joining Donohue's efforts was unmistakable.

Their goal, together, was to design a new financial management platform for all public schools in New York City. It would empower decisions by superintendents (and some principals), make it all transparent, and hold them accountable for student performance. They called the new plan "Galaxy."

Donohue's own reputation, or "brand," helped build trust among this core group. They knew her reputation for financial mastery, her passion for education, and her record of getting the job done in tough political climates. She also carried the chancellor's mace: Beverly Donohue spoke for Rudy Crew.

Donohue's job was to keep her team moving, and keep them protected during Galaxy's development. Even with the chancellor's blessing, Galaxy was still under the radar. The long knives at the Board of Education would surely be out if they understood Galaxy's true purpose: shifting power away from central and giving it to the districts. Galaxy would hardwire that reform. It would deprive the board of largesse it had long enjoyed as members wheeled and dealed budgets, "coordinating with cash" their political bases in the districts.

Like the information system Harry Spence discovered in Massachusetts, Galaxy, too, planned to be all-powerful—but not by accident, by design. The software would *embed* reform by executive decision. Galaxy was going to replace the profusion of local solutions with a single central fix and move the whole system from obscurity to transparency.

In New York City, "embed reform" and "make transparent" were dangerous moves.

The six core members met for a year and a half off-site, with topflight systems consultants, far from the prying eyes of the Board and Donohue's own central office budget executives. They compared notes with peers and translated their arcane knowledge into new business practices and a new financial reporting system for all districts and schools. Donohue's continued engagement signaled the urgency of their efforts.

"I spent a lot of time on this initiative," Donohue said. "The regularity of the meetings, the seriousness of purpose behind them, the level of engagement that we had—and it was quite a team—all contributed to a sense that this really mattered."

This was difficult leadership for Donohue. She was creating an insurgency, a parallel universe, even as she kept her own budget executives at Board headquarters at arm's length. Many on her staff were offended at the secrecy. Yet she kept the groups fenced off and focused on their respective tasks—one running today's operations, the other building tomorrow's.

A year and a half later, Donohue's core group saw the result: its best ideas were now built into a new financial control system that reflected the reality of practice at the district and school levels. Donohue was ready to bring her own budget staffs in from the cold. She formed a Steering Committee comprising central office and the core group of operations chiefs. She appointed a trusted, well-respected central office executive to lead the critical work of integration ahead.

Donohue instructed everyone to finish up: where core group proposals conflicted with central business practice, they should negotiate but resolve it in favor of the core group, and keep moving. Donohue made the core group the client of the system, and the budget office the provider. The design process, like Galaxy, flipped the historic power relationship on its head.

From that point forward Galaxy's implementation, now in the clear and with the chancellor's full endorsement, swept through the city schools. Galaxy today is the core financial reporting infrastructure of the New York City schools. Every principal is trained in Galaxy. Donohue reports that many principals tell her, "It is the way I manage my school."

THE CHANGE VANGUARD

Standing between your A-Team and the rest of the workforce is an important group of people. Harvard professor Steven Kelman, whose studies of organization change have brought together important lessons of psychology, politics, and management, calls them "the change vanguard."

The change vanguard are the constructive malcontents of any organization: they are hungry to break out, move up, and experiment. From executives to managers to employees at the point of service, Kelman's research shows 15 to 20 percent in any setting are ready to take up the cause and fix what's broken. Another 15 to 20 percent, Kelman says, are "early recruits."

Together, the "change vanguard" and "early recruits" make up the "change coalition": 30 to 40 percent of executives, managers, and front-line employees who stand more or less ready to move.

Members of the change vanguard need little wooing, inducement, or persuasion. They are adventurous: "When I go to a new city I prefer to explore on my own without a map" is the quintessential change vanguard attitude, according to Kelman. Keyed on the mission and idealistic, they're not set on going with the flow. You can count on their belief in the mission.

When it comes to people who are part of the change vanguard, Kelman says, you are not changing minds—you are unleashing change.

COLLABORATION THROUGHOUT THE ORGANIZATION

Change can make people uncomfortable. Adapting to anything new can take a lot of adjustment. Since collaboration changes how people work together, you may well see performance dip as employees acclimate to new approaches, technologies, and procedures.

If you can make it simple for those involved to be successful, you'll get to that tipping point when collaboration performance takes off.

There are things you can do to help get you there.

MAKE IT EASY: Don't ask for heroics from employees. Given the chance, most want to do well. Set up supports so that every employee, with ordinary resources, in ordinary times, can succeed in the new drill.

When facing tough problems, organizations often apply extraordinary resources and powers or call on extraordinary measures. That's fine for a time, but exceptional efforts can't be sustained forever. Put another way, heroics don't scale.

As you spread the innovations from an inner core more broadly and deeply throughout your network or organization, the new way of doing things will need to become standard operating procedure—the new normal.

Training helps. Think back to Bill Johnson's problem when the USS *Augusta* returned from its first ninety-day deployment with ARCI sonar, seeing no change. Johnson's master chiefs told him, "We have a training issue here." When that was addressed, performance improved, especially among the newer users who were not "endowed" with the emotion and habits wrapped up in the older monitors.

KNOW YOUR PATH: Often, collaboration changes the tools or products your people use, and the procedures that they follow.

When it comes to introducing new ways of working, success depends on how much change in behavior you are asking of employees. Professor John Gourville at Harvard Business School speaks of behavior change in terms of *smash hits, long hauls, small but easy sells,* and *sure fails*:

- **Smash hits** require relatively little behavior change. They provide a new set of tools that give a lot of benefit while requiring only small adjustments by users.

  Dee Hock's Visa platform didn't require customers, merchants, or banks to do much differently; all the behavior was in place, if they could just get back-office functions like authorization to work. When new technology reduced authorization time from twenty minutes to seconds, that "great leap forward" delivered a lot of value, with minimal behavior change for those involved, from banks to customers. It was a smash hit.

- **Long hauls.** Even when introducing "giant leap forward" tools with a great promise requiring significant behavior change, you can still gain widespread acceptance over time. But in a world of nonheroes, you are likely in for a long haul. Success will take time and persistence. If you don't have much time, long-haul collaborations are not the way to go.

  The change Harry Spence was bringing to the Department of Social Services would eventually pay off in a big way for social work-

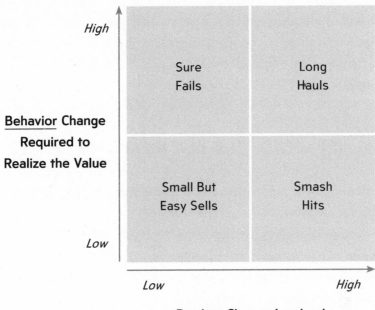

Product Change Involved
That Creates the Value

ers, children, and families. But moving from a compliance model to a strength-based approach was a major change requiring new tools and methods. The level of behavior change definitely forecast a long haul ahead.

• **Small but easy sells.** The easiest change of all is the one closest to status quo: a small change in tools, little change in behavior required, but solid value promised. Sometimes that kind of collaboration is best in order to get early, quick results.

Think of Mike Krieger's Community of Interest. The proof of concept was "simple in the extreme," as John Shea said. Everyone already knew how to tag terms and search. It was an "easy sell"— no new equipment, no huge behavior change—but delivered a lot of value, as shipboard officers could now see one another's vessels.

• **Sure fails.** Are you introducing a new tool with low value that requires high behavior change? You're in "sure fail" territory. Ever hear of the Dvorak keyboard? It rearranged the classic QWERTY keyboard, promising small gains in typing speeds. But the Dvorak required users to completely relearn how to type. That new product required a lot of work for a little gain. Sure enough, few people bought it.

INFLUENCE THE KEY INFLUENCERS

Hallway conversations and watercooler chat matters. In shaping opinion, some people are more influential than others.

At Google, the company runs what are called "prediction markets": for the fun of it, employees make "wagers" on matters such as new product rollouts, betting on which new products will be the winners and losers in the marketplace.

Not surprisingly, the employees closest to customers have the best track record at predicting new product success. The worst are those high up in the corporate hierarchy.

But Google went a step further. It turns out Google has geospatial locators on every desk in every office, so it knows who sits next to whom. When Google looked more closely at its data, the single best predictor of how a Googler would bet was how the person next to him or her bet. Physical proximity trumped all other factors.

The second best predictor was language. Googlers who spoke a common second language—as some programmers do, coming from overseas—often bet the same way. Together, physical proximity and cultural closeness were key influencers: they dominated other factors in shaping these opinions.

In other words, influencing the key influencers—knowing who they are and bringing them together—can work wonders in accelerating a collaboration.

WINNERS AND LOSERS: Those who stand to lose as a result of a collaboration usually can see their losses much more clearly than winners see their gain. That means defenders of the status quo who stand to lose from change tend to know vividly who they are. Folks who will benefit are rarely as clear-eyed.

Chances are that without some help many employees can't see what's in it for them. Having no strong opinion, they're open to the negativity of those who stand to lose—especially if they are (as Google found) physically proximate and culturally close.

That doesn't mean they don't have cares and concerns that your collaboration couldn't help address. Help them get jazzed by showing them that there's something in it for them.

SETTING YOUR COLLABORATION FREE: Sooner or later collaboration will fall into the hands of countless people you've never met. You can't anticipate every need, nor would you want to. Hand out the strategies; hand out the tools. Then set the networks free to invent, harvest, and share.

This approach helps you switch from "push" to "pull": from *selling* what you have, to having users *demand* what you have. You've put value in their hands—they want more. That's where you want to be.

CompanyCommand.com brought thousands of rank-and-file captains into the picture quickly. They added the content that created more value that brought more captains in that created more content. . . . That chain of collaboration anchored the innovation and gave it stature that made it prized by its many constituents.

In Canada, Doug Hull's initial groups didn't design everything. Hull used his platforms to turn networks loose to build more networks, customizing products and services as they went, getting passionate people into the game fast. When you're dealing with an entire *nation,* can anything but networks of networks spread the innovation outward?

Rally Fighter generated buzz and passion among the crowd of car enthusiasts Local Motors engaged for design and development. The result: an acclaimed desert-racer all could point to as "theirs."

Today, collaboration tools are everywhere. They take much friction out of search and find, engage and transact, collaborate and build. Think of Wikipedia, Intellipedia, and dozens of online platforms that help millions of strangers collaborate.

Digital platforms don't take people out of the equation. Far from it. People remain as important as ever. As we'll see later in chapter 9, at Wells Fargo one of the most impressive Internet collaborations in the history of global finance still requires steady face-to-face engagement. In the physical world or online, people who come together will always need care and feeding, to sort through conflict and confusion with a vision and plans, with a platform and partners, making collaboration pay for all.

Today collaborators can—and should—roll out that collaboration to the "crowd" much faster. The digital world now makes that possible. As Claudia Costin showed in Brazil, it takes a couple of seconds to tweet thousands of followers, a couple of hours a day to stay engaged, and days and months of hard face-to-face engagement to make collaboration real. But she changed the world for millions as a result.

BILL BRATTON's People

When I came onto the LAPD, Charlie Beck, now chief of police, was a captain and the commanding officer down at Skid Row. He and others like Mike Downing over in Hollywood were dealing with crime that had gone up under Bernard Parks, the chief who preceded me. Hollywood hadn't quite tipped back, but there was concern that it would. There was a tenseness, a shakiness to the Hollywood situation.

Before Parks, crime had actually gone down under Chief Willie Williams. Williams had more cops to work with, and brought community policing to LA for the first time. But I was astonished to learn that most cops weren't even aware they'd brought crime down, or understood how. They had no sense of their accomplishment—no awareness of having succeeded.

Parks wanted to return to the old days—the classic "LAPD way or the highway" days. He threatened to undo much of what Williams supported, disbanding the Senior Lead Officer program, for example—several hundred officers who were the heart and soul of community policing in LA, the go-to guys for neighborhood people.

Parks had had the luxury of riding Willie Williams's coattails for two years before crime started to climb back up. That was on his watch. By then the city was exhausted from years of that "LAPD way or the highway" mentality they'd lived through with Chiefs Parker and Gates; they'd had a breather with Williams. The city did not want to return to the old ways. Opposition formed up, and Parks was not rehired.

When I came on, I looked for people who, after all the conflict in LA, were not burned out or alienated from the community. Fortunately, there were still quite a few, from commanders to patrol officers. Downing and Beck, for example—both sons of men who helped build the LAPD—would become part of the fulcrum for leveraging change that I would rely on.

In each area, I looked for leaders who were comfortable creating and working in partnership, and understood that they could never be successful on their own. One of the characteristics that drew criticism of the LAPD throughout much of its history was the "leave us alone, give us the resources, and we'll take care of business" attitude. I sought out leaders who understood the need for change. I was fortunate to have them. They would have to be adept at not only motivating cops but also interacting with all the other partners—attorneys, civic leaders, business interests, community residents.

Downing was an ambitious, innovative, creative captain who was involved with the community in many ways. He was good with the cops; focused on quality-of-life issues; good at reaching out and getting other city services engaged; got along extraordinarily well with the gay community. There were race issues as well; the Holly-wood community was truly a melting pot, with every racial group imaginable. A huge tourist population was coming in and out. Gentrification efforts were under way. Within its domain venues such as the Hollywood Bowl attracted thousands of well-to-do people. All of these incredible dynamics could create conflict points, crises, and tensions. Downing was able to mediate between all of those worlds.

Jorge Villegas was the first captain in the newly opened Mission station in the San Fernando Valley. A Mexican immigrant whose parents came to the United States illegally, he spoke no English as a very young boy. Now, here he is the police captain in charge of an area that's going through rapid demographic changes and suffering from largely Latino-Mexican gang-related violence. No one was better than Villegas in that situation.

And Beck. Charlie did a phenomenal job. He got community policing. He was an activist. Cops loved him. He had a lot of specialized units down there—all officers who spent their time working with the most troubled homeless.

These were among my A-Team captains, the new leaders for LA policing. I needed to send signals across the city and the LAPD that this was the direction we were going in, and that I would rely on the LAPD itself to bring this change to the city.

I wanted the signal to be unmistakable—to the community, the commands, and the rank-and-file officers. All needed to step up and be part of the change. There were four elements that I used.

First, promotions. The chief of the LAPD, working off a promotions list, has total control over who moves up. During my seven years as chief, the 106 people in the leadership ranks of the LAPD became a handpicked team, like-minded, right for the job.

Second, resources. I would make sure the Safer City initiative in all five areas ultimately had what each needed for success. We would stake the areas to a large influx of cops to immediately stabilize the neighborhood and help draw other partners forward. I put fifty officers into the Skid Row initiative, for example. That sent quite a signal to the rest of the department and the city as to our priorities: collaboration is the way; partnership and change on the street and in the community are our goal.

Third, visibility. These were high-profile initiatives. Officers working in them were quite visible to me and the senior commanders, to city officials and workers, and to communities. It was a chance to show their stuff and be known as part of something that was changing LA for the better. That made it easy to answer "What's in it for me?"

Fourth, national stature. I brought in high-profile consultants like George Kelling. This helped raise the Skid Row efforts and all Safer City initiatives to national attention.

It worked to bring in the partners we needed, including the rank and file. With few exceptions, all officers working down on Skid Row had volunteered. They wanted to be there. For some, it was a busy district where they could make a lot of overtime. Other officers had great compassion: they cared about the people and were drawn to the opportunity to do good. There and across the Safer City initiatives I had the benefit of a workforce that did not prejudge the work. They wanted to see that they were making progress; that things were getting better; and that they and the LAPD received the public accolades they deserved.

The signals were clear: participants in the Safer City initiative were the LAPD's A-Team. That's where the promise, stature, and future were. I sought out those in the organization who would rally to the change that I wanted to make.

People are key: they signal, they support, and they deliver results. Having a strong team, enlisting the change vanguard, reaching out to executives and managers, the rank and file, and millions in networks of networks give you more than just prowess. They give you results. And in today's world, performance is everything.

PERFORMANCE

7

Ultimately, a successful collaboration comes down to performance. Performance is both the measure and the driver of collaboration. Everyone asks, "What's in it for me?" Performance delivers the answer.

Throughout this book we've seen collaboration's power, and the techniques that move it forward.

Bill Johnson and the ARCI sonar teams were *energized by emotion*—deep-seated patriotism, the press of the Cold War, the fearful price of failure, a passion for getting it right. Energized, they ignored the naysayers, and restored America's undersea advantage in an astonishing eighteen months.

The Obama campaign, for example, *pushed technology to its limits*. In state after state, Obama's team unleashed the new digital technology of social media upon the age-old goals of campaigning, tapped vast networks of partisans ready for action, and won the presidency of the United States.

The New York Stock Exchange's network failed when it needed it most: in the aftermath of crisis when the Wall Street trading floors were ready but the telecom wasn't. That *crisis made collaboration pay*—and brought forward a telecom network resilient as never before.

The *great urgency of "now, not later"*—a genuine impatience to achieve success—animated Mike Krieger and the overhaul of the US maritime domain awareness capability and bought him crucial support for his fast march to success.

Using CompStat, the NYPD turned *transparency in numbers* into crime-fighting efforts that yielded year-over-year declines in crime, brought neighbors out, and changed the look and feel of New York City.

So, what happens when you bring vision, right-sizing the problems, people, pay, and platforms together to achieve results?

You take performance through the roof.

SHOW ME THE MONEY

The bad news for Gary Loveman, Harrah's Harvard Business School professor–turned–casino empire CEO, was that Harrah's customers—*his* customers—were spending only 36 cents of their gambling dollar on his company. The good news was that they had another 64 cents left to spend. Loveman wanted it all.

For years Harrah's had been a sleepy lower-tier gambling house. By the 1980s its casinos just couldn't keep up with the big boys like MGM and their glitzy billion-dollar entertainment meccas that treated everyone from Durango or Duluth like the Sultan of Brunei. If fantasy was the name of the game, Harrah's nine dowdy casinos looked more like backdrops from a television special on "Vegas in the '50s" than a must-visit gambling destination.

Performance suffered. Quarter after quarter Harrah's missed earnings targets and bled cash. Phil Satre came on as CEO and immediately saw the problem: Harrah's wasn't so much a company as a collection of fiefdoms. It had no shared vision, no shared path nor plan to get there.

That was peculiar, Satre thought, since customer surveys told him that Harrah's best customers didn't care which Harrah's they gambled at. Whether they were in Tunica, Mississippi, Council Bluffs, Iowa, or Atlantic City, New Jersey, when it came to gambling joints, Harrah's best customers liked Harrah's not for its glitz but its game—and made a beeline for the nearest Harrah's casino.

Satre figured if he could inspire similar brand loyalty in the rest of Harrah's customers, and get hard-core loyalists to visit more and spend more, he could lift property performance *and* the company's overall results. Marketing the brand would pay for everyone.

First, Satre had to shake up some long-held myths and mindsets—that individual casinos "owned" their customers, for example, and were entitled to hoard their customers' data and run "go it alone" marketing campaigns. Harrah's own corporate practices helped fuel that mindset—

its compensation plans, for example, tied executive bonuses to property performance, not Harrah's overall corporate performance.

Satre needed to reclaim Harrah's customers from the individual casino managers and build loyalty instead to Harrah's *the company*. Satre shared his data with property managers, wooing them toward a better way and building a path there: a corporate-wide customer database. He pulled the plug on fortress-by-fortress "Castle on the Rhine" information systems and rewards programs. He moved all customer data into the corporate system and introduced a single Harrah's "Total Gold" rewards card. With that, customers could rack up points every time they played at a Harrah's casino, no matter where, boosting total property performance and the company's bottom line.

Harrah's seemed poised for greatness. Revenue was growing. It had sixteen million gamblers in its database. Satre began acquiring other brands, expanding from five to eighteen properties, and from five thousand employees to thirty thousand. But Satre was convinced that Harrah's still did not "get it." "We didn't understand how to market as a brand or how to run the operation in a fashion that created the image and impact of a brand for our customers."

So in 1998 Satre brought in Gary Loveman as chief operating officer and chief of marketing. By making all division presidents, property general managers, and marketing staffs report directly to Loveman, Satre positioned Loveman to lead the collaboration between floor and hotel operations and marketing that would take Harrah's to the next level. Loveman's mandate: market the brand first, deliver a consistent gaming experience that put the customer front and center at every Harrah's property, and boost corporate bottom-line performance.

Hiring Loveman was a gamble itself: a Harvard professor who taught marketing, he had consulted to Harrah's, but had never run a shop bigger than an academic office with a secretary and some grad students.

"They figured I was like a kidney stone," he mused. "Eventually, I'd pass, and everything would go back to normal."

Loveman fired the old-school marketing team and began reshaping operations and marketing. He relieved property managers of their individual profit-and-loss responsibilities and imported a topflight team of math gurus—a numbers-crunching A-Team—to run his analytics. From now on, data would drive every move in the collaboration.

FIRST UP: STRATEGY. Loveman recognized that Harrah's couldn't compete with destination properties like Bellagio or Luxor. It didn't have the war chest to build $1.6 billion pyramids and towers. But Harrah's could pursue a strategy like Taco Bell's—a case study Loveman had taught at Harvard Business School. Taco Bell, too, had been surrounded by competitors. Taco Bell mined its data, found a customer segment no one else wanted, and delivered on its simple wants: cheap, fast Mexican food.

SECOND: PLAY TO THE CORE. Harrah's own core customers, Loveman's data told him, were discards, too, of not much interest to the MGMs of the world. Harrah's players were older, plainer, little old ladies from Latrobe or doctors, mechanics, and accountants out for a weekend evening with the spouse or a visit on the way home from work. That "Plain Jane" core was 26 percent of Harrah's base—but 82 percent of its revenues.

Rather than jetting in, the data said, most customers lived within three hours of a Harrah's; they didn't need hotel room comps. They came to gamble. They wanted chips—and when they showed up, they wanted to get right to it—no waiting to park, no long lines for meals, no slow check-ins at the front desk.

THIRD: MAKE CUSTOMER SATISFACTION KING. Loveman knew he could deliver a satisfying experience to his core and other players at the casino level only through company-wide collaboration. All signs pointed then to a "same store" sales strategy—the retailer's classic move to increase loyalty and grab more of an existing customer's budget, whether for beauty, travel, or gambling. The lady from Latrobe had her hairdresser, her mechanic, and her drugstore. Loveman wanted to make Harrah's her gambling joint. "I'm in the business of fostering company monogamy," Loveman told a *Wall Street Journal* reporter. "Just like the Ladies' Temperance Movement."

Customer satisfaction would be king: Loveman's data showed that customers who walked away from Harrah's reporting "very happy" on surveys increased their gambling by 24 percent. Customers who said they were disappointed decreased spending by 10 percent. The data showed a direct correlation between customer service performance and financial performance.

Some customers were worth more than others. If Loveman looked to boost overall performance—deliver satisfaction, build loyalty, reap revenues—he'd have to know what made customers tick and which ones were worth spending more on.

FOURTH: KNOW WHAT MAKES CUSTOMERS TICK. Enter the Total Rewards card. Once on the property, you'd take the card everywhere you went, earning rewards by activating slots, dining at restaurants, shopping at retail stores. With every pull of a card-activated slot machine Harrah's added to its data store.

But this was more than a rewards card—it was a *loyalty* card, meant to be self-reinforcing: the more you spent, the greater your theoretical annual value to Harrah's, the more Harrah's would reward you with the things you wanted. You'd become even more loyal, get even better service and rewards, and spend even more. You could use the card and reap the benefits at any Harrah's property—whether in Topeka, Kansas, or Joliet, Illinois, or Vegas.

NEXT, APPEAL TO CUSTOMER ASPIRATIONS. Loveman made a point of activating customers' envy glands. That "no-wait" line over there? That's Diamond-level only, Harrah's highest-value customers. But they were average folks, not celebrity limo riders or blinged-up patrons. That was the message: use your card, gamble here, you'll be in that line soon enough.

"Marketing that appeals to customer aspirations," Loveman said, "works wonderfully."

In 2002 customers who held either a Platinum or Diamond card increased 16 percent from the year before, contributing to a 12 percent jump in Harrah's revenues to $4.14 billion and a 34 percent increase in adjusted earnings per share. That's some loyalty program.

DELIVER HIGHLY CUSTOMIZED SERVICE AND OFFERS. While the card was the visible trigger, behind the scenes Loveman turned each casino into a complex platform for collaboration between marketing and operations. It pulled data from floor operations, hotel and restaurant reservations, and Harrah's "patron database." That gave Loveman and his analysts a complete view of the customer. With that Harrah's wove together marketing offers by mail, in the hotel lobby, and on the casino floor—delivering on-the-money customer service, all focused on getting more of the customer's lifetime spending into Harrah's slots and tables.

The final link was the customer experience on the floor—and ultimately the employee. When the computers detected a newbie player having a run of bad luck, one of Loveman's "luck fairies" might wander by with an offer of a free dinner at Harrah's best restaurant. Eventually, Harrah's knew, the player's luck would turn. The fairy's job: deliver an offer to get her to stick it out long enough. Odds were, then, she'd walk away satisfied and be back.

It was all about revenue: the architecture of performance was so distinctive and so vital to Harrah's competitive advantage that Loveman patented the linkages.

DISPATCH OLD MYTHS. Data and analytics in hand, Loveman dispatched old myths and bad habits. Property managers feared getting stuck with empty hotel rooms, for example, and typically sold as many as they could as the reservations came in. But managers' anxieties cost Harrah's profits. Data showed that high-value customers often waited till the last minute to book. By being patient and holding aside rooms for them, Loveman consistently filled his hotel with the most profitable patrons. Harrah's-wide revenue increased from $178 per available room in 2000 to $268 in 2008.

KNOW THE LIFETIME VALUE OF YOUR CUSTOMERS. Loveman's analysts sliced and diced Harrah's customers into upward of one hundred different segments—each characterized by unique likes, habits, and dislikes. That let Harrah's estimate each customer's theoretical annual worth, not just what they'd spend in a single visit. That was potent knowledge: with it, Harrah's could do more than guess how much it should spend to keep a customer happy—it knew.

What would it take to keep customers who normally stayed for two days to stay a third, for example? Was it a $125 package of free room, steak dinner, and $30 in chips—or was it just $60 in chips? And which customers should get the offer because their lifetime value was high enough to justify it?

RUN EXPERIMENTS, PROVE THE BELIEF. If you had a hypothesis, Loveman directed, run an experiment. That process revealed the $60 chips offer, for example, and brought in higher-value gamblers. Harrah's canceled the $125 package, replaced it with a special chip promotion, and doubled its profits from those customers. The analytics were everything and every move, even if it started with a hunch, was validated by experiment.

FOLLOW THE DATA. Loveman's math gurus left little data unscrubbed. Myth had it that all slots were created equal. But Harrah's data showed that its top players preferred the end-of-row machines and disliked the crowded middles. Loveman's move: create more end-of-row machines by making more but shorter rows. Or put the machines in circles. The results: Harrah's got rid of 140 machines and boosted revenues from the remaining ones by 45 percent.

Data on low rollers persuaded Loveman to include a higher percentage of smaller-denomination slot and video poker games. That boosted revenue 12 percent from this segment. Overall, once the card program was tweaked for low rollers Harrah's per-floor sales grew at a 3 percent faster rate.

SCALE THE SUCCESSES, SHIFT THE CULTURE. By 2000, Loveman was pushing out twenty million highly customized offers each year and tracking them to see how they worked to energize customers and generate profits. The culture was shifting from the one Loveman inherited to the one he was creating. He expected managers to prevail in every metric of service—from greeting a customer to delivering a drink. "With the way we price the slot machines," Loveman said, "yield the hotel rooms, and procure things, we can be smarter than the local casinos in any market."

The new culture introduced a new language. Survival depended on getting fluent fast. Loveman explained: "I would come into an operating meeting at a property and say, 'Ok, what's wrong with segment 452 here in this city?' If they weren't using the right tools to figure it out, they were dead."

SYNCHRONIZE THE ENTERPRISE. Loveman began to orchestrate all of Harrah's systems so they played to the same score. Data told Harrah's that upbeat, positive employees were key to customer satisfaction, so Harrah's began to hire for that temperament—convinced that candidates who were already steeped in the right values made the best employees. But that was just the beginning. "We know how to describe what an upbeat positive attitude looks and sounds like," Loveman's director of customer assurance said. "We train for it. We certify observers to measure it. We score it in real time, and we give employees that feedback."

Loveman made sure choosing and retaining the right people drove every hiring manager's performance rating. Harrah's brought in a new HR chief and made its managers responsible for turnover rates. By 2003, they had taken turnover down from 48 percent in the late 1990s to 24 percent, a stunning figure for the service industry.

198 / COLLABORATE OR PERISH!

CREATE NEW PERFORMANCE PLANS. With financial performance off the property manager's plate—remember, Loveman had taken that on for himself—Loveman drove hard on nonfinancial results that he knew dropped to the bottom line. A property's customer satisfaction score counted for 25 percent of that manager's bonus, for example. And Loveman made collaboration pay: Harrah's tied all nonmanagement bonuses to unit and casino results. That gave individual workers incentives to lift each other up and encourage the right attitude and service. In 2002, Harrah's paid nonmanagement workers $14.2 million in bonuses.

REVEL IN THE RESULTS. The results were stunning. In 2000, 39 percent of customers gave Harrah's experience an A. A year later, it was 42 percent. In 2002, it was 44 percent. Loveman figured that every one-percent increase in a customer satisfaction score reaped a 5 to 10 percent revenue boost.

The changes dropped straight to the bottom line. Harrah's "same store" revenue grew 33 percent between 2000 and 2002—during seventeen consecutive quarters of growth. Harrah's share of its customers' gaming budget climbed from 36 percent to 42 percent. Earnings per share grew 110 percent from $1.28 to $2.90. The stock price climbed. By 2006, with further acquisitions, sales were forecast to reach $9.5 billion. Then Harrah's was taken private, purchased by Apollo Management and the Texas Pacific Group for $17 billion, making Harrah's the largest gaming company in the world, operating four of gambling's sterling global brands: Harrah's, Caesars Palace, Bally's, and Horseshoe.

"Our experience with customer service," Loveman said, "has shown us that meeting budget at the expense of service is a very bad idea. If you're not making your numbers, you don't cut back on staff. In fact, just the reverse."

SEEING WHAT IS

Great data and analytics point the way to high performance for every collaboration. Harrah's proves that you can achieve tremendous performance gains from collaborations by paying attention to the "signal."

Gary Loveman knew more about his customers and could deliver satisfaction better than anyone else in the business. He could get into people's heads and change their behavior because of corporate collaboration on the platform, finely aligned incentives, motivated managers and floor workers, a foundation of data and analytics, and a relentless pursuit of knowledge.

Make no mistake: the Harrah's "luck fairy" alights to rescue a losing patron not out of caring or compassion, but because computers have made the call. Group performance, future earnings, and this year's bonuses are at stake. In Harrah's world, the pathway to corporate riches is paved with satisfied customers. The plan is to understand those wants by data from the loyalty card, activate desires, satisfy them—and bind customers to you for the long haul.

We've also seen how to boost performance by unleashing the change vanguard waiting to mobilize. We've seen the power of reconnecting social workers and cops to the work they signed up to do in the first place, whether to save families or fight crime. We've seen medical technologists crunching seven hundred diverse data standards down to a handful in months, bankcard developers taking electronic authorization from minutes to fractions of seconds, and sonar teams hearing things they'd never heard before on gear installed and updated faster than ever.

After the vision and the planning, the right-sizing and the platforms, the talent and the inducements—what really makes these guys perform? What makes them *run*?

It's about the mission and motivational triggers—touching and activating deeply held values that define the culture of successful organizations. Just as Loveman activated the aspirational triggers of his customers, successful collaborations find, reach for, and act directly on collaborators' motivational triggers. Just as Loveman added data and analytics to activate these dreams, data can help break apart the crusty myths that define the culture, and day-in and -out suffocate blue-sky visions. When you speak the truth about real performance and the loss of the dream, share your plan to replace myth with reality and to restore the promise—you can trigger tsunami-like behavior change and boost performance across an enterprise. The secret is calling forth the passions all share.

THE LINDER METHOD

As a management consultant John Linder's passion has been helping leaders uncover the motivational linkages within workforces that can lift performance in collaborations. That process, Linder says, taps into what he calls "underactivated values."

Underactivated values hold the potent human energy that high-performance collaborations unleash for change. In the late 1980s, for example, New York City subway riders had fled the system. Ridership was down and spiraling to the bottom.

Starting in 1990, transit system leaders engaged Linder's "performance engineering" plans—and brought riders back with a campaign that didn't paint the subways as a rosy place. Riders knew better. Linder's "cultural diagnostic," rolled out in focus group and interview, made that clear.

Instead, the campaign acknowledged the truth riders all knew: the subways are tough. Then Linder got riders back to the subways with a highly visible campaign that played to a core value all New Yorkers shared: we're a gritty city and can handle it. Ridership rose 10 percent over three years.

In 1994, with new NYPD leadership in place, it was Linder's same theory and tactics that helped the NYPD lift crime-fighting performance, self-esteem, and public satisfaction.

The first step on the NYPD's road to recovery were focus groups that

Linder ran to uncover shared core values—the motivational triggers that leaders could activate. Not surprisingly, New York cops wanted to be real cops and catch crooks. That was the aspirational culture, the motivational trigger waiting to be pulled.

In focus groups, Linder discovered that cops felt frustrated, crushed not by the size of a problem, but by the loss of their aspirations: they couldn't be who they wanted to be, or do what they'd signed up for. Their supervisors, cops told Linder, told them to "stay clean, don't make waves. Don't cause problems."

That wasn't crime fighting—that was embarrassment management. It was a boulder crushing cops' aspirations.

Next, Linder had to pound the myth-versus-reality message into the command staff. "Here's the world you think you're sitting on top of," Linder told the NYPD's top cops. "And here's reality."

The NYPD's senior commanders protested. " 'We didn't tell them not to make collars.' Well, that's what they're *hearing* you say," Linder said. "That is the effect of your management on what they are doing or what they *think* you want them to do."

It was a hard moment. Linder called it "ripping the cataracts off." John Miller, then an NYPD spokesman, likened it to an AA meeting for bureaucrats: "You had to admit you had a problem, recount for everyone else in the group how long you'd had the problem, and how serious it was."

That's when Jack Maple grabbed commanders by the collar and waved the data: "You don't really think you fight crime, do you? These numbers say your narcotics people leave the stage at sunset when the players come on; your robbery squads work days and no weekends . . ."

Linder's process cut deeply against what he calls the "inherited culture": "all of the nice ideas we carry around about ourselves as members of an organization set against who we *actually* are as defined by what we are *actually* doing."

And it created a crisis of confidence; the data showed that the age-old beliefs in NYPD as a high-performance organization were mythical. It was time for every cop in the NYPD, from top to bottom, to acknowledge and recommit to core values they all shared—to the reason each had shown up for work day one at the academy, however many years ago, to make streets safe for New Yorkers.

That crisis can make life difficult for the status quo chieftains and risky for the message carrier. Linder had a top NYPD executive jab his finger in his chest at the next Police Foundation ball. " 'You didn't need to do that,' he said. 'You don't need to disrespect what we've done in the past,' " Linder recalled. "And I said, 'Well, I disagree. You have to define reality in a way that people already know it to be true. If you don't do that, they will not listen to you. They simply will not change their behavior.' "

With Maple's prodding, and with careful selection to the highest posts, the new NYPD command staff acknowledged the failures of the past and began building the NYPD's new path forward. The kitchen cabinet and senior staff rolled out eight strategies with 600 practical crime-fighting ideas. It gave the NYPD commanders their own new chance to make good on that same promise they made to themselves and all New Yorkers on day one of their careers. They were told, "You fill in the blanks." That forced commanders to turn to the lower ranks and say, "How should we get this done? Let's do it together."

The NYPD soon created CompStat, an accountability and best-practice forum, to keep checking on progress against the goal: to take back every building, block, and neighborhood.

To bring it all together the NYPD lined up administrative processes that touched cops' lives, like personnel management and internal discipline. Everything had to align: "speak the truth all know" and make good on the promise of reform applied not just to crime fighting, but to all facets of life in the NYPD.

Offering strategies, tracking performance, and aligning systems together transformed the streets of New York. But tapping the NYPD's underactivated values was key to mobilizing cops to be cops again, and to achieving record gains in crime reduction year after year for a decade.

———

What about an organization that marries the two approaches—a corporation like Alcoa, for example, that sought financial success by energizing a globasl workforce around a set of underactivated values that all shared, *but which had nothing to do with financial performance*? In fact, what if a corporation powers up collaboration—as Alcoa did—by *rejecting* financial goals as irrelevant if not practically subversive of the corporation's true aspirations?

That was Alcoa under Paul O'Neill, a collaboration that took a venerable hundred-year-old firm struggling through reinvention to performance that over ten years would claim for the company one-sixth of global aluminum production and nearly half of US output; a market capitalization of $29.9 billion, up from $2.9 billion when O'Neill started; and record profits of $1.5 billion on sales of $23 billion. All of this was accomplished through the single-minded pursuit of perfection in an area that wasn't about money at all.

It was about safety.

PAUL O'NEILL AND ALCOA

Aluminum is lightweight, highly conductive, workable, and easy to assemble.

Charles Martin Hall, Alcoa's founder, invented the smelting of aluminum in the 1880s; a century later neither the process nor the company, which was headquartered in Pittsburgh, had changed all that much. Take four tons of bauxite-rich dirt, refine it down to two tons of alumina powder, smelt that down to a ton of aluminum ingots, then on to can sheets, from there sixty thousand Pepsi cans, or seven Audi car frames, or planes, boats, and cars—whatever a customer wanted.

What Alcoa's customers wanted in the early 1980s was pretty much the same as what they wanted back in the 1960s, when the metal's last major consumer product innovation—the aluminum beverage can—hit store shelves. As an industry, aluminum was not exactly living on the edge of invention.

By the 1980s aluminum was in decline. Pin the blame on reduced trade barriers, moves by developing nations from bauxite mining into the manufacture of finished product, volatile world ore prices, and new substitute synthetic products like laminates and composites. The gleam had faded. Supply was up, demand was down: aluminum was a mature industry with a poor outlook.

When your product is commoditized, your company is "mature," and your prices are wildly cyclical, business strategists counsel you to "diversify."

In 1982 Alcoa's board of directors did just that. It promoted Alcoa long-timer Charles Barry to CEO and told to him to start acquiring companies that specialized in ceramics and composites, not aluminum. The board hoped that customers would come to know Alcoa as the "Engineered Materials Company."

But it didn't work. Five years later, Barry was fired, and Paul H. O'Neill was named CEO. O'Neill was an odd choice. He had grown up in government, not industry, rising from pavement to penthouse in the Nixon and Ford administrations as deputy director of the Office of Management and Budget. O'Neill had then served as an executive at International Paper. Having been on the Alcoa board for only one year and knowing little about aluminum, he was the first Alcoa CEO in a hundred years not chosen from the company's ranks.

Like a new sheriff in town, O'Neill rode in alone: he brought not one executive with him—nor did he fire any veterans.

His vision was clear. He said, in effect, "Forget diversification. There's plenty of horsepower left in this business and this company. Together we'll find a way."

Together was a weird word to use around Alcoa. The company and its union workforce had been mostly at war for a century. It was especially surprising because for the next decade, in the face of terrific economic challenges, O'Neill would mobilize employees at Alcoa not on financial performance but on workplace safety.

Ten years later, O'Neill had led Alcoa to a decade of unparalleled growth and vitality, raising revenues *and* making Alcoa one of the safest places to work in the world.

Understanding Alcoa's performance under Paul O'Neill starts with the word *shift*.

FROM SAFETY AS A PRIORITY, TO SAFETY AS A "PRECONDITION." In his first days on the job, CEO Paul O'Neill did three things. He announced safety as Alcoa's supreme goal. He invited Alcoa's safety director in for an hour-long chat. And he signaled that nothing—and no one—would be spared in relentless pursuit of zero workdays lost to injury.

"We're in the top third of all US companies on days lost to injury already," Alcoa's safety director said. "That's fine," replied O'Neill. "Everyone's done a great job getting us there. But from today forward, the only legitimate goal is zero."

Zero lost workdays? An injury-free workplace in a major manufacturing industry? Seriously?

At Alcoa's massive Knoxville, Tennessee, plant—the first stop on the new CEO's whistle-stop tour of Alcoa's facilities worldwide—forty-five union and management executives gathered for lunch.

"People," O'Neill told the group, "should not be hurt who work for Alcoa. It's not a priority. It's a precondition."

Turning to management, O'Neill said, "From this day forward we will not *budget* things that need to be done to improve safety conditions. If you have identified something that needs to be done, you should go and do it—not put it into next year's budget and in the meantime hope that no one gets hurt.

"I have told the financial staff, 'The first person who walks in here with a business case for safety gets fired.' Safety is not about money at Alcoa. It's a precondition."

Turning to the labor chiefs, O'Neill said, "If management doesn't follow up on what I just said to them, here's my home phone number."

He knew this would rile his executives. That was fine. "I was prepared to accept the consequences of spending whatever it took to become the safest company in the world."

FROM MYTHMAKING TO FACT-CHECKING. This was not pie-in-the-sky talk. This was O'Neill's vision of an institution that could no longer sit back and wait for the market to speak its verdict. Rescue by acquisition had failed, Alcoa's financials were stuck, and the firm now sat on the brink. Alcoa could save itself, but only by turning inward, wringing every last ounce of value from every facet of its business.

"Our financial goal is to earn, on average, a fifteen percent return on shareholders' equity—and to achieve growth by improving the way we use our assets," O'Neill said. Areas targeted for improvement included the speeds of machines, the amounts of energy used, people needed per task, waste material generated, and length of time on processes. "Financials," O'Neill said, "are a product of physical things you can measure. If we took care of those non-financial indicators," O'Neill said, "I had a really strong feeling that the financial result would take care of itself."

Alcoa's competitive advantage would come, then, from deep technical understanding of its process, what made the difference in firm-to-firm performance, and how far and how fast Alcoa could close gaps and then excel.

"The first organizational response," O'Neill recalled, "was 'Well, this is a tough business and Paul seems like he's a fairly bright guy. In time, he'll figure out it isn't possible to be any better than we are.'"

Alcoa's leadership had a bad case of that old-school pessimism, "This is as good as it gets," and that old-school arrogance, "Nobody does it better."

Echoing Gary Loveman's reception at Harrah's, many at Alcoa were hoping that Paul O'Neill was just a kidney stone that would soon pass. They were wrong.

Traveling around to Alcoa's plants O'Neill began "ripping the cataracts off," in John Linder's words. "How many hours out of every twenty-four are you producing class A product that goes to the customer," O'Neill would ask, "that perfectly satisfies their needs and lives up to the assertions we made about performance?"

The first answers always came back the same way: "Oh, we're really good at that. I don't know exactly, but it must be twenty-three hours a day."

That wasn't even close to true, and O'Neill knew it.

"Sixteen hours weekly maintenance downtime? You don't count that—even if you're actually touching the equipment thirty-two minutes. If the power goes down, you don't count that. If there's a snowstorm and people can't show up, that's not your fault—don't count that. If there aren't any orders, you don't count that. You don't count downtime associated with product changes."

Like Jack Maple pressing the NYPD's executive staff about how much time they actually spent fighting crime—could they spare eighteen minutes to update the precinct crime map?—O'Neill insisted Alcoa's executives calculate the true answers. Twenty-three hours of every twenty-four were spent creating product? No. It was somewhere between 50 and 60 percent of the time.

To O'Neill that gap was an invitation. "That's where we would make remarkable improvements in capital and human efficiency." But it had to be exposed first.

O'Neill sent teams to benchmark Alcoa against competitors like Reynolds and Alcan, and firms like DuPont, Xerox, and Florida Power and Light, identifying 450 measures for productivity, safety, and quality. How good were *they*? How did *they* do it?

The benchmarking was eye-opening for Alcoa's executives, and critical to shaking loose facts from myths. Every old performance assumption was subject to challenge, shifting from finger-in-the-wind mythmaking to documented metrics.

"We now know, for example, that the number of days an aluminum company can go before relining a smelting pot varies from 1,200 to a world's-best 3,200," O'Neill said. Having invented the smelting process, Alcoa learned that competitors had long since passed it by.

"If you're inside your own box," O'Neill said, "and never have a chance to look at how somebody else is working, you may believe you're excellent. The irony is that you indeed may be excellent by your past standard. You may even be improving. But in reality your work is not so impressive when compared to what is both theoretically and practically possible. Here are people who don't know anything about the damn business performing better than we are."

FROM GOOD ENOUGH TO PERFECT. How high should Alcoa aim? To O'Neill the answer was obvious: perfection.

"Benchmarking tells you, 'Find the best there is and be like that,'" O'Neill said. "We could have been as good as, say, DuPont, and stopped there. But they weren't perfect, so who wants to be like that? I didn't. If you're still thirty percent away from the theoretical limit, why the hell would you accept that as an appropriate resting place?

"The real standard" O'Neill said, "is not what somebody else is doing. It's what God tells us we can't go beyond, which is given by science and given by physical limits."

Like Gary Loveman looking for the theoretical limits of profitability of each customer, O'Neill was looking for what he called "the boundary conditions"—the theoretical limits of his own nonfinancial indicators.

"In an ideal organization, people are playing against the theoretical limit of perfect. If everyone does everything perfectly every day," O'Neill said, "you can beat any competition. And by perfect every day and everything, I literally mean everything."

Only an all-hands-on-deck collaboration could take Alcoa to performance at this level. Alcoa had never dug in the way O'Neill knew it had to now. O'Neill needed a rally point that would propel Alcoa into the "perfection" business.

FROM A BEACON OF PROFITS TO A BEACON OF WELL-BEING. The day laborer, the forge supervisor, and the plant manager wouldn't be swayed by cheerleading. In O'Neill's new world—lived in by generations of employees at Alcoa for over one hundred years—the one shared truth that bound all was the incredible complexity and danger of the Alcoa workplace.

"The wish to be injury-free isn't something people can debate," O'Neill said. "It was a good place to drive a stake into the ground."

From day one O'Neill forged a new compact: he eliminated cost as a reason to skimp on safety. "Don't ever bring me a business case for safety," he told his executives. "Spend what you need, and do it now. It's unacceptable to let things go more than twenty-four hours."

This would be the underactivated value energizing a new collaboration, mobilizing Alcoa to new levels of performance. "I needed to convince them that they mattered to me more than anything—and that they should matter to each other more than anything," O'Neill said. It was an appeal to the heart of every employee—that every employee at Alcoa mattered.

O'Neill believed it and lived by the Golden Rule. "The whole idea of diminishing marginal returns applied to safety is nutty," O'Neill said. "Think about it. 'We've reached the point of diminishing marginal returns and can't afford to get better?' Okay, let's kill a few people because we're honoring economic dogma. It's just garbage—a ready arsenal of excuses."

If a manager was told not to worry about money, what argument was left against a perfect injury-free work environment, against striving for zero workdays lost to injury? None.

As emotional fuel for high performance, a rallying cry for

collaboration, nothing was more potent than safety: "a direct, tangible way to connect with human beings on a non-debatable goal that is truly important to every human being."

As a business beacon, safety was unassailable; it was "the most important leading indicator of how good a company is or could be," O'Neill said.

As a standard of performance that could take performance through the roof, safety was unbeatable. "It introduced the idea of taking our reference point from something other than our past," O'Neill said, "or accepting as 'goodness' our performance against averages."

As an entrée to the world of not just "good enough" but perfect for *every* nonfinancial indicator, safety was . . . perfect. "The truth is you can't make safety better without having a profound understanding of your process," O'Neill said. That understanding would soon ripple through every process and lift Alcoa to unprecedented heights of performance—including financial.

FROM MAYBE TOMORROW TO THE URGENCY OF NOW. The whole enterprise ramped up. O'Neill gave his business unit presidents pagers and orders: call him directly within twenty-four hours of a workplace injury. Not just with notice, but with the cause and status. That meant the presidents had to hear from vice presidents fast. Vice presidents had to hear from plant managers even faster.

"This constantly engaged them about safety," O'Neill said. "It forced them to confront themselves: 'Why do I have to make this call I hate to make?'"

At the plants, safety programs ramped up. Managers created and filled new safety positions. Plants ran multiple audits of past safety incidents and new ones. Massive retooling of training programs began. With all eyes on them, safety managers addressed obvious problems that had been long ignored.

"You use statistical tools to see what the variation is, compare plant to plant, and tease out of the data those things that you ought to be focusing on," O'Neill said. "Then you can begin to distribute good ideas across the worldwide system so that people don't have to learn the lessons over and over again."

Not every fix was so nuanced. Following a fatal fall down a darkened pit in Davenport, Iowa, Alcoa spent $3 million to build fall protection against a danger that people had been walking by "for thirty or forty years," O'Neill recalled.

Change all started at the top, then spread downward.

"I'm convinced," O'Neill said, "that a company cannot possibly get this done if it skips any level of management. Everybody needs to understand not just the words but how to use the ideas behind statistical process control, benchmarking, and organized problem-solving—all concepts we're teaching to every employee."

Adding systems helped. The Alcoa real-time safety information system soon gave Alcoa employees at 340 locations in forty-three countries access to incident reports from near misses to injuries within twenty-four hours of occurrence—just as O'Neill had had from day one. Three Carnegie Mellon programmers built it in three weeks. This was in 1991, when few firms even knew what the Internet *was*. Yet O'Neill made safety his first major information systems investment, not marketing, not financials, not operations. He signaled, again, the urgency of "now."

"No one should be able to creep power by channeling information that other people don't have access to," O'Neill said. "I wanted everyone to have all the information—to understand that their responsibility was to take action, not wait for information to crawl its way up the corporate ladder."

Over time, the threshold for beeper notification became more intense. It was about "tuning up" the organization.

"Think about injuries as a triangle or a pyramid," O'Neill said. "At the base of the triangle are near misses. At the pinnacle of the triangle are fatalities. That's why airlines pay such unbelievable attention to the base of the pyramid. It's the preferable stage for learning—near misses give you prior warning of something that could have turned into something really awful.

"When you get an organization really tuned up for this, that's what people will report."

FROM "STUFF HAPPENS" TO "I OWN THIS." Six months after O'Neill took over, an eighteen-year-old worker died on the job in Arizona. O'Neill summoned everyone in the line of authority to Pittsburgh with diagrams, charts, and videotapes. The group mulled, considered, debated—and O'Neill gave his verdict.

"We killed him," O'Neill told the roomful of executives. "But it's my failure of leadership," he continued, "and all of you in this chain that caused this young man to be killed."

"They didn't like hearing that," O'Neill later reflected. "But if you're a leader, you're accountable. You don't have to be present when the incident happens. The leadership owns safety."

Alcoa was still learning. Stiffer penalties would come later. Shifting the mindset would take patience. "You can't get good safety results by beating the hell out of people," O'Neill explained. "If you want to see a dictator-style manager get frustrated, start holding his feet to the fire for safety.

"Until you've got all the pieces in place, and people know what their accountability is, people will hate you for taking what seems to them inhuman actions."

As for the rank and file, O'Neill felt he needed to shift that mind-set, too. The fact was that many in the Alcoa workforce could neither read nor use a computer; they couldn't read a safety sign, O'Neill found out: "Couldn't understand a sign on a wire fence that says, 'Do not pass this area or you will be electrocuted.'

"Employees exhibit so much habitual behavior," he said, "a kind of Western macho-ness that enjoys 'riding in the fear of danger.'" Here's how one employee described the culture:

This is tough work. It can easily reach over 100° F in the smelting department, and you're swaddled in long sleeves, sweat pouring down your face, ready to remove a flaming red anode. People
come from generations of Alcoans, grow up in the area, and expect
to sweat it out like their parents and grandparents did. This is real
work and you need to be mentally tough. Just look around; there
are no wimps out here. In the old days the elite workers in this
department were the guys who walked out on a grate right over the
top of the cell to break up the crust that sometimes forms during
smelting. That job took guts and skill and people got hurt. Now we
have equipment that takes care of that, but people still pride themselves on being tough. Burns, cuts, smashed fingers just come with
the territory; they make you part of the crew. Danger is like a rite
of passage.

O'Neill explained, "You have to convince your people that that kind
of behavior is not in their own interest."

FROM ADVERSARIES TO PARTNERS. The gains came swiftly. By late
1991, Alcoa could not yet deliver on zero lost workdays, but it had reduced its injury rate by 50 percent. These returns came from technical
engineering and plant rank and file, and went past safety.

Innovation and empowerment began to bleed over into other performance areas. Two employees at Alcoa's troubled Rockdale, Texas, plant
invented a new smelting process that reduced variation in a key stage by
80 percent, achieving the best "pot controls" in the plant's thirty-five-year
history. That idea added $80,000 of value to the Rockdale operation,
"maybe not a huge amount at the corporate level," O'Neill said, "but the
kind of initiative that will make the difference between companies that
are successful in the next century and those that aren't."

Alcoa's Addy, Washington, plant had dodged closure on a turnaround
but still faced one hundred layoffs. An hourly worker stepped forward:
his team had figured out how to reduce furnace downtime by 50 percent.

The plant manager said, "If you can train all nine furnace teams, we'll hold the layoffs." The new process saved Alcoa $10 million more than the layoffs promised—and preserved the jobs.

Texas workers found system fixes that clipped $400,000 off annual power costs. Brazilian employees devised new shipping containers that saved $150,000. Workers at a Tennessee plant reduced processing times by 40 percent for aluminum coils.

For the first time Alcoa was seriously listening to its employees, both salaried and hourly. "It's hard to do," O'Neill said, "especially with people who have been with a company thirty or thirty-five years and believe they know everything there is to know about the industry."

But it was essential if Alcoa was to hit new performance levels. "The people who know the work best and know best how it should be redesigned are those who do it every day," he said. "If all that creative problem solving falls on management, we'll never get more than fifty percent of a good solution."

It required a new humility that the future would not be the past. And the expectation that the rank and file not only had permission but were now expected to "think for themselves." That was new. "For too many years," a shop steward said, "people thought you left your brain in the parking lot and picked it up when you got off."

As employees emerged from their shells, the shift shocked union officials and made them rethink their role as well. "I'm never going to negotiate with you about safety," O'Neill told union heads. "I never want you to be in a position where you can legitimately say that we have not taken every step we know how to make sure that people don't get hurt."

O'Neill later observed, "It is inconceivable to me that any leader could be in a position where his workforce needed someone to represent them to reduce the hazards in the workplace."

O'Neill added financial incentives—a broad move to share perks beyond the usual elite ranks and shareholders. He brought half of Alcoa's wage-earning workforce onto a profit-sharing plan, up from 5 percent when he began. That put $1,500 into their pockets in 1989—serious money for workers with base wage rates of $12 to $15 per hour. "This begins to knit together the philosophical notion that we're all in this together," O'Neill said.

O'Neill's path to excellence transformed Alcoa labor relations. In 1996, Paul O'Neill reported this to his shareholders:

> Our focus on safety has been an important contributor to positive working relationships. Evidence of this contribution is the landmark contract we signed in 1996 with more than 10,000 U.S. employees represented by the Steelworkers union. This is the longest duration contract we know of—six years—which means all of us can concentrate on producing great results for customers instead of suffering the usual twelve-month productivity slump as we approach the end of the traditional three-year contract. Importantly, this new contract was negotiated by the Business Unit Presidents who have to live with the consequences, and it provides for a far-reaching partnership approach that can only succeed with their direct and continuing engagement. We believe the next stage of achievement in workplace relationships is an "evergreen" contract that leaves behind the outdated notion of hostility between employees and employers.

FROM REASONABLE GAINS TO QUANTUM LEAPS. August, 9 1991: Paul O'Neill stepped on the gas. The gains had been significant financially and operationally, and most of all in workplace safety.

But it wasn't enough. When a longtime Alcoa employee resigned as president, many expected O'Neill to hire a handpicked successor. Instead, O'Neill gathered Alcoa's top fifty executives and told them he was eliminating two management layers. Four senior executives had taken early retirement. Alcoa's twenty-five business unit heads would now report directly to him.

Each now had up to $5 million discretionary spending authority, up from $1 million—meaning no sign-off was required from headquarters.

But they had a charge: across all nonfinancial indicators, from safety to accounting, to close the gap between Alcoa and firms benchmarked as world leaders by a minimum of 80 percent in two years.

Madness? No, method. It was time for the great leap forward. "I am no longer willing to accommodate myself to the pace and direction of the organization when my own observations and instincts tell me we should be doing something different," O'Neill told a reporter.

To his team of executives he said, "If your calendar is filled up with people who want to see you instead of people you want to see, you haven't got a chance. You need to become creators, creating opportunities to add value in the business for the customer in a manner that is rewarding to all."

The results began pouring in. Within months there was a $75 million gain in first-quarter operating income. By December 1992, Alcoa's business units had hit 31 of 190 "quantum leap" targets. Inventory costs, ingot conversion costs, and long-term debt were slashed. Alcoa bookkeepers found ways to close their books in three days, down from nine; lawyers began filing patent applications in days instead of months.

As for safety, Alcoa's lost workday rate dropped by 50 percent. So did its rate of serious injury. The number of disabling injuries fell by more than half.

All in O'Neill's first five years.

By the end of O'Neill's ten-year tenure, Alcoa's lost workday rate had dropped to one-twentieth the US average. Not zero, but Alcoa was still learning. Along the way the company had gobbled up competitors, including Reynolds, and now controlled one-sixth of global aluminum output and nearly half of US output, and posted record profits of $1.5 billion on sales of $23 billion.

"This is a hell of a lot of fun," O'Neill said. "It's as though we've told everybody they can play ball."

Trade safety for profits? Many firms will. But O'Neill showed the opposite strategy worked better. He tapped deep into an underactivated value—to love thy neighbor as thyself—combined it with a clear-eyed focus on data, and brought his employees into a collaboration that drove safety and financial performance far higher than anyone at Alcoa thought possible.

Gary Loveman achieved performance breakthroughs with a laser-like focus on customers' aspirations. The NYPD activated mission values among cops and transformed crime fighting in New York. Alcoa gave new meaning to "mission values"—doing well by doing good.

Each collaboration had a vision, built the platforms, showed the path forward, got the right people involved, aligned personnel and other systems, and religiously applied data and analytics. The collaboration results were not miracles. Planned and systematic, they each appealed to some of our deepest wishes and achieved results by helping each man and woman realize their aspirations.

It all comes down to performance. But as we'll discuss in the next chapter, great performance also requires getting the politics right.

POLITICS:
THE GLUE AND THE GREASE

8

On June 30, 2008, two days before the scheduled launch of Operation Jaque to secure the release of the three American hostages held captive for five years in the Colombian jungle, it fell to Ambassador William Brownfield as chief of mission at US Embassy Bogotá to brief the president of the United States on final preparations—and get a green light to "go."

In a secure video conference from Bogotá, Brownfield addressed the president and his national security cabinet—the vice president, the secretaries of defense and of state, the chairman of the Joint Chiefs of Staff, the director of Central Intelligence, and the director of National Intelligence, among others.

"I had to walk them through this operation to get them to say 'Yes.' As you can well imagine, had we gotten those three hostages killed on the second of July, we would have been confronting a very, very serious political, legal, moral, humanitarian, military . . . you name it, it would have been a first class mess."

If Brownfield failed to convince the president—if he ran into resistance and could neither persuade nor negotiate the green light from Washington—nearly two years of painstaking work would be wasted. Brownfield's own legitimacy was at stake. If he could not deliver a green light, Colombians and Americans on the ground might conclude he had lost influence. That would be devastating personally, and a significant setback for any future American-Colombian collaboration.

Brownfield did not throw this on the president's lap at the last minute. For close to two years, and through the end-game of Operation Jaque, Brownfield had kept Washington informed.

"When working an operation from the field, share information to the maximum with Washington and the interagency community," Brownfield later said. "That gives you maximum margin for error. But keep your request for decisions from Washington to the minimum possible. The less you ask for permission, the more a small group of people can actually get things done.

"God, after all, did not give greater knowledge or wisdom to people who serve in headquarters in Washington," Brownfield mused. "He just placed our national capital there."

From day one in 2007 when he arrived in Colombia, Brownfield's mission stayed the same: carve out a zone of collaboration where he felt sure of support from Washington—and within which US operators on the ground could be successful. Provide cover to those operators so they could do their jobs. Maintain his own legitimacy with Washington *and* the government of Colombia by staying in the headlamps of his political support, holding everyone's trust, and regularly communicating the status of the mission.

The Americans had long since recognized that Colombians were in the lead on any hostage rescue, the stewards of the collaboration, and expert at this game.

"We had our 'first team' on the ground," Brownfield said, "the very best that we have in this sort of stuff, and these guys came out saying, 'The Colombians are probably the best jungle fighters in the world today.'"

For their part, the Colombians had learned the Americans were strong in some things—satellites and sensors, for example—but also learned to bring the "gringos" in only at the end lest they slow everything down.

Early on, for example, the Americans were riven by discord, deeply divided on how best to free the hostages.

"One side was saying, 'The only way we're going to get these guys out is by talking them out, so that the FARC will eventually release them,'" the ambassador recalled. "The other half was saying, 'Under no circumstances whatsoever do we talk to hostage-takers. It only encourages more hostage-taking. The way we're going to get these guys out is a rescue—and to shoot them out.'"

The ambassador took a deep breath. "So there was a bit of a split," he said. "One side was saying, 'Only talk, no shooting,'" and the other

222 / COLLABORATE OR PERISH!

side was saying, 'Only shooting, no talk.'" Without an agreed-upon strategy—a plan everyone could put their shoulders against—the Americans were gluing up the collaboration.

But to Brownfield's surprise and delight, the Colombians had devised an extraction plan that resolved the deeply conflicted US interests. It was a third way, the ruse—the extraction-by-deception.

The plan: close in on the FARC, putting so much pressure on them that eventually they would be open to discussing a hostage release. That would please the "only talk–don't shoot" faction. Alternatively, the FARC would be in such a vulnerable position that a rescue operation could be successfully launched. That appealed to the "don't talk–only shoot" side.

With the Colombians already in motion, Americans could either come along or watch. In fact, Colombian ingenuity kept the American faction intact and in the game. "Better to have a simple strategy with different people giving it different interpretations," Brownfield said, "than to have no agreed-upon strategy whatsoever." Resolving those differences, the Colombians inadvertently helped Brownfield keep his own support strong in Washington and in Colombia.

At the final hour, as Brownfield briefed the president and his national security team, everything made sense internally to the operators—the vision, the plan, the people, the platform in the jungle where it would all go down. President Bush authorized the mission. It proceeded, and achieved astonishing success. The all-Colombian extraction-by-ruse team on the ground, backed up by some of America's most sophisticated technical teams around the world, rescued not only the three Americans, but also twelve Colombian hostages, and for good measure captured the FARC's local front commander and his deputy.

All with neither shooting nor talking—but by a third way, a ruse.

MANAGING THE POLITICS

Collaboration requires getting people to move with you, as fast as you need, as far as you require. Since often you will lack the formal authority to direct or control others, this is a profoundly political challenge. But whether you have the authority, money, or other currency to get people going, chances are you'll be using the classic tools of politics to mobilize them: persuasion and negotiation.

Managing the politics of collaboration requires first and foremost organizing your support. That means knowing what you are expected to produce and how far and how fast you can move before you stray too far or move too slowly to hold that support.

When you deliver on the promise, you build legitimacy, and everyone wants to back you. You likely have some legitimacy at the start—you've got the expertise or a mandate of the board or the boss to get the job done. Deliver results on the first round and support is even easier to come by on the next.

While you worry about your results, everyone else is worrying about theirs. Managing the politics of collaboration also means holding your coalition together as others do the same, keeping support for collaboration with you intact.

Some may question whether the organization is really backing your vision and plan. You may need the support of a respected outsider or someone higher up to confer legitimacy.

You may need to make adjustments in roles and contributions, fine-tuning to keep weak supporters close, or inducing hold-outs to join.

Some may not have the time to participate. If you really need them at the table, you may need to reduce the time they're needed, or persuade a boss or supervisor to free them up so they can work with you.

Politics is both the glue of collaboration, binding people to a shared future, and the grease of collaboration, making it run smoothly. Bungle the politics, and your collaboration may fail.

A BRUISING IN SAN DIEGO

Anthony Alvarado was, for many years, the darling of public school reform in New York City. Through the 1970s and '80s he had become
something of a hero, first as superintendent of schools in District Four's
East Harlem—where he raised test scores and made the schools so attractive that families who had once fled to private education clamored for
admission—then again as superintendent of schools in District Two,
which ran from lower Manhattan to the Upper East Side. District Two
included fifty mostly elementary and middle schools serving twenty-
two thousand students, who were 60 percent white or Asian and 30 percent black or Hispanic. Half the students came from families living below
the official poverty line, but the census tract itself was astonishingly
wealthy: average family income was in the $160,000 range. It was a true
mix. Alvarado would use District Two as his canvas for all the reforms
he'd pioneered in Harlem, and more.

Alvarado, the savior of schools, was a professional educator strongly
committed to raising up teachers and principals, a man of action who
produced results most superintendents could only dream of through his
collaborations with teachers, parents, and administrators. He built and
maintained a strong working relationship with the United Federation of
Teachers and the Council of Supervisors and Administrators.

Among Alvarado's innovations were small schools-within-schools,
school-choice programs, and a methodology called Balanced Literacy for
reading—a teaching drill halfway between traditional phonics and the latest "whole language" methods. Alvarado mandated the reading pedagogy—
and an approach for math that similarly combined the best of new and
traditional methods—for all schools.

The changes required a relentless focus by teachers and principals on
instruction. Staff was retrained; principals rescripted their roles to become leaders of instruction, not just building administrators.

"The original idea of a principal was that of a principal teacher," Alvarado said. "That's where the word principal comes from. It then moved in

the American historical term to being the person in charge, the manager of the building, and it lost its foundation in knowing what teaching is, and being able to lead its improvement."

Throughout, Alvarado stressed collaboration and prized invention at the school level. He recruited new teachers and principals who believed in the reforms and tapped into the change vanguard already under way in the schools. "Eighty percent of what is now in the district I could never have conceived of when we started this effort," Alvarado told Harvard researchers. "The initiative and energy of the people we've brought in . . . produce a constant supply of new ideas that we try to support."

Those who didn't buy into the changes were encouraged to find work elsewhere. Over Alvarado's eleven years in District Two, many of his principals and teachers moved on. Some superintendents accused Alvarado of simply moving his problem teachers and principals elsewhere. So be it, Alvarado said dismissively. There was no shortage of parents, teachers, and principals backing him. "Teachers are interested in colleagues who carry their weight," the president of the United Federation of Teachers said. "I'm absolutely thrilled with the work we're doing with Tony in District Two."

During Alvarado's tenure, District Two rose from middle of the pack to the second highest performing district in the city. "You have to be fearless, visionary, and imaginative to get results like that," one of the city's education advocates remarked. "That's what Alvarado is." Harvard researchers championed Alvarado's methods as a model for schools nationwide. Reformers in government, civic groups, and foundations seized on his approach as a potent brew for urban school district reform.

The District Two approach created a complex platform for educational reform. It arrayed numerous groups, individuals, and organizations, all delivering services to and for children. Alvarado began looking for a larger canvas, and soon he found it in San Diego.

Through the 1980s and '90s, San Diego's public schools were themselves exemplars of reform and innovation, the envy of many cities.

But in 1996 teachers went on strike for higher wages and won. San Diego was a conservative town, and to business leaders this looked like caving to organized labor. They supported a slate of candidates to overhaul the district school board and bring in a new team to run the schools. The board hired Alan D. Bersin, an ex–US attorney for the San Diego area, Brooklyn born and trained at Harvard, Oxford, and Yale, as superintendent.

Anthony Alvarado, the renowned educator and man with a method, would come on as Bersin's deputy for instruction.

The selection of a school superintendent is, of its nature, a highly political event. Two facts stand out about the hiring of Alan Bersin. First, he came in on a 4–0 vote (with one abstention) of the school board—a moment of near unanimity for San Diego education that would soon become as rare as snow there. Second, the teachers' union felt excluded from the process. Though in the eyes of the business community the union had by its strike showed itself unfit for partnership, this was a difficult way to come into an already tough job. Schools chancellors have a notoriously short life span, and need everyone on board if there are reforms afoot.

Alvarado rapidly introduced the mandated reforms of Balanced Literacy and other elements of the Alvarado package—changes it had taken him eleven years to implement in New York's District Two. Over two years in San Diego, the school district flattened central administration, cutting out layers, downsizing staffs, and reinvesting in instruction coaches, staff developers, resource teachers, and content administrators— just as Alvarado had done in New York. Foundations funded and established a principal's training academy at the University of California at San Diego. Alvarado drove the instructional agenda relentlessly; he focused on professional development, adding summer school, extending the school day, and providing other supports for children and teachers who needed it.

It all added up to what became known as the San Diego Blueprint for Student Success in a Standards-Based System. The blueprint was expensive. The Gates, Hewlett, and Broad foundations provided over $50 million; the district raised another $20 million from savings taken from staff reductions.

As he had in New York, Alvarado considered anyone who did not stand up in front of a classroom fair game for downsizing. Six hundred aides lost their jobs, with the savings plowed back into mentoring and training. Numerous principals were removed and demoted, sometimes to public outcry.

In New York, Alvarado had spread the pain and the gain over eleven years and thirty-one other local school districts: there were lots of places to stash District Two's "discards." He had nurtured families back, built coalitions spanning the middle class and the poor, and insisted on results. Teachers couldn't wait to win a chance at a District Two position.

"In District Two," Alvarado said, "we had not only an internal community, meaning the professionals committed to doing it, but we worked hard to get the board's support, and to have the larger community understand our work, particularly at the school level. Each of the principals was able to bring the neighborhood along. We had a deeper culture and a deeper set of supports for the reform. That was not the case in San Diego."

In San Diego, Alvarado's pace and regimented approach left key partners—teachers in particular—gasping in the dust. While many in San Diego, including some teachers and principals, felt good things were happening for their city and their schools, others experienced the Alvarado "reforms" as a loss, a downgrade from professionals nurturing children to components in a production line teaching the Alvarado way—or no way.

The superintendents lost the support of the teachers' union. In the rush to transform education, the urgency of "now" in San Diego had opened a legitimacy gap. The comprehensive reform package required the full and willing participation of all: teachers, principals, and parents. Alvarado had taken ten years to develop that in District Four and eleven years to achieve it in District Two. He came to San Diego with none of those relationships in place, yet moved faster than ever.

"It was a fundamental disagreement," Alvarado said, "and underneath the fundamental disagreement was a lack of trust about the implementation of the reform."

Bersin and Alvarado were nonetheless passionate about the vision and the mission. They offered an ambitious array of initiatives and programs, believed the performance of the reforms would soon show results, and felt little need to apologize for their pace.

"You've got to jolt a system," Bersin said. "If people don't understand you're serious about change in the first six months, the bureaucracy will own you."

Within two years the school board had fractured 3–2 in support of the reforms. Candidates emerged to unseat trustees who supported the superintendent. Countering, and hoping to unseat the superintendent's opponents, business interests raised nearly $1 million for what was customarily a $40,000 race. All incumbents won, leaving the board as it was before, only now more riven than ever. The next round of elections in 2002 brought out more big money, another vituperative campaign—and still no change.

That year also brought test scores that the superintendent and his supporters could now champion as proof that change was getting results. But the two antireform trustees scoffed at the data and continued to vote against nearly every proposal offered by the superintendent. Open board meetings were appalling. The *San Diego Union-Tribune* reported that the superintendent sat "stone-faced" during a rowdy meeting where an angry crowd demanded the resignation of an anti-Bersin trustee who had sent an e-mail suggesting that the pro-Bersin trustees be shot.

It was that bad.

Alan Bersin worried that the rancor was starving his reforms of support. Alvarado acknowledged as much. "The 3–2 vote on the board essentially gets mirrored in the schools," he said, "in the willingness to participate or not, to accede and to co-construct the reform or to oppose it. The reform [acquires] opposition both at the policy level and at the implementation level."

"You can't let those situations develop," then-interim superintendent of Los Angeles Schools Chancellor Ramon Cortines said later, speaking of the virtual estrangement of two of five trustees from the reform effort. Early on, Cortines had offered this advice to his old friend and colleague Tony Alvarado.

"I told him, 'Take care of them and they will take care of you.' "

J ust after the 2002 election Bersin and Alvarado parted ways. Alan Bersin bestowed greater decision making on schools and principals. But it was too late. In the 2004 school board election Alan Bersin lost his majority and resigned.

And what of results? The evaluations of San Diego continue to this day. There were significant gains in test scores. But the improvements came too late to mend fences. Having come to San Diego elbows up on a fast-track strategy for what was a long-haul mission of reform, leaders missed the opportunity to engage their full spectrum of support, and ran out of time for changes that no doubt many had been waiting for.

"Ultimately, people at the leadership, teaching and staff development levels did not get enough practice at it," Alvarado said, "so that it could generate the kind of results that we would expect over time. In part, that did not happen because politics in San Diego from day one were split in terms of the nature of the reform and the support of the superintendents.

"I should have realized that you need to be grounded with the people, particularly a community in which you have no history. What happens is that an outsider brings in reform that is opposed, and the outsider had no relational ability to convince, cajole, communicate, listen and work through the difficulties of the reform. It's a problem. In hindsight I would have said, 'Not a good idea to do that under those circumstances.' "

A PLACE IN THE SUN

How far and how fast can you move? You'll need to take stock of your political support and look ahead to the terrain you have to cover.

Your support comes from both inside and outside, near and far: from bosses, managers, and employees who know what you're up to; from boards and committees; from analysts, legislatures, and even the media, all of whom can make life easy or hard.

Your terrain will inevitably be filled with bumps and potholes. To keep on track, you'll need to maintain your support with both inside and outside authorizers. You'll need help. "Needing help," Harvard's Philip Heymann wrote, "always means sharing power."

Tony Alvarado led, shared power, and held support in New York for close to twenty years. In San Diego, his efforts revved the engines of change, seeming to start San Diego at the end point of a process that had taken New York many years to reach, inserting a platform for collaboration that was imported and delivered rather than homegrown and discovered. Alan Bersin and Anthony Alvarado were the A-Team. But was there time or room in San Diego to build a consensus for change, unleash a change vanguard, or mobilize teachers?

The San Diego superintendents had what the presidential historian Richard Neustadt once referred to as a "hunting license": they were commissioned to bring about change in San Diego. That commission is never permanently given, Philip Heymann writes—it's on loan only so long as "the great currents of legitimacy" remain strong: "A manager's approach to legitimacy shapes every aspect of strategy, from external support to the deeply held values of the staff. Above all, it determines the alliances to which the manager can turn."

When leaders lose legitimacy, crucial support fades, alliances crumble, and even supporters pull the plug. Legitimacy buys you time to negotiate your move forward, persuading doubters to join as you go along. But in San Diego, where Alvarado needed time to gain buy-in and support, and produce results, he didn't have enough time for either.

"When building a complex agreement, trouble results if any party forgets this rule: the first negotiation is with your own base," writes the political strategist David Steven. In any school system, that base includes teachers.

MAPPING YOUR SUPPORT: Political support is dynamic. The pace and scope of your collaboration must be as well. With many parties arrayed around your platform, some for, some against, the glue and grease must constantly be adjusted to hold your coalition together—moving neither too fast nor too far in front of your support, nor so timidly that you lose legitimacy with supporters who expect change now.

When collaborating, how do you find the bright lights of support?

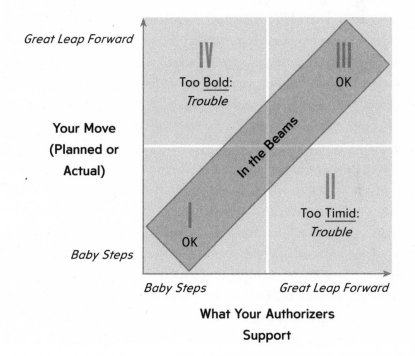

On the graph above, you can see that there are two safe quadrants and two risky quadrants. The safe quadrants—I and III—are where you and your supporters are pretty much aligned on how far and how fast you can move. That keeps you in the bright headlights of your support. In quadrant I, for example, you are planning on baby steps—and that's just fine with your supporters. In quadrant III, you are planning a great leap forward—and that's just fine, too.

There are two problem quadrants, as well. In Quadrant II, you are planning baby steps, but that's not moving fast or far enough for your supporters. They support a great leap forward, but you have only baby steps in mind. You have legitimacy to move further and faster—if you don't, you may lose support.

Quadrant IV is a problem as well: you are planning a great leap forward but it's too bold a move for some—they will support only baby steps. You might have to slow down or shrink the scope. You're not authorized for a move past the reach of these lights, and your support will trail off.

Notice that your supporters might not all be of the same mind. When conflict arises among them, you need to regain alignment: slow things down to give you time to persuade or negotiate to reduce the scope, for example. Without adjusting your pace and direction, you risk moving ahead of support from some, and even losing it.

In San Diego, teachers and the business community differed on how far and how fast Bersin and Alvarado could move. The reformers moved way out in front of teachers' support, and lost it. That put the superintendents in a risky quadrant where conflict ultimately brought their efforts to a halt.

Managing your political environment so that you maintain support is crucial. Dynamic as that environment is, it may pay for partners to play one day and bolt your collaboration the next. When times change and the make-it-pay equation slips, political management can help you keep your coalition together, ready for collaboration and for achieving together what no one can achieve alone.

TAKEOVER

General Motors go bankrupt? Preposterous. Not the soul of America, the heart of the auto industry, the giant of the factory floor. Never.

In January 2009, General Motors was riding a $17 billion gift from the American taxpayer, courtesy of outgoing President George W. Bush. Bush overruled his own free market counselors like Treasury Secretary Henry Paulson and Vice President Dick Cheney who had urged, "Let General Motors fail."

One million auto industry and supply workers out of work? The onset of a second Great Depression? That didn't strike President Bush as the legacy he wanted to leave. "Here's a $17 billion lifeline," Bush seemed to say to Chrysler and General Motors. "Godspeed and good luck. I'm outta here. Be sure to turn out the lights when you leave."

As Bush departed and the Obama team arrived, GM chairman and CEO Rick Wagoner had faith in his numbers and his future. Despite having burned through $82 billion in cash since 2005, with a little more time, and a little more help, Wagoner felt confident GM would ride the wave of the global financial meltdown crimping his and his customers' credit lines. GM would no doubt take its turn in the winner's circle once again.

But Rick Wagoner failed to see the political shift coming. Wagoner and your grandfather's General Motors were already history. They just didn't know it.

In the fall of 2008, Secretary Paulson had secured $350 billion from Congress as initial bailout money for the banks. The Big Three auto manufacturers, with their sales and cash fast disappearing, were pitching hard for a share of it.

Even in the midst of a gargantuan spending spree, the US government had an astonishingly frugal streak, as Obama's "car czar" Steven Rattner soon discovered. Rattner was a well-regarded investment banker on loan to the White House. Tasked to figure out a rescue plan for the auto industry, Rattner figured on a team of fifty lawyers and bankers—

that's how many he would have used for such a monster task on Wall Street. But Obama's chief economic adviser, Lawrence Summers, told Rattner to hold the team to fourteen.

They worked incalculable hours. They sat on threadbare chairs, toiled in dingy basements, met in ratty windowless conference rooms. Rattner winced at fake antiques everywhere—and pulled $100 bills out of his own wallet to buy guests sandwiches. They ate on paper plates. Rattner noticed even the president's telecom gear crackled and popped—*in the Oval Office.*

Rick Wagoner and Team GM got the announcement of jaw-dropping bailouts just fine, but somehow missed the "frugal government" memo. Flying into DC on private corporate jets, the chief executive officers of Ford, Chrysler, and GM beseeched senators for a $25 billion slice of the bailout. The optics of jet-setting in with tin cups at the ready made national headlines. When senators asked how the sums would be allocated, Rick Wagoner testified, blandly, "Proportionately." When asked how America's Big Three had come to this crisis, the CEOs blamed fuel prices and the economy, skipping over well-known problems within the companies themselves. Asked about their estimates of recovery and repayment, they waved charts with trend lines pointing skyward—provided they got the money they were requesting.

But these were fantasies, independent analysts said, built on overly optimistic assumptions. Moody's chief economist told Congress the CEOs' estimate of sums needed for recovery and repayment was off by as much as a factor of four.

It was all so blithe. That was the world—the political environment—Rick Wagoner had long inhabited. High up in the Renaissance Center overlooking broken Detroit, General Motors executives occupied a space where numbers like $300 million were rounded to "0.3" in budget documents, decisions moved glacially, and time stood still—a slow-motion, consensus-driven culture more like the United Nations than a firm running lean and competitive on the global stage.

Wagoner would soon have a pitiless new partner: the US government.

Within months the government would do what GM had for years failed to do for itself: clean house, clear out the deadwood, and bring the automaker into the world of global competition leaner and ready for the tough times ahead.

Steven Rattner, Lawrence Summers, and others on the Obama auto rescue team felt enormous urgency. GM's January 2009 auto sales had plummeted 49 percent. Auto parts suppliers were already starting to fail, putting another 650,000 jobs at risk over and above the Big Three's own 350,000. GM was inhaling cash—$21 billion in and out in 2008, and another $13 billion funded by the taxpayers in the first quarter of 2009.

Rattner and Summers needed GM and Chrysler to step up and present their restructuring plans (Ford dropped its aid request)—a first version by February 17, and a final by March 31. That's when the automakers would be out of cash, and the first $17 billion would either get repaid or rolled over—and more cash injected. Bankruptcy or liquidation: those were the choices ahead. With the global credit markets frozen by financial collapse, the US government was the only game in town; there was no other capital available.

As the investment banker-on-loan, Rattner would subject GM's finances and assumptions to withering scrutiny. Summers, an economist, a past president of Harvard, and now Obama's chief economic adviser, would shape the government's terms for GM and get them in front of the president. As for Obama: a White House aide once described him "as the most unsentimental man I have ever met." The president would await the recommendations of his staff, then decide.

Rattner soon discovered that General Motors—now sitting on its "proportionate" share of $17 billion of the US taxpayers' equity—felt little of that same urgency. Worse, GM executives were ignorant of crucial financial aspects of their own business: the sum of their global cash reserves, for example, or even how many accounts they had.

As Rattner and his team gasped at the magnitude of management

236 / COLLABORATE OR PERISH!

failure at GM, few at General Motors headquarters thought anyone would seriously consider GM bankruptcy. To their way of thinking "GM bankruptcy" equaled "GM destruction." The company would dutifully submit its plan and, no doubt, get more taxpayer money. Everything was cool.

That was not how Barack Obama saw things. True, Obama, like Bush, never considered letting GM die. But from the Oval Office vantage "GM bankruptcy" did not equal "GM destruction." Handled right, bankruptcy could just as well equal a leaner, stronger GM and a softer landing for the American economy. If GM bankruptcy worked to serve the nation—and perhaps preserve the Obama presidency—so be it.

attner had long believed that GM was a viable automaker. It just needed to get into fighting trim for global competition: eliminate wasteful brands, close hundreds of dealerships, shutter production lines. Cut the fat.

Rattner also became convinced that bankruptcy was the only way to rescue GM. Its thousands of creditors would be hard to mollify except under bankruptcy protection. If it came to it, Rattner's team figured it would take $50 billion to keep GM running until it emerged from bankruptcy, less for Chrysler. But if handled wrong, cleaning up the mess the previous administration left for Obama could cost a million jobs and send the country into the second Great Depression.

Through February and into March, frustration with GM's management grew. Even with Rattner's continuous prompting GM's first crack at a restructuring plan, submitted in mid-February, lacked the hard-nosed discipline of data and sacrifice Rattner knew GM needed now. The market expected better as well. Upon its public release, GM's stock fell another 19 percent.

GM had already burned through its new owners' cash at a mind-boggling pace. With March 31 approaching, there was no way Rattner could recommend pumping billions of dollars more into GM as long as Wagoner held the company's reins. No decent hedge fund manager would. "We had to address GM's dysfunction head-on," Rattner wrote, "and a key to that was upgrading its leadership."

As Obama navigated to rescue first Chrysler and then GM, he faced treacherous political shoals. Michigan's senators and representatives were watching like hawks. The United Auto Workers was all set to say no to any further concessions. Republican leaders and right-wing editorial pages voiced disgust at any US government involvement in the markets.

Bondholders like JPMorgan Chase—with $6.9 billion sunk into Chrysler—were lining up to be first in any payouts, and looking for dollar-for-dollar payback. Rattner knew that was laughable: Chrysler's corporate paper was trading for 15 cents on the dollar and its total liquidation value was $1 billion. But if dealing with the lenders was a thorny issue, there were dozens more on the horizon.

On the evening of March 29, 2009, Obama and his aides huddled around the Oval Office speakerphone as the president made the obligatory calls to the Michigan delegation and governor, informing them of the announcement he would make the next day. Obama would fund Chrysler for thirty more days to give the company time to work it out with bondholders and the UAW, or to see if it could arrange a marriage with the Italian carmaker Fiat. Obama would give the more troubled GM sixty days to work it out with investors and labor before taking more drastic action, including forcing the automaker into bankruptcy.

Meanwhile, the administration tossed a bone to the Michigan delegation by helping to stimulate new car demand with its "cash for clunkers" trade-in program.

Rattner informed Rick Wagoner he was out. Splitting the ousted executive's duties, Rattner appointed GM's president, Fritz Henderson, as the interim CEO, and Kent Kresa, a GM director, as the interim chairman of the board.

As for Chrysler, by the end of April the UAW had signed on to concessions including exchanging an $8 billion existing claim for $4.6 billion in notes and 55 percent of the equity in the reorganized company. Some auto suppliers would get 100 percent of their claims paid.

But bondholders like JPMorgan Chase balked at Rattner's best offer of $2 billion (30 cents on the dollar)—twice the market valuation of the bonds or Chrysler's liquidated value. By rights, the bondholders said, they should get a better deal than labor or suppliers. Rattner countered: car companies first and foremost need workers, suppliers, and customers. The deal collapsed, and Obama announced Chrysler would now proceed with bankruptcy. "It was the Golden Rule of Wall Street," Rattner wrote. " 'He who has the gold makes the rules.' " Let the bondholders sue. Which they did. And lost.

The deals proposed by the US government went into force with the UAW, suppliers, and bondholders. Allocating $2 billion to the bondholders, Obama saw to it that they did better together than they would have on their own in a liquidation. Fiat could now proceed with its courtship. And Chrysler would be preserved.

Chrysler bankruptcy proceeded quickly. To everyone's amazement a "new" slimmed-down and married-up Chrysler was slated to emerge from bankruptcy in midsummer 2009.

Over at GM, Chrysler's bankruptcy and Wagoner's departure finally got their attention. The "B" word was now not only mentionable but likely. Still, it was one thing to try for agreement with Chrysler's forty-five major lenders; it was another to coordinate agreement with GM's thousands.

Meanwhile, new GM management was putting finishing touches on an aggressive restructuring plan. They had bargained a new arrangement with the UAW. But US government support was still needed to close final gaps. That would come in the form of stock, not cash. Cash would have created new unmanageable debt for GM. Instead, the US government would take an equity position in GM, becoming for a time its principal stockholder, planning to sell its stake as soon as it could get its money out.

By June 1, 2009, Obama had done his round of obligatory consultations. He announced GM bankruptcy. Supported by another US investment, General Motors underwent the largest industrial bankruptcy in the nation's history, shedding assets and leveraging strengths.

A scant five weeks into bankruptcy, GM emerged from protection. The company soon announced net quarterly earnings of $1.3 billon, its second quarterly profit in a row and its best since 2004. On August 18, 2009, the "new GM" proffered an initial public offering of stock, an event greeted by the *Economist* with the headline "Rising from the Ashes in Detroit: General Motors' Return to the Stockmarket Heralds a Remarkable Turnaround for America's Carmakers." The US taxpayer now owned 60.8 percent of GM, but was on track, soon, to be paid at least in part, if not in full.

A second Great Depression had been averted. The Big Three auto companies were preserved. There were fewer jobs, yes, but jobs all the same. Two companies were smaller, leaner, and ready to compete. Everyone was arguably better off together than alone under a liquidation.

The Obama team had made it pay for collaborators to stick together, providing the glue and the grease—and the cash—to make it happen.

THE READINESS GAP

Keeping your supporters happy with the pace and direction of the collaboration is key. But your political chores don't stop there. You have to get your collaborators ready for the shared journey ahead. That means closing gaps and filling in where you can, and negotiating the remaining distance.

No one, finally, could help the San Diego superintendents fill in the *legitimacy gap* in time to rescue their reforms. But Obama could help GM's lenders, creditors, and workers close the *make-it-pay* gap by injecting US capital into the mix. That reduced the distance each had to go, made a hard negotiation easier, and helped persuade all to make the final shared sacrifice under a tough bailout plan.

THE (NOT SO) GREAT PHILIPS FIRE

It started with a great flash of lightning; fire raged through Fabricator No. 22 and in less than ten minutes on that night of March 17, 2000, every tray of silicon wafers in the Philips chip factory in Albuquerque, New Mexico, was baked, soaked, or otherwise rendered a useless gelatinous mass.

Halfway around the world at a Nokia mobile phone plant just outside Helsinki, the supply chain hiccoughed. An employee who was monitoring systems noticed that Nokia hadn't received an expected signal on the next chip batch due from Philips in Albuquerque.

Both Philips and Nokia had transparency when it came to the chip flow, the heart and soul of their collaboration. Nokia knew what to expect—what "normal" was. Their collaboration platform was loaded with sensors that would trip signals when something was amiss.

In fact, Nokia had a good idea what Philips's capacity was generally, just as Philips had long-term visibility into Nokia's business plans. In those days, the consumer electronics world was starved for chips. Laptops, cell phones, and other devices flew out of factories, 40 percent more year over year. Chastened by global chip shortages, Sony, Dell, Sun, and others were backing off production schedules and changing forecasts. There was huge demand and zero excess capacity anywhere in the global system to make more. In that time-critical, resource-short environment, close collaboration helped Philips and Nokia assure correct levels of production.

How did Nokia, the towering giant of Finnish telecommunications, react when that Philips input from Albuquerque didn't show up? The company was in a hot cell phone market and chips were its lifeblood. Let's just say Nokia did not respond like a security guard who slaps a video monitor that suddenly goes scratchy.

On Monday, Philips began notifying its customers. A Philips executive called Tapio Markki, Nokia's top component purchasing manager, and told him to expect a one-week delay in chip delivery. Philips made the same call to its thirty other chip customers, including Ericsson, the giant Swedish cell phone manufacturer. Fierce competitors, Ericsson and Nokia together accounted for 40 percent of the Albuquerque plant's sales.

Philips was determined to get this problem fixed and give priority to Nokia and Ericsson once it restored production. Cor Boonstra, Philips's CEO, had done a magnificent job turning the electronics giant around in recent years; relationships with firms like Nokia were the cornerstone of Philips's future.

For his part, Nokia's Markki doubted Philips could restart its chip flow in a week. He'd worked in the business long enough to know that Philips was going to have its hands full. But he wasn't fazed. Nokia could draw on its own "rainy day" chip supply stockpiled for just such predictable surprises. Markki had confidence in Nokia's ability to handle the situation as he understood it.

Nevertheless, Markki passed news of the situation up to Pertii Korhonen, the senior vice president of operations, logistics, and sourcing for Nokia mobile phones. Korhonen put Albuquerque on a watch list, elevating checks on that plant's status from once-weekly to once-daily calls.

After a week, Nokia had learned little that assured it Philips had the problem under control. Nokia offered to send its engineers to Albuquerque; Philips declined. Nokia continued to press, launching a concerted campaign to increase Philips's sense of urgency. "Get involved, do something," senior Nokia executives communicated to their Philips counterparts. "You need to take stronger action."

In Helsinki, Matti Alahuhta, president of Nokia's mobile-phone division, took an unscheduled moment in a meeting to raise the fire with his Philips counterparts. "We need strong and determined action right now," Alahuhta said. Philips executives noticed Alahuhta's tone now had traces of something they recognized as *sisu*—a Finnish term meaning guts, resolve, and tenacity, the traits Finnish armed forces showed in the face of the invasion by the Soviet Union in World War II.

"It was clear they were angry," a Philips executive said. "You got the idea this was a matter of life or death for these guys. We respected that."

Two weeks in, on March 31, Philips called Markki with its worst assessment to date: it would take weeks to restore the Albuquerque clean rooms, and months to catch up on the production schedule. Now, Nokia saw, its customers and sales were at stake—as much as 5 percent of its annual production at a time of booming demand.

Nokia secured alternative sources in Japan and the United States for as many chips as it could muster. Suppliers went out of their way to accommodate Nokia, a prized customer. But certain chips only Philips produced, and only at the Albuquerque plant. Nokia dug even deeper into its supply chain data to be sure it understood exactly what alternatives Philips had. Then it moved.

Korhonen, Markki, and Nokia's chairman and CEO, Jorma Ollila, flew to Philips headquarters. This was Nokia's A-Team coming face-to-face with Philips's A-Team, including its semiconductor division chief, and Philips CEO, Cor Boonstra.

With their A-Teams, both sides were signaling concern for the situation, awareness of its potential impact on Nokia's sales, and the high value placed on the relationship. In that meeting, Nokia was relentless and demanding. "We cannot accept the current status," Nokia's team insisted. "It's absolutely essential we turn over every stone looking for a solution."

Nokia had done what it could to close the chip gap. Now it was up to Philips to move as well. Nokia would redesign some of the unique-to-Albuquerque chips so Philips could produce them in its other factories. But Philips had to commit to shift production to those factories no matter the inconvenience and get those chips flowing again. Now.

"We asked them—told them—to replant," Korhonen said.

Philips seemed ready. "It was exactly what we expect from a customer," a Philips executive later said.

"Philips didn't go into denial," Korhonen said. All agreed, he said, that "for a little period of time, Philips and Nokia would operate as one company regarding these components."

Nokia and Philips looked to the past, to the present, and to the future—and did together what neither could do alone. For a limited time, over a well-defined problem that was core to their businesses, they would stretch the relationship to get over this bump and leave each partner better off than either would be going it alone.

Soon Philips's Eindhoven and Shanghai factories roared into production of ten million of the highly specialized Albuquerque-type chips. The benefits kept rolling: Nokia shared a new chip process it had developed that would help Philips boost production. In the aftermath, Philips embraced the new process at its Albuquerque plant and rapidly made up for another two million chips.

How did Ericsson react? While Nokia raced to deal with the crisis—and saw opportunity in this narrow window if it could get Philips to move with it—Ericsson slept through the entire adventure. It had none of Nokia's awareness, action, or involvement with Philips until it was too late. Waking up to the true nature of the disaster, Ericsson found itself starved of chips, with all of Philips's excess capacity already consumed by Nokia.

It was a financial disaster for Ericsson—a $400 million loss and write-off that year—and drove the company out of the cell phone business. As for Nokia and Philips, their collaboration was so successful they both took it in stride: there was no mention of the fire in either firm's annual report.

ARE YOU READY?

Your overall readiness to collaborate depends on your *capacity* to move, meaning the people, the platform, and the plan at the ready; the *value* of your move, meaning you have a vision and what it takes to make it pay; and your *support* to move, meaning you have the legitimacy and the authority you need.

Let's look at the readiness graph on page 244. Nokia had high urgency to move, for example. It was practically ready to reinvent chip production to keeps its phones flowing to the overheated marketplace.

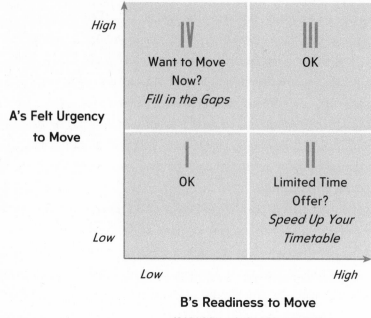

A's Felt Urgency to Move

B's Readiness to Move
(CAPACITY + SUPPORT + VALUE)

Philips wanted to move: it had *support* to move at the highest levels, and it definitely saw the *value*. But its *capacity* to move was low. As a result, Philips's overall readiness was low.

That created a mismatch: with Philips having "low" readiness, and Nokia feeling "high" urgency, their collaboration was sitting in quadrant IV. That's not where Nokia needed it to be. Nokia needed the collaboration moved into Quadrant III. There, Philips would have high readiness that matched up well with Nokia's high urgency.

The mismatch was conflict-prone. It would be easy to see lawsuits or other disasters arising if Nokia couldn't relax—and lose tons of money—or Philips couldn't ratchet it up.

Understandably, Nokia wanted to move this collaboration from IV to III in a hurry.

That would take negotiation and persuasion: Philips would have to boost its capacity, the missing link in its readiness. On its own, Nokia took extraordinary measures and narrowed the distance Philips had to go. With a little Nokia *sisu* thrown in, it didn't take much negotiation or persuasion for Philips to close the remaining capacity gap by shifting production to Eindhoven and Shanghai. With that and some sharing of new advanced production methods, Nokia and Philips moved their collaboration to Quadrant III, right where Nokia needed it: Nokia highly urgent, and Philips highly ready.

Quadrant I is a sleepy quadrant. Everyone is aligned on moving slowly, and not really ready to do much. You might think of General Motors in the months before Wagoner's removal. What's the rush? GM didn't even know its cash position; it was hardly ready for collaboration.

But when that new partner—the US government—arrived, the relationship shifted to quadrant IV, a trouble quadrant. Something had to give. Either the US government had to relax and settle into Quadrant I, or GM had to step up the pace. As Nokia did with Philips, the Obama administration felt nothing but urgency: it wanted to get to III with GM in a hurry.

In Quadrant II, A feels no urgency to move, but B is definitely ready. This might be a situation where B is holding its support together for a limited time, as when Obama pressed GM for action. Or A might be riven by disputes, as the American side found itself in the months before the FARC hostage rescue. The clock is ticking. If you want B's collaboration, you'd better speed up. Otherwise, B might lose its support, or throw its support behind some other collaboration, or go it alone—without *you*.

In Quadrant III, A feels real urgency, and B is definitely ready. All systems are go. Think of Nokia and Philips moving together "as one company."

Politics is a game of timing. As circumstances change, even from news cycle to news cycle, what seemed impossible today becomes inevitable tomorrow. Knowing when, where, and how to move means patience, readiness, and, at the decisive moment, action.

BILL BRATTON on SWAT

The culture of the Los Angeles Police Department was even more entrenched than that of the NYPD. I had been in LA for a while before I felt that we would be ready to make moves on some of the greatest symbols of LAPD's culture and direction.

In 2005, the SWAT unit was trying to rescue a nineteen-month-old infant named Suzie Pena from her father, who was holding her at gunpoint and had been firing at the police. In the ensuing rescue attempt, a SWAT officer was wounded. Both the father and child were hit by SWAT bullets.

It was the first time in its thirty-eight-year history that SWAT had killed a hostage. But it wasn't the unit's first crisis. During another recent operation a SWAT officer had been killed and another severely injured. It was time to raise questions that had needed asking for a long time.

SWAT was one of the most prestigious entities within the LAPD, wielding influence well beyond its numbers, and among the best known outside the LAPD. It was also, for my purposes, the most significant representation of an LAPD whose go-it-alone culture many wanted to change, including me.

In a department not known for collaboration, SWAT was even more insular than other units, with no tolerance for outsiders. It had never allowed a woman into the unit, was in many respects— because of its elitism and mission—isolated within the department, and was not out on the streets engaging with the community, except during tactical operations. If you were SWAT, you expected to be in that unit for your entire career. And SWAT had always been left pretty much on its own; no one had ever questioned how it did things. Even within the LAPD, leadership often did not question SWAT. They were the unchallenged experts.

In this environment, I would have to move strategically to gain political and organizational support for change.

I convened a Board of Inquiry—not specifically to look at the Suzie Pena case, but to examine in a larger context SWAT's operational practices, policies, and procedures. It was part of the overall effort of changing the culture of an organization that was resistant to criticism, particularly from outsiders. If I could show through the Board of Inquiry that no entity within the LAPD was above examination, above being controlled by the department, immune to the same transparency I was bringing to the rest of the LAPD, it would go a long way toward breaking down the last of the old LAPD. That was the LAPD that was in some respects so harmful to the department's reputation and its relationships with the various communities in Los Angeles.

For most of the units in the department I had already found ways to challenge how they had done things. It was a matter of targeting areas to go after, pacing change correctly, and then always being prepared to use a crisis to accelerate the process. It's about staying in your political headlights—knowing how far and how fast to move, and where to start first.

We might call it the artichoke approach—start at the outside, work methodically toward the core. If you get to the core too quickly you risk outrunning your own process, losing all the benefits and support you pick up on the way as change spreads. When you reach the core, it won't make sense in the larger context—you won't have paid your change tolls. It will look instead like you're attacking the heart of the organization. That was something I knew not to do.

And there were elements of the culture that I didn't want to change. I didn't touch the "black and whites"—the classic LAPD cruisers with understated three-inch-high lettering on the side that said "Police" and the famous motto "To Protect and to Serve." Most police departments had fifteen-inch-high letters emblazoned on their cars.

The wool uniform was in some sense impractical for California's climate and the police mission. But it's part of the LAPD culture's focus and cops' intense pride in their appearance and professional image.

Also, the LAPD was the only police department in California that didn't wear intricately designed, city-identifying patches on its shirtsleeves. That was the way they uniquely identified themselves in the police profession. It was part of the ego that I opted not to tamper with. It was in furtherance of the culture of pride in appearance.

The cars were always spotlessly clean. The uniforms were always spotlessly clean. Those were positive and important. I left them alone. I intended to use that platform of appearance and professionalism in furtherance of other goals.

The Board of Inquiry was a tool that could be used to examine an operation or an entity. It was accepted as a time-honored, appropriate, and legitimate vehicle for the kind of scrutiny we were putting SWAT through.

Unlike with previous boards, however, we were very deliberate in bringing in outsiders to sit with insiders. An LAPD three-star chief chaired it, but it included Seattle's second-in-command, who had a SWAT background; the head of the LA County Sheriff's office SWAT unit; senior LAPD commanders with deep SWAT experience; and several attorneys, both from within and without the department.

That took away the insularity. With insiders only you may get a board that is too in awe of the people they're listening to. They may not have the expertise to ask the challenging questions; or they don't want to embarrass themselves by asking a question they don't have an answer to. Outsiders are beholden to no one. They're going to pick up and leave at the end of the day and go home to their respective jobs.

With SWAT, the whole process took a year. This was about the fabric of SWAT—its policies, procedures, and practices. Its process was slow and deliberate. There were tensions within the board as it wrestled with issues. It was controversial within the LAPD because of the outsiders. (At one point, when it looked as if we might have a runaway board on our hands, I was even considering issuing a minority report.) The board needed to maintain its legitimacy: this was not a hang-'em-high inquiry, looking for scapegoats. This was to be a thoughtful, deliberative process.

Though the board was not specifically focused on the death of Suzie Pena—there were other commissions and panels meeting to investigate that—the tragedy did give us the ability to question SWAT tactics and training. In the incident, four SWAT officers with rifles set on full automatic had fired dozens of rounds. Few actually hit the target. One killed the child.

The death was a crisis for a number of SWAT policies and procedures, many never before questioned. SWAT commanders didn't have adequate answers to many of the questions that we were asking. For example, why did they train with their weapons on full automatic? They insisted that they could still control how many shots were fired. We asked, "Well, if you want to control shots, why don't you have it on semiautomatic, which would ensure that control?" The answer was "Well, now, that's not the way we do it." Why not? Because that's not the way we do it. This was an ego rather than an operational issue.

I moved on the automatic fire issue right away without waiting for the board to make its final report. Some things are so blatantly problematic you change them right now; the safety of officers was at stake. You can't afford to wait a year.

When that kind of thinking was challenged, the defenses began to crumble. This was a crisis that created doubts about how SWAT had been run, doubts within the department and in the community and within the SWAT unit itself. And that crisis created an opening—a shift in the political environment—for beginning to change the unit's culture.

We challenged the tradition of excluding women, for example. We questioned the admission standards and challenged their relevance to SWAT performance. And we changed them without diminishing the skills requirement. The first woman soon joined SWAT.

We required that SWAT officers spend 40 percent of their time on patrol. They were like fighter pilots, wanting to train all the time. And they were all in great shape. But the unit was standoffish from the rest of the department. To make them pull their own weight and break down the insularity, we put them out in the field with patrol.

As much as they moaned and groaned about it, an incident occurred in which a female officer was shot, critically wounded, and ultimately paralyzed from the waist down. But for the fact that SWAT units were in the field that night on patrol, likely she would have passed away by the time an ambulance got to her. Many SWAT officers are trained as EMTs; they saved her life by stabilizing her.

There were no major personnel moves or disciplinary actions taken as a result of the Board of Inquiry. That was not its purpose. This was not a matter of gross negligence or gross lack of command. We found that accepted policies and procedures had been adhered to. We found, however, that the policies and procedures themselves were deficient.

Just the fact that we were questioning SWAT was a major move. We took advantage of the crisis to not only make SWAT better, but to signal a new era of collaboration throughout the LAPD. The inquiry demonstrated that no one is above review or reproach. No one—alone—has all the answers.

LEADERSHIP

9

Throughout this book, we have met leaders who made collaboration happen . . .

Doug Hull rescued some broken-down desktop computers bound for scrap, linked them together through two schools, and gave Canada its first move to the Internet.

Claudia Costin brought tens of thousands of teachers, students, and parents into collaboration for Rio de Janeiro's schools, starting with her personal Twitter account.

Dee Hock's vision of a global payment platform created Visa.

Rudy Crew gave principals the power to make decisions about money; Beverly Donohue hardwired it into a computer platform that shaped the schooling of children for a decade.

Paul O'Neill of Alcoa saw that with the right business discipline, safety and financial success could both soar.

William Brownfield kept the collaboration between Colombians and Americans within the headlights of political support from both nations' militaries, intelligence organizations, and foreign services.

Leadership of collaboration demands seeing above the fray to victory—and then returning with that vision to create a plan that helps everyone feel as if they are bound for success, holding one another to account and garnering support to the finish line.

Not everything will happen on time or according to plan. Leaders must be resilient so that in times of crisis the balance in the trust bank is high. Chances are, you'll need to make a withdrawal.

Even when collaboration appears headed for the rocks, true leaders do not abandon their core values. Secure in their vision, buttressed by plans, people, and support, they derive strength from those values, confident that, especially on the most difficult days, collaboration is not just the better way—it's the only way.

BILL BRATTON: MacArthur Park

MacArthur Park is one of LA's oldest parks, and probably its best known. Right in the heart of the city, adjacent to downtown, MacArthur Park has been featured in practically every movie and television show ever made about Los Angeles. Iconic in stature, it is also extremely visible. Leaving or getting to downtown on the freeways, you use Wilshire Boulevard. Thousands of Angelenos passing through see this area every day.

By the time I arrived in LA as chief in 2002, the area around MacArthur Park had become one of the poorest, most densely populated of the city—largely immigrant, El Salvadoran, and home to several of the worst gangs: 18th Street, the Mexican Mafia, and MS-13. The park itself was still beautiful but neglected. It was widely perceived to be under the gangs' control, overrun by drug dealers, people selling counterfeit licenses, illegal peddlers of all stripes.

The park had symbolic imagery as well. It was the epicenter of the Rampart Police District and thus of the Rampart scandal, in which a number of officers in the Rampart antigang unit had been implicated in crimes ranging from drug dealing and framing suspects to bank robberies and shootings. That had been the final straw in bringing about the federal consent decree under which the department operated when I came on as chief.

Less than three blocks away was the resurgent downtown business district. Money was coming free to restore many of the great old buildings; people were moving in. Development was starting to leap across the freeway, moving toward MacArthur Park.

On the other side of the park, moving out on Wilshire Boulevard toward Beverly Hills, after a couple of blocks, the same thing was happening: it was getting cleaner. MacArthur Park was a troubled spot in what was becoming a revitalized area.

Even in the midst of the turbulence in and around the park, there were positive elements: a heavily used subway stop; a vibrant street economy that made you feel like you were walking around in a Latin American city. On its periphery was the Mexican Consulate; Loyola University still had a campus there; a couple of businesses were still surviving. Several restaurants, including Langer's Delicatessen, had been there for years.

And there were plans. When I came on as chief, the city councillor for the Rampart neighborhood, Ed Reyes, took me on a ride through his district. A number of investments were being planned for the park, he said. New lighting, refurbishing of the concert stand; maybe even a new artificial turf soccer field. A grand vision, considering the dilapidated state of the park we were riding through.

The investments were important—but could they turn around the park? MacArthur Park had become a platform for drug dealing, disorder, and crime. Our idea was that it would become a platform for collaboration around community renewal, a highly visible place where we could make change happen fast. Like Hollywood, Skid Row, Baldwin Village, and the Mission Area in the San Fernando Valley, MacArthur Park would become one of our five Safer City initiatives, pilot programs that would use our minimal resources in partnership to maximize the benefits and make the case for growing the department.

We couldn't be everywhere at once. But we could showcase what more cops and more partnerships could achieve. We would prove that even in the midst of a gang-controlled area, with all its serious crime and quality-of-life issues, you could use the police as a catalyst to bring it back.

But we had a problem. Our potential partners were distrustful of us. The business community had lost faith in the police; even the political community and city council had not had much luck with the police in addressing these issues. The media had spent years reporting on the Rampart police scandals, and now the LAPD was under the watchful oversight of the federal government and its consent decree.

We would have to build trust fast with short-terms gains and long-term plans. You buy trust with wins; trust buys you time, and more support. But as we set out, trust was hard to find: after years of conflict, no one trusted anyone.

Trust that we're going to be there over the long haul. We would stay long after the cameras had gone. This would persist.

Trust that even as we're working on those longer-range plans we're doing something together *now*, creating value fast.

Trust that this was possible. We've done this before wherever I've led departments: coming together, we could make this happen.

The beauty of MacArthur Park was that there was something in it for everyone. It was so far gone it wouldn't take much to get a sense that something was changing.

One of the things that would give that sense was energetic and responsive police presence. Because of his successes on Skid Row, I moved Charlie Beck to the area. Beck was great with the community. He was very good with the cops. He proved that collaboration was good for communities—and good for careers. Charlie is now chief of the LAPD.

We gave Charlie a few extra bodies, not a lot. But he also went across boundaries, reaching out to the business community and neighborhood residents, gaining their support for putting cameras into the park. The cameras were monitored live back at the police station; officers in and around the park could be directed to activity identified through the cameras.

The cameras had a psychological and practical, force-multiplying effect. But they also introduced the idea that in the neglected park the LAPD was going to embrace technology and leverage every asset we could in trying to secure the city's public spaces. It was going to become a city priority, not a liability.

The cameras showed, further, that nothing on this platform

could work without political support. To have the cameras work effectively at night there had to be enhanced streetlighting. That's where the mayor, through his ability to influence the Water and Power Department, the city council member who used some of his funds to help pay for some of the cameras, and Motorola all got involved.

It was a matter of building alliances.

Alliances

I wasn't tied down by the controversies that had diminished the creativity and success of my predecessors.

For years LAPD's chiefs had had endless wars with mayors and the city council, and been unable to increase the number of police officers. LA was huge—nearly five hundred square miles. If you were an officer responding to a call you could be alone for an extended period of time. You had to be able to control a situation and the threat of force had to be credible.

For the most part, white Angelenos had little interest in supporting more policing. So long as they were safe in their homes, what happened thirty miles across town was not of strong interest.

That created the "go it alone" LAPD culture that permeated the organization in the 1960s, '70s, and '80s. "If the political leadership leaves me alone," Chief Bill Parker would say, "I'll take care of business." He used a term that became very popular, "the thin blue line." Many thought that meant a few police trying to keep the forces of anarchy at bay, to keep the law-abiding community safe. It really meant "a thin blue line to keep whites separate from blacks, to keep the poor separate from the rich." Taking care of business in the LAPD really meant controlling the poor and the racial minority groups.

Policing, meanwhile, had become much more difficult in every American city. There was more drug-related violence, more social disorder and breakdown, and a growth in racial tension even as the civil rights movement brought an end to segregation.

Rather than trying to adapt to a changing world, the LAPD was becoming increasingly driven by a culture of control and separation—from the community, political support, and business leadership.

The LAPD was changing, but it was moving in the wrong direction. With the city and the country becoming more violent, the police became aggressive, and in some neighborhoods more abusive. And you could understand that. With ninety-three hundred cops for five hundred square miles and four million residents, with the country's worst gang problem, in LA cops had to go without—without support, without backup. They felt threatened. LA had starved its police force. In New York, I had had thirty-eight thousand cops. On a comparative basis, LA was understaffed by half: it was like working New York with nineteen thousand cops.

The "go it alone" culture fed on itself. Police conduct was constantly an issue. Daryl Gates, chief of police in the 1980s and early 1990s, wasn't speaking to the mayor, Tom Bradley. The department wasn't getting any resources. Cops were angry at the community. "You're not giving us anything. We ride around in six-year-old cars. The police stations are a mess. There are not enough of us. You don't care about us, so why should we care about you?"

"Go it alone" and a "culture of control"—in the hands of individual police officers, that's a potent brew.

Now, as a leader, you want pride in your organization. You want a culture of confidence. You want a culture of optimism. You want a culture of can-do. You want a culture that stresses partnerships: there's no way in LA, pressed as cops are, you can "go it alone" and succeed.

But you don't want to be in an emperor-has-no-clothes situation. And that is exactly what happened, finally, during the Rodney King verdict riots in 1992. The LAPD, which had prided itself on never giving up, never backing down, on its *competence* to handle any situation, effectively abandoned motorists to the mob at Florence and Normandie in South Central Los Angeles. Literally retreated. First time in its history. This shook the department to its core. And it ultimately led to Gates finally being forced to resign.

Reform chiefs followed. Willie Williams came in after Gates with a great burst of energy, hope, and optimism. He captured the community's interest and brought crime down by working with cops and neighborhoods in community-policing initiatives.

But Williams never was able to get a hold on the department. It's almost as if nobody, cops included, could understand *why* crime was going down—or that it was because of what they were doing. He was the LAPD's first outside police chief. The cops didn't like or respect him. Eventually he lost the support of his mayor and police commission, and the *Los Angeles Times*.

At the same time the drumbeat of criticism against the LAPD was incessant. The old guard used the drumbeat as a rallying cry, safe in their silo fortresses and resistant to the best efforts of chiefs to reach in and change. Patrol, detective, narcotics, administration, and special operations were all under independent command by and large. SWAT, Metropolitan Division, and Helicopter/Aviation were the iconic LAPD units, smaller entities within the larger organizations, highly resistant to change, with influence well beyond their numbers. They demanded and received prideful allegiance. They accepted advice or guidance from no one. They epitomized the old philosophy: "The LA way is the only way," everybody else be damned.

Despite all the books that have been written about change and leadership, the reality is that most organizations are still locked into the old silo overconfidence: "We don't need to change really. We'll continue to do more of the same thing."

Arrogance—"nobody does it better"; pessimism—"it doesn't

get any better than this." Those attitudes ensure that an organization stands still while the world moves forward around it.

The LAPD was operating without sharing, without transparency, without inclusiveness. It was operating on a structure of exclusiveness, resenting anybody, whether outside or inside the organization, who questioned what they were doing. The whole structure was weakened; there was nothing but vertical beams running deep into the organization, rising high, with nothing connecting them, no interactions, joined only at the top at the chief's office. The situation was completely unstable.

Chief Bernard Parks came after Williams and undid his community policing work, losing public support in turn. He uncovered the Rampart scandal but then was consumed by it—and by his poor relations with the police union. His style of leadership just wasn't getting anything done. The union spent almost $1 million in an advertising campaign tearing him down, helping to drive him from office. Unfortunately for him, he provided them with a lot of fodder.

I came in as the LAPD was entering a very difficult period—operating under a federal consent decree that mandated certain reforms as a result of the Rampart scandal, which had caused grave damage with the Latino community. The African American community was incensed that it had lost its second African American chief. Each of my three predecessors had been forced from office, and crime was back up. And still the LAPD was starved for resources.

At the same time, I was able to use the consent decree, which had been seen as a negative by my predecessor and by the union—by just about everybody—as a positive. It *required* change, and it funded the change.

What was new about this was that, unlike in Chief Bill Parker's time, where the ideal was "Leave us alone and we'll take care of your business," we were saying that we recognized we could not do this alone. That *even if you resource us with more cops*, etc., we still need partnerships. We need collaboration. We need to be working with the city attorney's office, the district attorney, the city council, the mayor, the Feds, the immigrant community, the gay community—entities many of my predecessors were constantly ignoring or fighting.

I had a unique opportunity to open the tent and welcome people who had not been allowed in before. Citizens more used to clashing with the police than cooperating with them welcomed the invitation to collaborate. Many came forward, and we were able to take advantage of that.

In MacArthur Park, for example, we worked with an ambitious city attorney who saw the park as an opportunity for visibility and press conferences about the successes. One of the issues in the park was the sale of counterfeit licenses and documentation. Those were misdemeanor offenses, something his office had jurisdiction over. We needed that enforcement. He wanted publicity. We both wanted success. There was something in it for everybody—most important, the public.

I worked with the union, instead of against it. Union support was absolutely critical. I wrote a regular column for its newspaper. We fought, but we agreed on more than we disagreed about even in the midst of the consent decree, which was widely unpopular with the rank and file.

There had been historical tension with the civilian bosses—the mayor and the police commission. The commissioners had seen their powers increased again and again over the years to the extent that they now had an inspector general. My predecessor wouldn't let the inspector general into meetings. Basically, I opened up everything to them. The police commission and the inspector general were actually empowered during my time. The department and I benefited from the support and guidance they provided.

Same for the federal monitor. The consent decree was thought

by many to be an albatross around our neck. I saw it as an opportunity to build a collaboration with the federal monitor. Instead of
fighting him, we worked with him and his people. I'd been part of
the federal monitoring team for the year before my appointment;
we understood each other.

I had the benefit of partnerships with two great mayors. Jim
Hahn brought me on, at great political risk; Antonio Villaraigosa
reappointed me. Both were strong advocates for a strong LAPD.

Now, I had my share of fights. Working with the mayors, we constantly fought with the city council to grow the police department.
But you choose your battles; you don't fight with everybody at
the same time; and you don't quarrel to the extent that you break
off the relationship so you can't come together and find common
ground when the tides shift. Councillors came around when they
started hearing from the media and constituencies: "We want more
cops." That was the idea.

Success stories helped: "Look at what we did with these fifty
extra cops and Skid Row. See what we did with the new police station out in Mission—how that turned that area around. Look at what
we did with these eighteen extra cops down at the Baldwin Village.
Just think what we could do with fifty extra cops up in Hollywood."

I understood that I needed to market smaller successes as we
built toward the ultimate accomplishment: citywide crime reduction
and national attention for the achievement.

Without tabloids like the *New York Post*, the *New York Daily
News*, or *Newsday*, the media in LA were not anywhere near as per-
vasive as in New York, particularly in covering crime, especially in
the minority neighborhoods. Baldwin Village, which had extremely
high levels of crime and serious gang violence, got little media
attention. There was plenty of other crime around the city to cover:
being far away in South Los Angeles, Baldwin Village was off the
radar; television stations didn't like sending camera crews down
there unless it was a true "bleed to lead" incident. The half-dozen

shootings a day or the hundreds of murders a year, largely of blacks and Latinos, just didn't draw the media in.

We attempted to *attract* attention to the crime problem. My leadership team and I made ourselves very available to the media. We talked constantly about the gang and crime problem, what we were doing about it, and the help we needed. We acknowledged the truth everyone in the black and Latino communities knew.

We investigated officer-involved shootings so thoroughly and reported them so openly to the police commission that you have to go back to 2005 for the last time there was any significant, widespread community outrage over a police officer taking a life. This transparency was unheard of in a city with a fifty-year history of hostilities between black and Latino communities and the LAPD.

We didn't run from incidents. The idea was to get the information out; if we were wrong, we were wrong—admit it, fix it, move on.

As a result, people eventually got the sense that (1) we're focused on these incidents; (2) we're not trying to hide anything; (3) we're not going away. And hey—crime is going down. Things are getting better and they're getting better throughout the city. No one could miss 50 to 60 percent crime reductions.

These were collaborations that I would describe as the spokes of the wheel. The Safer City initiatives were five spokes that helped to strengthen the wheel. For each of these initiatives—the pilots, reaching out to the union, the police commissioners, and the inspector general, even dealing openly with LAPD critics like the ACLU in terms of attending their meetings—each of these spokes of the wheel was strengthening the department by improving its image and its working relationships.

With widespread media reporting and documentation from ourselves, the civilian police commission, the *Los Angeles Times*, and our federal monitors, we showed that the department—when properly resourced, properly led, properly focused, and properly partnered—had the capability to do very good things.

By 2005, the turnaround in MacArthur Park was so significant that the owner of Langer's Delicatessen would tell you that the park was safer than it had ever been—and he'd been in the area for over forty years. The owners of Mama's Hot Tamales said the same thing. For the past few summers, there's been a concert series at the park that attracts eight hundred to a thousand people a night. That series has never had an incident. They refurbished the band-stand and stored tens of thousands of dollars of equipment there—none of it was ever stolen, and the bandstand itself has never been vandalized. That is reflective of the community watching out for this thing they all value.

The city put in artificial turf for the soccer field and the park is used day and night. You won't find drug dealing, the homeless hanging out, gangs, illegal licenses being sold. The cameras are still up and running. The real estate push from downtown has been stalled somewhat by the recession. But the mix of people in that area is changing also to include more dog walkers. That's always a good sign.

Fifteen years ago, when Jeff O'Brien moved to MacArthur Park, near the city's downtown district, the neighbor-hood was run-down and notorious for crime, drugs and poverty.

At the time, though, it was all that he could afford. He was making a living as a messenger and a part-time bass player and sharing an apartment with a group of art students.

Although he left the neighborhood many years ago, he decided to return three months ago.

"If you told me 15 years ago that I would be living in this neighborhood now, I never would have believed you," said Mr. O'Brien, a prop-master in the film industry. Two women joggers passed by. "A few years ago jogging around the

park at night would have been suicide. That's not the case anymore."

With increased police patrols, the crime rate in the park and the surrounding area has dropped dramatically. Homicides in the Rampart Division, the police district that includes the MacArthur Park area, have declined from about 140 in 1994 to 27 last year, according to police statistics.

The park itself has been revitalized, and the surrounding historic buildings are being restored, mirroring the renaissance in the park.

—From the *New York Times,* April 17, 2005

By 2005, the transformation of MacArthur Park was a powerful symbol of what collaboration could achieve. Two years later, that same park would be the site of a crisis that could have either destroyed that collaboration or helped it become stronger. Once again, leadership would make the difference.

The MacArthur Park May Day Confrontation Begins: LAPD Report, October 9, 2007

During the spring of 2006, immigrants' rights groups across the nation called for protests to take place on May 1. In Los Angeles 500,000 took part. Participants marched and rallied in Central Area during the first half of the day, and then marched into Rampart Area for the final rally at MacArthur Park.

The May 1, 2007 marches and rallies were expected to be similar [but smaller]; a morning march and rally in Central Area, and a final rally at MacArthur Park.

[On the day of the march,] the crowd, estimated at between 15,000 and 25,000 people, was peaceful. While a small group of individuals described by officers as "anarchists" were spotted that morning, they were contacted·by

*officers during the event to ensure they understood the
police were aware of their presence.*

*The May Day events in Central Area occurred without
incident.*

*As the crowd dwindled, [LAPD chiefs on the scene,]
comfortable with the success of the morning events, decided
to [release] three of the four Metropolitan Division Platoons
that had been on standby for the Central Area event to other
duties.*

*By 5:00 p.m., the majority of the demonstrators, esti-
mated at 6,000 to 7,000, had reached MacArthur Park and
were entering. With no officers or sound truck in place to
guide the marchers into the park, however, many individuals marched onto Wilshire Boulevard. The crowd that gathered on Wilshire Boulevard soon grew to approximately
300; officers were faced with an impromptu march, heading
westbound.*

*Police employed several strategies to encourage the
crowd to move into the park. First, a skirmish line of officers
deployed to stop the crowd from crossing [streets] and to
direct people into a park entrance. Then, event organizers
were asked to use the Department sound truck to ask the
crowd, in Spanish, to move into the park. Finally, a team of
Motorcycle officers drove the crowd eastbound on Wilshire,
compressing the crowd.*

*As events unfolded in the park, a group of 20 to 30
individuals, whose intent appeared to be to provoke a confrontation, threw objects at police, including wooden sticks,
water bottles filled with water, ice and gravel, and pieces of
cement.*

*At 6:17 p.m., Metropolitan Division B-Platoon formed a
skirmish line on 7th Street, and without a dispersal order
being given, moved the crowd northbound, pushing and*

striking some individuals in the crowd, including some members of the media, and firing less-lethal impact munitions. As officers continued to report objects being thrown by individuals in the crowd, the skirmish line continued north across Wilshire, driving the small group of disruptive individuals from the south side of the park into the thousands of peaceful demonstrators gathered in the north side of the park for a rally.*

From the *Los Angeles Times* (October 10, 2007):

The melee left 246 journalists and protesters as well as 18 officers with injuries, and more than 250 legal claims have been filed against the city. Los Angeles County prosecutors and the FBI are continuing to investigate the case.

Officers shot 146 less-than-lethal rounds, including foam projectiles that were fired directly into the crowd rather than at the ground as LAPD policy mandates.

Police also used batons to strike protesters and journalists more than 100 times. Many of the baton strikes were inflicted on peaceful demonstrators.

Gerald Chaleff, LAPD Special Assistant for Constitutional Policing, at LAPD Police Headquarters, Tuesday Night, May 1, 2007

We were at the Parker Center. It was late; people were very unhappy. About 20 commanders, the deputy chief who had been in charge of the command, captains. People from Metro, people from the media. The inspector general. All LAPD executives and officers, except for the inspector general.

---

*Chaleff and Hillmann, *Los Angeles Police Department Report to the Board of Police Commissioners: An Examination of May Day 2007.*

*The gravity of the event was not yet fully absorbed.
I think Bratton certainly understood it as did I and some
others. When he'd gotten to the park there were rubber
rounds all around; nobody could tell how many were really
fired.*

*Bill was outraged. He immediately realized what had
happened and the problems created. We'd spent almost
five years building up trust in the community and the police
department. That was all at risk.*

*As Bratton has always said, "You know police work isn't
pretty. It's never going to look pretty." But the appearance of
what happened and the reaction of the community? Some of
the events that we saw that night were far beyond the pale
of what's "pretty" or not. Pushing TV cameramen over, things
like that. . . .*

*For Bill, the next steps were to get out there. Talk to the
community. Do as much of the stuff that he's really good at,
which is getting out in front of stories. We started arranging
meetings with the immigrant community, the communities
that people represented, particular areas of Los Angeles,
the news media, police union, and the rank and file cops.*

*But the deputy chief in command that afternoon? He
didn't seem to get it still—the gravity of what happened. The
next day he got on a plane to go to some memorial cere-
mony somewhere, leaving the rest of us still dealing with this
mess—as we would be for months.*

Deputy Chief Mike Hillmann in Bill Bratton's Office, Wednesday, May 2, 2007

*The next day, Wednesday, Chief Bratton summoned me
to his office. "I want you to look at something," he said. He
showed me some of the video footage. "What do you think
of it?"*

He was animated. So was I. "I'm pretty ashamed of what we did," I said. "I'm disappointed with the response of Metropolitan Division."

"What do we have to do to fix it?" he asked. I said, "Well, I have to think about it. There's a lot of things here that I think are in question."

Chief Bratton was pissed, to say the least. Extremely hot.

"Whatever you need—I want you to stand up a new command. Figure it out, name it, build it, shape it, put it in place, and tell me what you need to do with training."

"Okay," I said. "I'll figure it out."

Jerry Chaleff was sent off writing the reports—and I was sent off to stand up a new command for crowd events.

Press Reports from May 1 to May 20, 2007*:

Late Tuesday, Police Chief William J. Bratton, speaking at a hastily arranged news conference at MacArthur Park, promised a department review "to determine if the use of force was appropriate."

He said police responded after "certain elements of the crowd . . . began to create a series of disturbances." During that activity, Bratton said, "Missiles were being thrown at the officers, and officers [were] responding." Still, Bratton said, the demonstrators creating problems were few and "that the vast, vast majority of the people who were here were behaving appropriately."

It was hard for Bratton—who expressed "grave concern"—to see why it was appropriate for officers to fire 240 times while arresting none of their targets.

. . .

Los Angeles Times dispatches.

Police Chief William J. Bratton, who promised an investigation, said at a news conference Wednesday that a key part of the inquiry into the officers' actions would focus on why they used force against members of the media. "We should never be engaged in attacking anyone in the media," Bratton said.

"The treatment you received yesterday from some Los Angeles police officers . . . we can't tolerate and won't tolerate," Bratton told reporters at a City Hall news conference, extending his remarks to members of the public also caught up in the incident.

. . .

Three Los Angeles Police Department and Police Commission investigations have been launched. Bratton's decision Thursday to ask the FBI to launch an independent investigation comes as a needed reminder that cops should be held accountable.

. . .

Police Chief William J. Bratton escalated his criticism of the officers' tactics and said the department's three investigations would focus on the actions not only of line officers but also of the top brass who gave the orders.

"There were mistakes made here all the way up and down the line. I want to make that clear," Bratton said. "Was there lack of supervision? Was there lack of leadership? What were [the line officers] directed to do?"

. . .

Telemundo anchor Pedro Sevcec, who was broadcasting from under a canopy, was pushed to the ground while on live television as police shoved through. "Here you have a tent clearly [for the] news media," Bratton said. The anchor "wears a suit and tie and there [are] clearly cameras . . . and the knocking over of cameras in the tent—that behavior is not under any circumstances justified."

Bratton said he was troubled by reports that police used force on women and children who had gone to the park to play. "The idea that officers would be firing—some of these devices send out five or six projectiles with one shot—that is a concern," Bratton said.

. . .

On Friday, after meeting with the mayor and other community leaders, Bratton continued to criticize the police actions, in which officers in riot gear fired foam bullets and used batons on demonstrators and reporters during the May Day immigrant rights march at MacArthur Park.

"A lot went wrong," he said. "I'm embarrassed for this department."

. . .

[With] City Councilman Ed P. Reyes, who represents the district that includes MacArthur Park, and Police Chief William J. Bratton, the mayor promised a full investigation into Tuesday's altercation involving police, protesters and the news media.

"The events of May 1 should not be seen as any reason not to come back to the park," Bratton said. "I don't want the events of one day to take away from the successes we've had at this park."

For his part, Reyes indicated that crowds have remained. "They're still here. For the most part the feeling was what happened here last week was an anomaly," he said.

. . .

Los Angeles Police Chief William J. Bratton on Sunday offered his strongest apology yet for the actions of an elite platoon of Metropolitan Division officers who swarmed a May Day immigration rally in MacArthur Park, and said that those officers are off the streets until he finds out what went wrong.

"I feel comfortable apologizing. . . . Things were done that shouldn't have been done," Bratton told a group of journalists who gathered at the KTLA-TV Channel 5 studios in Hollywood. "I'm not seeking to excuse it. . . . As one human being to another, there were things that shouldn't have been done."

Bratton said the 60 or so members of the Metropolitan Division's Platoon B have been "stood down" and won't return to active street duties until they have undergone retraining that meets his level of comfort.

The chief made it clear that incident commanders would be just as accountable.

He said the officers in the Metro unit, an elite corps of men and women trained in various crises including crowd disturbances, had 15 to 25 years on the force and are among the most highly trained of the LAPD's 9,500 officers. "This was my best, and that was what was extraordinarily disturbing about this," Bratton said.

• • •

Bratton said commanders know they must keep order among the officers. "One thing I know about them [police] is you have to control them, because they go out of control faster than any human being in the world" because of the traumatic circumstances of the work, he said.

• • •

On Monday, Bratton announced that he had demoted and reassigned the head of the Operations Central Bureau, Deputy Chief Cayler "Lee" Carter, who was the highest-ranking officer in MacArthur Park during the melee. He also reassigned the bureau's No. 2, Cmdr. Louis Gray. On Tuesday, Bratton announced that he had promoted Cmdr. Sergio

Diaz to the rank of deputy chief and asked him to take over for Carter.

. . .

"I think most police officers who look at those images are concerned they were disturbing," Bratton said. "At the same time, what I am committed to is that there is not a rush to judgment as it relates to the actions of the officers and the use of force."

On the "out of control" comment, Bratton said it reflected a reality for police organizations, that strong supervision and management were essential when employees have the power to use deadly force.

"I'm a cop. I love being a cop. I enjoy working with cops and I think after all this time I understand them. I understand as a police leader you have to control them," he said.

That said, Bratton plans next week to attend roll calls at various police stations so he can talk directly to concerned members of the rank and file.

"Cops are hurting. They are wondering, 'Why isn't the chief defending us?'" Bratton said. "I have to be frank about it. There are certain things I can't defend. Where I can defend officers, I will."

A Crisis of Confidence, an Opening for Reform

MacArthur Park created a crisis of confidence not only on the part of the city's huge legal and illegal immigrant population, the media, the political leadership, and the public, but also among the men and women of the Los Angeles Police Department. It was an "Oh, no, here we go again" type of situation.

The Metropolitan platoons were the most involved in the incident, seemingly out of control and indifferent to people's rights.

This gave us an opening to move on the Metropolitan Division and break apart the silos even further. Metro was the last remaining vestige of the old go-it-alone LAPD. Operating under the consent decree and the Board of Inquiry we had already made progress on SWAT in the Suzie Pena case. Now, for the Metropolitan Division, MacArthur Park was the tipping point.

In a crisis, the division's leadership looked around and saw that in their isolation they had lost all support, including from the LAPD rank-and-file officers. I had to capitalize on that fact, and very quickly share a vision that all who wanted change could rally around—that we could turn this crisis into a positive experience.

I'm a great believer that crisis is opportunity and accelerates change. There's something wrong in what used to be a comfort zone, and it can be a jumping-off point to make real progress. You have to move quickly to find people who will see the need for change, show the way, and then go for it. It's that search for common ground that John Linder talks about—underactivated values—that you can tap into and rally around together to get out of crisis and into a better place.

I had to find allies quickly. I was out there, going to different people, enlisting their support, getting them to buy in. We'd earned their trust; now we were going to spend some of that trust capital.

For the inside work, which was critical, I turned to Jerry Chaleff and Mike Hillmann.

Chaleff, as a leading civil rights attorney, had been the conscience of the city. But as part of the department, he appreciated and understood the organization. *He* believed that this could be used as a positive experience.

Mike Hillmann was a forty-year veteran of the LAPD. On critical incident management and crowd-control issues he was one of the best. He understood how badly the department had screwed up. Its *leadership* had screwed up. Hillmann loved the LAPD. We used to joke that like the LAPD cruisers even his underwear was "black and white." But he was horrified by what he saw, because it was not his LAPD that day.

As pitiless as Chaleff was in his overall assessment, Hillmann was even more brutal in his. He was scathing in his *self*-criticism because he had commanded the Metropolitan Division for so many years. He had now become a believer in the need to reform the division.

So I had an opportunity to engage all of those people in the LAPD and the community in creating the changes they had been demanding: turn this crisis into a positive, tip the organization, change the last vestiges of the old LAPD culture and operations, and move forward.

And the buy-in after the May Day melee was extraordinary; at the outset it was almost impossible, if you think of it. The media had been attacked by the police, so they weren't looking too kindly on us. The immigrant and Latino communities were not looking too kindly on us. Political leaders were beside themselves: "Here we go again with the lawsuits."

The report that we wrote—it was one of four investigations we initiated—went beyond questioning skills and capabilities or the ways we had always done things. Hillmann came out of this with a totally new Incident Command and Control System that we used to retrain the whole department: each commander and officer of every command within the Metropolitan Division. Train, retrain, refresh, clarify—and resolve policy conflicts we had never fully addressed.

To ensure that the department would never forget these lessons, and to emphasize that we would train, and retrain, on how to handle such matters, I created a new bureau to deal with nothing but incident policy, training, and liaison, and put Mike Hillmann in charge.

The new ways that were being proposed turned out to be much

better. In the old silo structure, the commanding officer of the area—a captain—was the incident commander, and his bureau chief was the overall commander.

As we had seen, that captain might not be our best person for that particular event. He might be a brand-new captain. He might never have worked an event like that before. That was part of the MacArthur Park problem: we had deployed a number of people who had never worked such large rallies.

Hillmann designed a system that defined all the positions that had to be filled in an incident command. He trained teams of six or seven to work together. An incident command would then be filled from those teams drawn from across the department.

The next year at MacArthur Park, the bureau chief and the captain of the area in which the event was going to be held were not in the incident command. We brought another team in that worked *with* them. This helped us bring in a fresh perspective or a more seasoned perspective.

Since that time, we have never had an incident involving loss of control or command of the situation.

By holding to our values, and never losing sight of the vision that drove us in the first place, by tapping into that trust account we'd built up and turning to the allies we'd made before the crisis, we emerged from the potentially disastrous MacArthur Park incident with an even more powerful collaboration.

The Metropolitan Division remains smaller, wiser, more capable. But having failed to embrace collaboration, it had already lost support; isolated, arrogant, and not nearly as capable as it thought, it had no idea that the LAPD had moved past it. When crisis hit, Metro could easily have perished.

The LAPD as a whole had the same experience—in reverse. MacArthur Park could have undone all the years of hard work and reform. Without the trust and support of our partners and critics alike, it would have been impossible for us to have survived the MacArthur Park confrontation. Instead our response and that of the city reaffirmed the direction we had taken—partnership and collaboration. Collaboration created a great resiliency to deal with crisis—not just the LAPD's, but the city's. Everyone was in this together.

As the mayor, Councillor Reyes, and I strolled through the once-again crowded park the next Sunday, even with the memories fresh, it was clear that the city was getting on with its life, resilient through crisis, confident that its police department, which had stumbled badly, was picking itself up, dusting itself off, and getting back on track.

The LAPD finally came out from under almost all components of the consent decree by 2008, when it was lifted by the federal court. I don't think most people fully appreciated what this meant for Los Angeles and the LAPD until it finally did happen. The city was almost like a person who's been struggling to catch his breath, gasping for air, and finally breathes freely again.

THE BILLION-DOLLAR BET

When you are leading a collaboration, you are dealing with hierarchies, crossing boundaries, and making common cause with leaders who have their own agendas, issues, and baggage.

To deliver on the promise, leadership of collaboration requires single-minded pursuit. But if it's "all about me," a crisis will bring out the worst in everyone.

On the other hand, leaders who are single-minded about making the pie bigger for everyone create a "yes we can, together" attitude. This kind of single-mindedness can lead collaboration out of crisis; these leaders touch those whose faith in change is rattled. They reassure partners who have stuck their necks out that it is still safe. They assure all: we are who we said we were.

But what about a collaboration that straddles two worlds—the brick-and-mortar bureaucracy and the new digital world of bits and bytes? It is one thing to lead men and women across the boundaries of an institution in the name of some greater good; it is another to lead men, women, and *machines* in a global collaboration.

In the age of the Internet, successful leadership of a collaboration relies on successfully navigating both the brick-and-mortar world of bureaucracy and the digital world that is in our pockets and on our desks.

WELLS FARGO AND THE WHOLESALE BANKING INDUSTRY

Not many of us care much about our bankers. We've come to love direct deposits, electronic transfers, and ATM withdrawals. The banker and the branch have become superfluous, and for many of us who prefer our banking online, that's just fine.

But there exists a world of banking few of us see, where the relationship between bankers and their customers is positively existential; bankers grease the cogs of billions of transactions between companies, moving hundreds of trillions of dollars every year. It is the world of the small-business owner buying and selling goods, of a corporate treasurer making payroll, of the chief financial officer of a Fortune 10 titan wondering about her cash position in a hundred different checking accounts around the world.

Banks pump data like blood through the veins and arteries of these businesses. And in recent years, practically every piece of that data, every binary 0 and 1, every single byte has come to be the digital representation of money. The better, faster, and cheaper a bank can pump money-as-data into the corporate tank, make it visible and usable anywhere, anytime, keeping it utterly secure at rest or in transit, the faster corporations can move in the marketplace, lower their cost of business, and satisfy customers and shareholders.

Monte dei Paschi of Siena, Italy, the earliest chartered bank still in existence, opened its doors in 1472. Today, digital technologies and the Internet have transformed the Florentine *banca*—the medieval banker's countertop—into a global digital platform supporting millions, billions, and trillions of transactions and dollars daily. Data *is* money. And today wholesale banking, as it is known, resembles its antecedents of just a decade ago about as much as an iPhone looks like a corded wall phone.

Getting from 1472 to 2012 in the space of a decade or so has been an exercise in collaboration between customer and bank that has straddled two worlds: the staid world of risk-shy bankers, operating on timeless banking principles, and the wild west of twenty-first-century Silicon Valley, where the "first one in the valley gets the best view"—and the billions. All of this is complicated by the fact that just as banks finally adjust to some new technology, it all changes again.

"Technology," Sun Microsystems's Scott McNealy once said, "has the shelf life of a banana."

At the epicenter of this collaboration has been Wells Fargo Bank of San Francisco, neighbor to Silicon Valley. Ground zero at Wells Fargo has been the Wells wholesale banking shop and its executive vice president, Steve Ellis. If you had to pick a date and place when Silicon Valley turned global corporate banking on its head, it would be April 12, 1999, at a bank industry session in Atlanta that Steve Ellis attended. That was the day Scott McNealy, then CEO of Sun Microsystems, framed the position of banks as nothing short of collaborate or perish.

Wells Fargo built its fortunes in a mad dash to service the unbanked settlers and farmers of California's Santa Clara Valley, and soon the miners of the California gold rush. Since 1852, Wells has forged its reputation on hard-won security and trust, deepened relationships and lured customers with new products and services, and built all on a foundation of the latest technologies. Before Wells Fargo's stagecoach carried its first gold coin, dust, and bullion overland from San Francisco to St. Louis, for example, money and gold were shipped by river and sea.

That took six months. Wells covered that same distance by stagecoach in four weeks.

But by 1998, when Richard Kovacevich came on as Wells Fargo's CEO, Wells was behind the times. It was missing in action on the Internet. Not on the consumer, or "retail" side—where individuals and small businesses could use a dial-up service—but on the "wholesale" side, where industry banked.

Wells moved cosmically huge sums for its fifteen thousand largest business customers—as much as $650 million at a pop. Small as this customer segment was, it brought in 30 percent of Wells's revenue.

"*Everybody* in the business world had access to the Internet," Kovacevich mused. "But not every consumer, by any means. A lot of people didn't even have computers."

What was Wells *doing*?

With twelve years at Wells and roots in Philadelphia, Portland, and now San Francisco, Steve Ellis, an executive vice president in the Wells wholesale shop, was wondering the same thing. Ellis could see and feel Silicon Valley all around him—perhaps better than most bankers. At a personal and professional level Ellis was used to operating in suited banking worlds, but seeing things differently. Happiest surfing and snowboarding, Ellis, at age forty-six, stood out dressed in a suit and Birkenstocks and sporting shoulder-length hair and an earring. But he was successful wherever he went, from San Francisco to Tahoe to Maui, in operations centers, office cubicles, and company boardrooms.

Scott McNealy, a giant of the digital age (*Fortune* magazine once likened McNealy's appearances at industry gatherings to "Jesus showing up at a tent revival"), had the stage in Atlanta at a banking industry function and Ellis's attention. These were Ellis's people, after all: payment systems specialists, mostly back office "ops and sys" guys, the pocket protector crew. But McNealy was Ellis's kind of guy. ("Am I a computer scientist?" McNealy once replied to a reporter's question. "No, I'm a golf major.") And Ellis listened.

You've made progress, McNealy told the bankers. You're dealing with e-commerce and servicing customers. That's good. But make no mistake—Internet banking is not just another ATM or telephone call center. The Internet channel is potent stuff and you need to attack it differently.

"I will tell you," McNealy said, "that I've explained to every telco that either they become a destination site, or the destination sites will become a telco. And I will tell you that either *you* become a destination site, or the destination sites will become a bank."

Banks worried. What if some Internet-only bank or brokerage raided Wells's best customers? On the wholesale side alone, Wells figured it had a billion dollars a year exposed. That "click click click" from a desktop mouse might be the "tick tick tick" of a time bomb.

Wells Fargo wholesale needed to get with both clicks, and bricks, fast.

Back in San Francisco, Steve Ellis took five people off projects and said, "Go find out everything we know about the Internet and figure out how we approach this thing, alright?"

A few months later, in June 1999, Ellis had enough of a vision and a plan that he was ready. Standing before a Wells wholesale unit strategy session in Phoenix, Steve Ellis made it as simple as he could in a presentation that influences Wells's strategy to this day.

We're under attack, Ellis said. The threat is real. But our brand is strong. Our customer base is loyal. They are ready for the Internet. But we are not ready for *them*—yet.

But we know how to do this. We've offered the Internet to consumers since 1995. Now it's wholesale's time. Either we get the Internet to our wholesale customers first—like we got the stagecoach to the California gold rush—or others will.

It was McNealy's Law: "Eat lunch, or be lunch." Collaborate, or perish.

THE CUSTOMER. Ellis's presentation lit the path with vision and a plan. Our customers have done business the same way for decades—maybe even centuries, he said. Now, the digital world is in their face. They want what it promises. But with all the choices, they're confused.

That's good for us, Ellis said. We can take the complexity out and put the risk on us. We've always done that.

By helping our customers, we'll help ourselves. Wholesale is challenged to deliver over 10 percent earnings growth annually. With a single sign-on for the entire wholesale side, we can cross-sell every unit's products. Just by cross-selling better into *current* customers we'll hit those numbers. There's something in this for everyone.

It's about a *portal*, Ellis said, where everything Wells has comes together for its wholesale customers. They'll *have* everything they need here; they can *do* everything here. Real transactions, Ellis said. Trades. They can see cash position. They can execute payment instructions. They can move balances. Let them do it on their schedule without having to call Wells Fargo every five minutes.

"Wait," someone in the room said. "We're going to let them *move* money? We're just going to give them information, right?"

There was no turning back. If people are just going to look at things, Ellis said, if they can't *do* things, there's no value there. They won't come back.

"The portal," Ellis began, "is built the way the customer does business."

Ellis called it "A Day in the Life"—a concept that helped doubters understand his vision. "The first thing a cash manager, a payroll clerk, or a chief financial officer likes to check in the morning, that's the first screen that comes up. Easy, intuitive access."

A single sign-on. A dozen products from across Wells appearing with the same interface, the same navigation. We'll rinse complexity from the user's world. No matter how fractured we are, the customer signs on once, and sees one cohesive bank.

Data will be precise, exact to the minute, as close to "real time" as bank data gets. The treasurer can see it formatted as he or she prefers, over whatever channel the treasurer prefers. That's value and comfort, trust and security. That's banking on the Internet.

THE BANK AND THE INTERNET. McNealy had said of the big software shops, "Our vision couldn't be more different. Theirs is to put a mainframe on everybody's desktop. We want to provide dial tone for the Internet."

That's how Ellis saw it. If Wells could provide a "dial tone" for global banking—a browser-based portal—all a customer needed was web access and an Internet jack. The key here, Ellis said, is building the connections end-to-end from the customer into bank systems, then back to the customer. That's heavy lifting for us.

But for the customer, Ellis said, it will be light. No loading up Wells's software on customers' machines. The Internet lets Wells build "once for all"—a common infrastructure, then customize exactly to the business and the customer. On the Internet, that happens fast.

We'll create and put new services on the web as quickly as a customer needs them. Even before they are needed, as technology shifts. They don't need a manual. When was the last time anyone used a manual for Google or Yahoo?

Lightness. Quickness. Exactitude. That was the vision. Visibility. Multiplicity. Consistency. This was the Internet world Wells would have to build to.*

There was only one small problem: Steve Ellis worked for a bank.

THE REAL BRICK AND MORTAR. A rule of thumb from software developers—dubbed Conway's Law—says that the architecture of any system will mirror the architecture of the organization that built it. That meant a bank would design its Internet presence to look like . . . a bank: stovepiped, name-plaqued, and bureaucratic.

---

*A vision articulated beautifully by the essayist Italo Calvino. *Six Memos for the Next Millennium.* New York: Vintage Books. 1988.

Ellis figured it had to be just the opposite. He wasn't sure what Wells's corporate customers wanted on the Internet—but he was pretty sure it wasn't a *bank* bank. They wanted information and action. They'd want a button that said "Transfer Now." They would want transactions, not just staring—the same experience they had when surfing the net at home.

Ellis was also pretty sure that whatever Wells customers wanted today, with fast-changing technology in everyone's hands, it would likely change tomorrow. No way around it: Wells would have to ask the customer, "How are we doing?" With the world changing so much so fast, Wells would have to *keep* asking the customer. "That's now how the game is played," Ellis would later say. "It's about how people are doing things, and that evolves very quickly from what I see."

"The Internet," he would say, "is about customers, not products."

The solution? Conway's Law. If customers were involved in design, then the Internet bank would be all about customers.

A network to design a network, a collaboration to design a collaboration. Customers collaborating with web designers collaborating with bank operations—forging a new platform, with Wells as its steward.

That's how Ellis intended to play the Wells game—with one foot in Wells's brick-and-mortar culture, the other in Silicon Valley, a foundation of bank systems as secure as Fort Knox beneath a Christmas-in-July portal for digital banking that would make every corporate customer's wish come true.

THE GENERAL ON THE MOUNTAIN. Five minutes before Steve Ellis presented at the June 1999 Phoenix session the new Wells Fargo CEO, Richard Kovacevich, dropped in unannounced. At his side was Dave Hoyt, head of wholesale, and Steve Ellis's boss.

The CEO was in the house.

Ellis kept stride. "Whether they bought into it or not," he said, "what I said was just obvious. Hopefully, it would become obvious to other people."

Dick Kovacevich, it turns out, had already parsed the Wells position and was ready to move. Kovacevich didn't know much about the Internet. But he was used to dialing up the big picture, making bold bets, and winning.

He saw his business customers using the web for personal needs. But their companies had to e-mail Wells, or phone the bank, use paper reports, and operate on bankers' time. As consumers his customers managed their accounts directly, 24/7. This should work on the business side for corporate accounts, too.

Kovacevich saw Wells, heavily invested through its venture capital companies, making a ton of money on Internet start-ups—a hundred times revenue. Was everybody dreaming the same Internet-Gone-Wild fantasy? Not likely. There would be winners and losers, to be sure. But if worst comes to worst and the whole bubble bursts, Kovacevich reasoned, Wells will be selling its investments on the one side and funding a move of wholesale to the Internet on the other. All bets are covered.

He saw a management plan, a path forward: bring all of Wells's Internet operations under one roof and put one person—the trusted and proven Clyde Ostler—in charge. Give the consumer, small business, brokerage, and wholesale businesses their own Internet heads, but make sure all the architectures were seamless, there was no duplication in infrastructure, and the platform was developed once for all four units. That was savings.

Kovacevich saw customers loving the cost-cutting and convenience ahead, just as they loved the move to ATMs. For the bank, applications were cheap to develop; branches and call centers were expensive to staff. Customers taking care of their own business would think they were getting a better deal—and the bank *knew* it was. "We could just see how important we could become to that treasurer with a gazillion accounts scattered around the country," he said. "The ability to move money and work with it? They never had that before."

Kovacevich saw huge cross-selling opportunities. Add wholesale products to the mix, get exactly the right ones in front of customers who were already using the Internet for their personal banking, and let the cross-selling begin. "I was convinced that the stickiness of the Internet and our ability to cross-sell would absolutely be a terrific combination."

Kovacevich knew these would be great customers: anyone with an Internet account carried 20 to 30 percent higher balances, used 30 percent more products, would stay two and a half times longer, and had 30 percent lower attrition. "This had to result in either getting more business with that customer or tying them to the company," Kovacevich said. "They couldn't do without us."

"When you think about how uncertain this was, I can't think of ever spending a billion dollars without calculating," Kovacevich said. "But all these things convinced me that at least we'd break even just on the self-service side of things. It was just obviously the right thing to do. I considered it just as important as putting ATMs out there."

Analytically, it all worked for Kovacevich. But it was what Kovacevich *heard* that clinched it.

He heard Steve Ellis.

TRUSTING THE SIGNAL. "Steve Ellis was a technologist who grabbed that it's all about the customer," Kovacevich said. "And he knew the wholesale business. Here he is, very enthusiastic, really believing this is something the customers are going to want. 'We can do it for them. It's the right thing to do. We will gain business.' There was never a doubt in his mind that we should move forward. I found his relentless customer focus in everything he and his team did just very reassuring.

"Steve's influence was therefore much greater than just the Wholesale side, at least from my perspective as the ultimate decision maker," Kovacevich said. If this was as good as Ellis believed for Wholesale, Kovacevich reasoned, the same should hold for all Wells's corporate banking.

The consumer side of Wells Fargo was in. Wholesale was in. Kovacevich next turned the screws on small business, the lone holdout.

"Put them all together to allow the seamless transfer from their business needs to their personal needs to their investment needs," Kovacevich said. "It just makes all the sense in the world."

There was push back from some Wells business heads, each of whom would have to contribute. Clyde Ostler was predicting a $1 billion price tag—$250 million a year for four years.

" 'We don't know what the savings are,' " Kovacevich heard. " 'We don't know what we're gaining from this. There's no profitability plan. How much do we spend here?' "

The CEO had a "penguin problem." His answer: "We'll all jump together—it's the only way.

"Each agreed they would do their part, they would give people to Clyde from their various businesses, they would pay for it, and there would be give and take where Clyde would interact with the businesses, set goals and budgets."

A month after Phoenix, Clyde Ostler offered Steve Ellis the reins of wholesale Internet, a step down in grade but a chance to soar. It was 1999, the Internet boom was on, and this would be Steve Ellis's start-up: he'd bet his career on it.

"Not that either of us knew what the hell that meant, of course. . . . 'Do you want to run this Wholesale Internet stuff?' " Ellis said.

"People said, 'Why would you take that job?' I had four or five hundred people reporting to me, and here I was starting this little thing."

"I said, 'Wow! That sounds like fun.' Failing never entered my thinking," Ellis said. "Honestly, not once did it cross my mind. It was so obvious that it was going to be fun, to me."

Kovacevich, too, made his move. Knowing little of the Internet, he stayed close to Ellis. "He's just a very interesting guy," Kovacevich said. "I had a great respect for him and his thought process." And with the voice of the customer soon streaming in from Ellis's initial forays—"seeing the first functionality come in," as Kovacevich put it—he knew the call was right and put his money down.

"Whatever it took," Kovacevich said, "we were going to do it."

A billion-dollar bet.

The vision was aligned. The plan was clear enough that people could move against it, even though no one was quite sure "what the hell that meant." A billion dollars invested over four years to cover—and then riches.

It was "a big, hairy, audacious goal," according to Danny Peltz (quoting Jim Collins's phrase from his book *Good to Great)*. Ellis would soon bring Peltz and Debbie Ball on as his top consiglieri.

"We had the keys to the Porsche, but no Porsche—yet," Danny Peltz said.

The people—Kovacevich, Ostler, Hoyt, Ellis—were Wells Fargo's biggest guns. And they had all the latitude of a dot-com in the heart of San Francisco in 1999 backed by one of the most powerful financial services brands in America with plenty of funding and a huge embedded customer base.

Steve Ellis was soon to have the best time of his life.

THE PLATFORM *IS* THE STRATEGY. But soon wasn't fast enough. Something had to happen tomorrow—which was not exactly at bank speed. With Wells's customers ready and dot-coms moving at Internet speed, waiting for "perfect" was not an option. Start small, go large, Ellis figured.

"Functionality soft—deadlines hard": that became Ellis's Law. Get value in the hands of users fast. As customers adopt and adapt, get the feedback loops going. Do it again.

"We figured with that approach whatever we built, even if we built half of what we wanted, it would be twice as much as what anyone else had," Ellis said.

He pulled his team together and moved out of Wells's downtown headquarters to a hipper San Francisco neighborhood that was teaming with dot-coms. Wells had no trouble attracting top talent: web developers, product specialists, operations gurus, risk management, services professionals.

"There was no real playbook; we built our own, which we wanted to do anyhow," Ellis said. "We couldn't be the way the bank was, take two, three years, go through all these steps to get big projects done.

"The world was different—customers changing all the time. You have to start thinking differently." Think like a dot-com.

"That's why we built the open space," Ellis said. "That's why we didn't have offices; that's why we let people dress however they wanted to. Why we started with small boutique vendors and we stuck with them. It was much more of building a culture, and a concept, trying to make it feel real where you were working.

"This entrepreneurial stuff is not that easy in a big company—it's a whole different world than the space I'm in—getting people to act in concert together around a common goal—especially a goal that was very hard to articulate."

The Commercial Electronic Office platform, or CEO, was where it would happen. With money now data, Wells's systems and its customers could easily cross each other's boundaries thousands of times a minute. Together, Wells and its customers could design new, digitally powered work flows; kill paper; speed processes; and converge on Wells's product mix. That was the idea; design with customers right from the start, innovate faster, cross-sell products, and deepen dependencies.

"Our core organizing principle around treasury management," Ellis said, "is that we want to get *everybody* we can in front of the customer. Not just Sales. Not just us, in Services. It's product management, it's our systems people, it's ops, it's our risk management people. It's everybody.

"The more we know about the customer and we get it in our DNA, the better we are going to be able to unlock the value of what we can do," Ellis emphasized. "As customers *adopt*, they will *adapt*." And create the greatest of opportunities for Wells.

"If that's the guiding principle," said Ellis, "then you can never sit still."

One year from the Phoenix off-site, on June 24, 2000, Wells Fargo rolled out version 1 of the Commercial Electronic Office, a portal for Wells Fargo's industrial and commercial customers. Within the decade, the Wells wholesale platform went from boundaried, cylindered, and stovepiped to practically seamless. By 2010, "customers are now accessing our core systems directly," Danny Peltz explained. "It's difficult to see where our bank systems and business processes end and where theirs begin."

VERSION X.X. Getting there was half the fun. Ellis led the version 1 CEO build in 2000 with a team of seventy. It was a total custom job—nothing canned, off the shelf, proprietary, or generic. Built from scratch. But in that first design, the "voice of the customer" could hardly be heard.

"Customers could not see how this would change their lives yet," Danny Peltz said. Wells was actually ahead of its corporate customers. After all, only 3 percent banked online.

When version 1 hit the street, with three services offered, customers gawked, laughed—and then oohed. They began talking to their bankers about it, building buzz within the organization.

"Wells folks started saying, 'Hey, what's this CEO thing?' " Ellis said.

In year one, two thousand firms enrolled. With Wells's customer antennae raised and feedback pouring in, version 2 followed, then version 3 . . . a new version every sixty to ninety days, getting value in the hands of users fast, adding services, streamlining clicks, building, and customizing.

By 2001, forty-three hundred firms were enrolled; by 2002, thirteen thousand. From 2002 to 2003, revenue on the channel leapt by 54 percent. The average number of products per company doubled.

"The longer a customer has been online," Danny Peltz said, "the more of our products he is likely to have."

Wells was feeling on top of its game—even while the post-9/11 recession hammered other big banks and corporations. CEO was tapping into a marketplace filled with anxious, overworked treasury and finance shops desperate for what Wells was selling: simplicity and efficiency. Most had ten or fewer full-time staff. Each was handling billions of dollars in revenues.

By 2004, Wells wholesale was handling $5.9 trillion in payments on-line, up from $930 billion in *all channels* in 2000. Ellis and his team had rolled out seventeen CEO versions. Eighteen thousand firms now used CEO, and it was tied in with thirty-five Wells products.

The customer tide was pulling powerfully—and Ellis made sure Wells felt every tug. He scrapped early plans to create Internet market-places. Instead, his ethnography teams made forays to customers' sides, watched them at work, helped redesign work flows, rinsed out handoffs and sign-offs, and substituted clicks for bricks.

"We spent a lot of time and built up a lot of processes and feedback loops to get the voice of the customer inside our heads," Ellis said. "With the right feedback loops you figure out a lot faster that you don't have a good decision. You get twenty people in the room: if they're saying, 'Gee, what am I going to do with this?' and they're confused versus, 'How am I going to use it to get things *done*?' you know right away.

"People think that Internet banking makes customer relationships less personal," Danny Peltz said. "That's not the case at all. By making so many more services accessible to customers, we're actually *increasing* our interaction with customers."

There was that day in September 2001, for example, when terrorists leveled the World Trade Center in New York, and the FAA grounded all planes for days. Forty-seven billion dollars' worth of paper checks lay in hangars waiting for clearance to fly—signed, sealed, but not delivered.

The financial industry was grounded. Congress changed the law to let banks exchange check *images*, not just paper. No planes flying into towers would ever grind image exchange to a halt.

Although some banks had for years wanted to get rid of paper and ex-change only check images, several years passed before all the big systems began converting. In the meantime Wells saw how it could seize the day for its customers and its bottom line.

In came Wells with a little scanner box that sat on a customer's desk. Plug it in, power it up, log on to CEO, download a driver, and you'd be scanning checks—*payments to you*—into your corporate account ten minutes later.

Competitors offered products that came with all sorts of third-party software to run—the bane of corporate information security folks, as we've seen. Updates required more downloads, further complicating life for treasurers. Wells handled its scanner updates online. That made life simple for the treasurer—and for her corporate information security officer.

For Wells's treasury customers that desktop scanner was a godsend. They could deposit checks from their offices—skipping the dreaded run to the bank—even *after* the local branch closed, and still get same-day credit. A customer who had twenty business sites could image all checks and deposit to a single Wells account online—instead of running to twenty branches—or paying an aggregator to do the same. If you were 7-Eleven you could set up kiosks in 1,050 stores, cash payroll checks 24/7, and ship the images to Wells for processing.

Wells's desktop scanner made every clerk's desk a teller's window. It blew away the boundary between bank and office. Wells Fargo could be everywhere and anywhere there was a customer with an office and an Internet connection.

The platform *was* the strategy; every customer *a branch*. Wells built infrastructure and processes so *adaptive* that Wells could turn on a dime to meet customers' business needs, seize opportunities, grab fast-changing technology, and anchor it all to solid, secure, dependable bank systems.

By 2005, five hundred firms had signed up for DesktopDeposit® Service Release 1.0—and scanned 1.4 million checks. By 2010 the scanner had became an award-winning beachhead of remote capture for Wells, with 13,000 firms signed up, 306 million checks scanned, and over *$1 trillion* deposited.

"Fastest uptake I ever saw," Ellis said.

Wells pushed out more innovations, collaborating with customers on design and development, with benefits to all. At every turn—every law change, every advance in computing and communications—Wells was ready to push the technology to its limits, faster, better, cheaper. It understood its customers' processes. It stewarded the shared platform to include the latest technologies.

In mid-decade, for example, Wells made the move to "web services" technology. That enabled Wells to unbundle its applications, and let customers pick and choose whichever ones they wanted.

Then came mobile. "In '06, I went to my boss," Ellis said, "and said, 'This mobile thing is a big deal. Everyone's got a phone, devices are more intelligent, people are more connected, they want better information.' I said, 'We've got to get really focused here.'

"He said, 'What are people going to do with it?'

"I said, 'I don't know but I just think it's really big.'

"He said, 'Well go do it.'

"I get room to move," Ellis said. "But I don't ask my people to build me really complicated business cases. We sit down and we work it through."

A year later Wells offered CEO Mobile, a mobile-ready version of desktop CEO. Wells was the first major US bank to provide browser-based mobile banking for its commercial customers.

"Our customers told us they wanted to handle wires and check exceptions without being at their desks," a Wells wholesale spokesperson said. "And when our customers give us feedback, we act."

By 2010, customers looked forward to being part of the Wells development cycle. Two dozen advisory councils met several times each year, each comprising ten to twelve customers from different industries. Thousands of customer suggestions came in. Ellis himself spoke with five thousand customers every year.

"The world ahead? It's like mobile," Ellis said. "Who knew what it was really going to be? Or even today, what it's really *going* to be?

"I have no idea," he admitted. "But I can create a process that lets us grow. We get our customers involved early. 'You have this phone, you'll be walking around with this phone. How would you use it?' People spit out ideas, ideas we never thought of. That's what we build. Eighty percent of things we built, the ideas are our customers'; twenty percent are ours."

Today, Wells is prospering. Its site has four million log-ins a month. CEO, which started with three products, now offers eighty. Wholesale customers of Wells, which is now merged with Wachovia, move $11 trillion online per year.

"When you think about what we were spending on an unknown technology, I guess you would say we were pretty lucky," Dick Kovacevich said. "We did pretty well. I guess you would say, in hindsight, we probably did about as well as any mere mortals would do."

LAST WORD. In Steve Ellis's world, the platform *is* the strategy.

The Wells wholesale platform is where banking meets the digital world: safe *and* available for transactions anytime, anywhere, by anyone authorized. Individuals can find and come onto the platform with ease. It makes the world of accounts wonderfully visible to those authorized to see it. They can move, shape, and fix their financial positions as needed. Power shifts to the edges. Hundreds and thousands of data points are brought together—a huge multiplicity, consistent across channels, with astounding exactitude.

It is perfect Internet fare built upon a traditional foundation of brick and mortar.

Leadership of such collaborations has special obligations and opportunities: Ensure that collaboration forms up to design the collaboration. Protect that enterprise at its fragile start by removing it—physically if need be—to a walled garden where it can move fast and light, just like the platform it is designing. Early collaborations of new ventures need that, whether Beverly Donohue's Galaxy at the New York City Board of Education, or Steve Ellis's CEO at Wells Fargo. Flatten decision making for quickness and simplicity; keep the bureaucracy outside the wall, if at all possible.

As always, get value into the hands of users fast. Start showing doubters and partisans alike how "this works." That keeps you and the platform squarely on the good side of your sponsor's support.

Once the platform is operating, keep it safe, available, and trusted. Probe, test for, and fix problems that keep the right people out, or that let the wrong people in. Make sure everyone understands the rules of the road.

Most important, leadership of collaboration ensures platform readiness for a world of constant change. That's the world customers live in, and the world technology makes inevitable. Ellis's leadership across the CEO platform engaged customers as a new way of doing business, not just once but continually. The platform kept Wells, the bosses, Ellis, the troops—and the customers—happy and competitive.

Customers could always leave. Most never did.

As a leader Ellis relinquished power: he let Wells became the "mere" vehicle of the customer. As the DNA of bank and customers melded, Wells's systems, the CEO platform, and the customers' own business processes became extensions of each other, indispensable to each other, almost at times indistinguishable. It is collaboration for a networked world, reaching across boundaries at its best.

OUT OF EGYPT

On Friday, December 17, 2010, in the market square of Sidi Bouzid, a threadbare county seat of thirty-nine thousand in central Tunisia, 120 miles south of the capital city of Tunis, a twenty-six-year-old fruit seller set the world on fire where he had been born, and where on January 4, 2011, he would be buried.

Since the age of eight the fruit seller had picked and sold vegetables and fruit, earning a meager living from his wheelbarrow stand in the square, enough to support his mother and young siblings—even to send his sister to the university. He was also known, from time to time, to give free fruit to the very poor.

That morning, the municipal inspector grew impatient. No money for her bribe again? She would teach this fruit seller a lesson. Where was his license to peddle fruit from his wheelbarrow? "I don't need a license." Whose scales are these? "They are borrowed from a friend." Where did you get these bananas? "I purchased them with a credit of 300 dinars. I am here every day."

The fruit seller suddenly found himself slapped and spat upon; he heard his father, who had died when he was three, cursed by the inspector. Her "aides" seized his fruit, took his scale, and for good measure tossed the fruit seller to the street. Perhaps, also, he was kicked or beaten.

Angered, the fruit seller walked to the regional governor's office to see if he could get his fruit and scales back. The governor refused to see him or hear his case.

Disconsolate, Mohamed Bouazizi, the fruit seller, purchased a can of gasoline or solvent—some flammable liquid—and returned to stand in the middle of morning traffic where in full view of the governor's office he doused himself with the fuel, yelled, "How do you expect me to make a living?," lit a match, and set himself ablaze.

Dying, the fruit seller Bouazizi was soon removed to a hospital. Astonished, aggrieved, and infuriated, Sidi Bouzid's street vendors and citizens gathered around, joined by Bouazizi's mother and cousins. A crowd of several hundred stood in front of the government building. Some sellers dumped their wares on its stoop in protest. An attempt was made to storm the locked wrought-iron gates. Bouazizi's mother raised her voice. The YouTube videos recorded by cell phone cams are astounding; the camera searches for its subject, but there is no crowd leader. There are many voices; a man holds his bananas aloft; anger and bewilderment are all around, as much for this sorrowful day, perhaps, as with this remarkable occurrence in Tunisia: a protest, and in that, a brief gasp of the exalted air of freedom.

After the protest Bouazizi's relatives posted the cell cam videos to YouTube. Minutes or hours later Facebook had consumed them and they moved quickly among a few veteran activists. Fear of reprisal from state security froze others from "sharing" on Facebook, or even "liking." But with one-third of Tunisia on the Internet—3.6 million users—there was plenty of viewing.

Al-Jazeera's "new media" team, searching the web, found the videos. That evening, December 17, 2010, al-Jazeera broadcast the day's cell cam videos around the Arab world.

Later that night, the national police chief arrived in Sidi Bouzid. A peaceful march to honor the fruit seller was held the next day. Tear gas flew; clashes followed; arrests were made. Police reinforcements arrived Sunday—one hundred on motorcycles. Rioting in this desperate desert dust-hole resumed on Monday with hundreds of young people—most so young as to have known only the twenty-three-year reign of Zine El Abidine Ben Ali—confronting the hopelessness of their lives.

The children of the regime, it was said, were turning against it, with "a rock in one hand, a cellphone in the other."

The news, at first denied by official spokesmen, suppressed by state organs, or spun with a smiley-face by state-controlled media, traveled by other circuits: four television networks—al-Jazeera, France 24, al-Arabiya, and CNN—Facebook, and Twitter. An established blogosphere operated "offshore," keeping information alive.

It might have been a blessing that until the end only activists had posted to Facebook. As the pharaonic regime in Tunis responded with digital suppression of the web, then physical repression of web partisans, they literally passed over Facebook, deeming it irrelevant, an Old Testament–like reprieve in this twenty-first-century story of liberation. The Facebook viewing continued unabated. The revolt spread.

"The hashtags on Twitter," al-Jazeera reported, "tell the tale of how the uprising went from being local to national in scope: #bouazizi became #sidibouzid, then #tunisia."

Video imagery transformed Sidi Bouzid from local backwater to global spectacle, revealing the truth all knew but no leader spoke, igniting passions and activating the aspirations of millions.

"We could protest for two years here," a YouTube poster said, "but without videos no one would take any notice of us."

In 2011, the 24/7 news cycle had a voracious appetite for content. Once on the Internet, images went "viral," reverberating across broadcast television and social media like Facebook, YouTube, and Twitter, amplifying effects and accelerating change.

On January 14, 2011, a scant thirty days after the protests began, Zine El Abidine Ben Ali was gone, having fled to Malta under Libyan protection, then to Riyadh, Saudi Arabia. His country—a dynasty of the few, by the few, and for the few—was no longer "his."

Ben Ali had played by the same ageless bloody rules of despots around the world—repress fast and win, or go away. All other strategy would be improvised.

But Tunisia was different. In this opening salvo of the "Arab Spring," like-minded grievants and partisans searched for, found, and saw each other—in seconds. Isolated by distance of miles and chasms of culture, they needed only a few bytes to connect, and two or three clicks of a mouse for a picture and some words to ignite their passions.

Television networks like al-Jazeera gained outsized reputations. Upon seeing its studios in Qatar, Egyptian president Hosni Mubarak had once lamented, "All that noise from this little matchbox?" In reality, al-Jazeera scooped up the great storm of signals from original reporting, blogs, Twitter and Facebook, and YouTube and blasted it to the world.

Knowing they were being seen globally—not just on al-Jazeera, but on Twitter, where partisans could see #Tunisia trending in the United States—many gained courage. Tunisia surged; events moved from clicks to bricks far faster than Ben Ali, armed only with the crude tools of truncheons and torture, could extinguish.

Two thousand miles to the east, in Tripoli and Cairo, Sidi Bouzid's signal beamed clear. With millions of antennae raised, web browsers opened, and smart phones on ring, a new Internet age of the "many to many" received and rebroadcast Sidi Bouzid's unmistakable message.

"Now is *our* time."

"People, have some shame."

The speaker was a pudgy-faced young woman wearing a striped shirt and head scarf. She sat, staring calmly and speaking steadily into a web cam.

Her name was Asmaa Mahfouz. It was January 8, 2011, four days after the death of Bouazizi.

"Four Egyptians have set themselves on fire to protest humiliation and hunger and poverty and degradation they had to live with for 30 years. Four Egyptians have set themselves on fire thinking maybe we can have a revolution like Tunisia, maybe we can have freedom, justice, honor and human dignity. Today, one of these four has died, and I saw people commenting and saying, 'May God forgive him. He committed a sin and killed himself for nothing.'

"They say, 'These guys who burned themselves were psychopaths.' Of course, on all national media, whoever dies in protest is a psychopath.

"If they were psychopaths, why did they burn themselves at the parliament building?

"I'm making this video to give you one simple message: we want to go down to Tahrir Square on January 25th. If we still have honor and want to live in dignity on this land, we have to go down on January 25th. We'll go down and demand our rights, our fundamental human rights."

By 2011, such a call to action was nothing new. In Egypt blockages, work stoppages, and sit-ins to protest this and that government policy were common enough. It was how average citizens had come to litigate their grievances. Block a street, claim an intersection, close a shop—these outbursts did not shock the Egyptian conscience.

From time to time street actions turned confrontational and bloody— Egyptians were not concerned with that, either. "Doing politics out-doors," as Barnard professor Mona El-Ghobashy wrote, gave citizens a good grasp of the monotone response of police to control by force and fear. It was part of the rulers' game of rope-a-dope perfected and played by the Mubarak regime. Give some room for expression, let leaders ex-pose themselves, ruthlessly lop off some heads, denounce the rest as anti-Egyptian agitators, and kill off any thought of revolt.

Go home, all. And they did.

By late 2010, the tidal bore of sentiment built up over three decades of agitation, repression, and response was now at the seawalls of Cairo, Giza, and Suez. Over the years it had crested and retreated, the bitterness of vast unemployment and a median income of about $1 per day, cramped living, repressive security, and deeply corrupt government smoothed over with gifts of bread and wages (offset moments later by higher taxes), laced with stern warnings about the bogey-men of disorder or foreign elements and the necessity of the state-as-protector.

Egyptians were by 2010 well practiced in their opposition, having developed dozens of trade, social, and political groups, opposition parties and leaders such as Mohamed ElBaradei, and organizations of varying stripe such as the religious Muslim Brotherhood, the neutered but visible Wafd reformist party, and others—Nasserists, Islamists, Greens, liberals, Marxists, and secularists.

Each had run the regime's gauntlet of repression. They also shared a recent history of loose collaboration and coordination, called the Kifaya movement, embracing a vision of democracy and reform and, specifically, urging direct presidential elections with competing candidates.

While dismal in outcome, their campaigns in well-controlled elections helped build networks, training, and experience in dealing with the state's repressive guises. A sophisticated political culture of commentary and blogging arose, providing anyone with the Internet a view to the Arab street, dialogue with fellow partisans, and a steady visual and verbal diet of government abuse.

All was built upon a widely shared foundation of grievance. Egypt had become a nation of deep and wide resentment. "Mubarak's regime," the Egyptian blogger Sarah Carr wrote, "has stripped the act of earning a living of its nobility and cheapened the currency of dreams."

In June 2010, the most common of occurrences—the brutal, senseless beating and slaying of a young man whom police dragged from an Internet café—splashed across blogs and Facebook. In response Wael Ghonim, a thirty-year-old Egyptian Google executive for the region with experience building websites for ElBaradei and an MBA from American University in Cairo, created a Facebook page named after the poor soul: "We Are All Khaled Sa'id."

Covering his digital tracks with the nom de guerre "El Shaheed," Ghonim plastered the Facebook page with photographs of Sa'id's beaten body and face. None could mask that before the feet and clubs of Egyptian police had rearranged them Sa'id had once been a perfectly ordinary man with a nose, mouth, teeth, and eyeballs all in the right places and pointing in the same direction. Like Mohamed Bouazizi and millions of others across the Arab world, that was practically all Sa'id had. Now that was gone, too.

Enough. "Those photos killed me," Ghonim said. "I felt in pain. I wanted to do something. It happened that I created this page, and it happened that 375,000 people 'liked' it.

"Once you are a fan, whatever we publish gets on your wall," Ghonim wrote. "So the government has no way to block it—unless they block Facebook completely."

Antiregime sentiment began cresting. "We Are All Khaled Sa'id" attracted cell phone cam pictures and videos, messages, and testimony recounting the corruption and beatings. By January 25, El Shaheed's page was at 450,000 "likes"—a staggering number.

Ignoring the Facebook rumbling, Hosni Mubarak announced in September 2010 that the great progress of Egypt would continue with the planned succession of his son Gamal.

As the Egyptian novelist Alaa al-Aswany put it, Egypt was to be handed down from father to son "like a poultry farm."

Some Western commentators saw this as Egypt's best hope. "If a democratic revolution is unlikely," Harvard's Tarek Masoud wrote in September 2010, "so too is a military coup. Thus, we are really left with two choices: Gamal or his father."

The effect was to remind many Egyptians that not only had they no present, they had no future. In November the regime dropped all pretense at democracy and declared that in the general election just held, it had won 97 percent of seats to Parliament.

With opposition seats reduced from one hundred to fewer than ten, Egyptians' fear of reprisals and even death seemed nothing against the fear of living another day, let alone a generation, without a voice or a vote. The only Egyptians who now had a stake in Egypt's future were the members of Mubarak's close circle, the military from whom Mubarak arose and drew strength, and the thousands of poor men and boys recruited from agricultural backwaters of Egypt to police its great cities.

On December 2, the Lebanese newspaper *al-Akhbar* published Wikileaks documents that exposed leaders across the Arabic world to be as corrupt as was generally believed.

On December 12, demonstrations and street battles broke out in dozens of Egyptian cities, protesting the sham election.

In early January, Coptic Christians—10 percent of the population and despised by Islamic fundamentalists—fought police in Alexandria after a church was firebombed.

Days later detainees at a police station in a working-class neighborhood of Cairo rioted and set fire to the jail; hundreds of relatives, believing their loved ones were trapped, swarmed the station, shouted their protests of innocence, and battled the police for hours.

This nation was wired to blow.

On January 14, the deposed Zine El Abidine Ben Ali fled Tunis for Riyadh, sending fresh currents ripping through Egypt. There were no circuit breakers left to blow. The Arab Spring was on.

THE FACEBOOK REVOLUTION

"The delusions of dictators," David Remnick wrote of Hosni Mubarak in *The New Yorker*, "are never more poignant—or more dangerous—than when they are in their death throes."

The regime had declared January 25, 2011, the first "National Police Day" and gave everyone the day off from work and school. "We Are All Khaled Sa'id" had promoted numerous protests over the summer and fall. Seeing the page's 375,000 Facebook "likes," veteran activists contacted El Shaheed. Might he or she—for no one had penetrated the Facebook page's nom de guerre—promote a small protest they had planned for that day on the Facebook page?

The protest's goals were clear: get rid of the security chief and the emergency laws, set a minimum wage, and establish term limits for Mubarak. Within days fifty thousand people had clicked "Yes, Will Attend" to El Shaheed's invitation. By January 25, the number had climbed to eighty thousand. Ghonim later said he'd had high hopes but no illusions. Translating clicks on the mouse to feet on the pavement was tough. He posted links to flyers anyone could print and hand out.

A Google exec by day, a writer of web copy by night, and passionate for Egypt, Ghonim was angry, but he had options. If the protest failed, it would be no big deal. "I'd learn from the lesson, move forward and do something else," Ghonim said later.

The veteran activists who had approached El Shaheed saw this as something more. Having trained together and run previous campaigns, they had serious organizational and street skills. Even so, they figured the day would go fast—"like usual, we'd go out to protest and get arrested in the first ten minutes," said Ziad al-Oleimi, one of the organizers.

The normal state of affairs. Or was it?

"It was on the Saturday night before these protests," recalled Eric Trager, an American researching his dissertation in Cairo. "I actually heard a number of Egyptian friends who never in a million years would do anything political—because they were elite, or because they're scared, or because they have friends who've been imprisoned—say, 'Actually, January 25, I'm going to the streets.'

"All of a sudden, these opposition movements had started sending out tons of text messages to even random Egyptians. Facebook messages, YouTube videos: telling people where to go, how to behave at the protest, what they should wear, what they should not do—specifically, they should not attack the police."

Police higher-ups later said their preparations had been quite usual. They'd briefed the plans the day before; orders were clear not to tangle with the protesters. Cairo chief of police Ismail al-Shair issued the customary warnings against congregations of five or more. Riot trucks were deployed on major thoroughfares and the streets around Cairo University, all announced as march routes by organizers. The Interior Ministry, designated as a target of the protest, was further secured; all avenues leading to the ministry were sealed. Routes inbound to Cairo were checkpointed to block the flow of partisans from the provinces.

Everyone was ready for the 2:00 p.m. start.

Except it began at noon. And protests started not at mosques in announced neighborhoods but at different ones. Facebook and the press carried the correct rally points, but with the feints carried off, and start time and routes all different, security forces were out of position.

Marchers went down side streets, undisturbed by police, beckoning to the tenements and balconies, waving Egyptian flags, picking up people along the way—with messages not of democracy but wages and food. "They are eating pigeon and chicken and we are eating beans!"

Dozens of such marches wove through Cairo's tiny picturesque lanes, picking up a thousand bystanders here, a thousand there, streaming toward rally points in central Cairo. By cell phone and text they learned that crowds were gathering steam in working- and middle-class neighborhoods alike—all marching toward Tahrir Square.

Police sought to bottle up the side streets and keep the groups from becoming one. New streams arrived, thousands of chanting activists, Greens waving flags, liberal party youth sprinting down the Nile cornice, adding bystanders as they went. They paused in front of the ruling party's headquarters to denounce Mubarak and promise him Ben Ali's fate. Joined by still another group coming across the Qasr al-Nil Bridge, the roiling brigade headed for the state radio building, circled it once or twice, then headed off for Tahrir Square.

By 4:00 p.m., security forces in the square had gathered themselves up and were resisting new surges in. Soccer fans led chants of "Egypt! Egypt!" and battled police as they were chased and beaten. But the day was not half over. New marchers coming from farther away were now arriving by the hundreds and thousands. A former ElBaradei campaign chief entered the square from underneath the Qasr al-Nil Bridge. "It was one of the most profound moments of my life," he said. "The sight of the square filled with tens of thousands heralded the long-awaited dawn. As we entered the square the crowds installed there cheered the coming of a new battalion, greeting us with joy. I wept."

COMPRESSION. And so it went for four days and four nights as police in uniform and plainclothes battled protesters for Tahrir until finally demonstrators seized Tahrir for good. The same in Alexandria, Ismailia, Mahalla. . . .

The government of Hosni Mubarak fell eighteen days later. The

Egyptian military, Mubarak's guarantor, withdrew its support when it became clear that Mubarak could not stem the spreading protest, nor would protesters relent. Everything he tried, all the ruses, pandering, violence, and appeals, failed. Mubarak cut off cell phone service and the Internet, but the protests continued a cappella when the music stopped. They even multiplied: cut off from the digital world, protesters headed for the squares.

Wael Ghonim, kidnapped and held for days blindfolded, returned to enrapture throngs and energize millions of Egyptians. During a tearful television interview Ghonim apologized to parents for the deaths of their children in the square. Egyptians learned then that Ghonim was in fact El Shaheed. Television began to sway toward the protesters. Hugely popular news anchors Shahira Amin, Soha al-Naqqash, and others walked off sets rather than lie on demand.

The sympathies of any still-quiet Cairenes for Hosni Mubarak faded. Mubarak sent thousands of plainclothes security men to beat, shoot, and crush the protesters. Bloodied but persisting, protesters multiplied in march after march that stymied Cairo. Marches after prayers went from five thousand to forty thousand within blocks. The regime seemed unaware of the lessons learned by brutal Rome two thousand years earlier—perhaps even at Egypt's expense. "Repeated punishment," Seneca wrote to Nero in *De Clementia*, "while it crushes the hatred of a few, stirs the hatred of all."

Tear gas blanketed cities. Parties and individuals once on the sidelines joined in, seeing history in the making and not wanting to be on its wrong side. The Muslim Brotherhood brought its thousands and its discipline to the fray. Mohamed ElBaradei, late to support the protests with a tweet that made him sound a little like the *Doonesbury* character Roland Hedley ("Fully support call 4 peaceful demonstrations vs. repression"), was dutifully anointed by water cannon, captured for news cameras as a result of planning between protesters and the press. Fifty thousand blockaded a highway and provincial government building in Tanta; twenty-five thousand did the same thing in Kafr el-Dawwar. And the ruling party headquarters burned—most spectacularly in Cairo.

"The situation here is beyond belief," transcripts from Alexandria police communications show. "We are still engaging very large numbers coming from both directions! We need more gas!" In town after town, police stations, provincial government buildings, and party headquarters were being surrounded, torched, and burned to the ground. In all, ninety-nine police stations and three thousand police vehicles were destroyed.

All this compressed into eighteen days.

Police fought with live rounds, bricks, whips, and pipes, but were encumbered by crowds so dense officers could not maneuver. Protesters stayed calm and resisted "eye-for-an-eye" violence. "No Stones! No Stones!" was a frequent cheer. Battles took shape that will now be forever part of the Egyptian memory. On the Qasr al-Nil Bridge police sought to keep surging crowds away from Tahrir. In Matariya Square in the Cairo suburb of Heliopolis crowds from several neighborhoods struggled to breech police lines and became an unstoppable human mass; fifteen protesters died.

One night, Mubarak in a feint withdrew security and sent in his paid looters to refresh the imagination and fear of Cairenes—then brought in his "community safety patrols" to beat activists. The theater of lies was spectacular, inventive, and deadly.

Mubarak's promises of reform and his efforts to divide and conquer by concessions here and there were nothing against the single-minded vision that soon emerged to bind them all: Mubarak must go. That was it: one vision compressed to one demand. "The people . . . want . . . to overthrow the regime!"

With a single demand binding all, no negotiation was possible. With no obvious leaders but millions in the streets, any effort to fracture and deal with one group would be tweeted to "trending" in moments; none could possibly tamp this down. With millions activated by deep passion and mobilized around a single goal, it was a fire that would burn until all fuel was gone—or Mubarak left, whichever happened first.

With no political solution possible, the police battled. Outnumbered by a million, in pitched battles ten thousand at a time, the solution came only when the military said, as so many Egyptians already had, "Enough."

In Washington the events staggered the Obama White House. In Cairo in 2009, President Obama had promised the people of Arabia a new day. That day was now, but America was caught flat-footed. Mubarak the oppressor was also Mubarak the stalwart ally. Even on January 25 itself, the American secretary of state declared the Egyptian regime "stable." Egyptians in the streets missed that memo.

Obama finally told Mubarak, "Change is needed *now*."

" 'Now,' " Robert Gibbs, Obama's spokesperson, explained, "means 'yesterday.' "

Even if Mubarak played hard to get, Egyptian armed forces chief of staff Lieutenant General Sami Hafez Enan, on a long-planned visit to Washington, got the picture. With $1.3 billion in US military aid at stake, and perhaps less than certain about all those lieutenants and captains the generals left back in Cairo sitting in tanks, the delegation caught the first flight home. The generals were among Egypt's wealthy few; the army's middle ranks knew the pressures of the middle class. Those tank turrets were built to swivel.

THE FACEBOOK REVOLUTION? It is said that Egypt's was the first Facebook revolution. Wael Ghonim called it Revolution 2.0.

"I want to meet Mark Zuckerberg one day and thank him," Ghonim told CNN. "This revolution started online. This revolution started on Facebook. This revolution started when hundreds of thousands of Egyptians started collaborating content. We would post a video on Facebook that would be shared by 60,000 people on their walls within a few hours. I've always said that if you want to liberate a society just give them the Internet."

We cannot know for certain what this means; history is not yet finished. We can say that worlds clashed between tradition and bureaucracy, netizen and citizen, Facebook and state-controlled television and newspapers. Social media was no doubt a rallier, a force multiplier, and an echo chamber. Between tweets and al-Jazeera with forty million viewers, information was not hard to find, whatever efforts were made to suppress it.

Alya El Hosseiny, a twenty-one-year-old Egyptian student who as @alya1989262 sent the first tweet using the #Jan25 hashtag, told Twitter's own "Hope 140 Blog" that Twitter kept Cairo current on news from Tunisia even with a general media blackout.

> **#Tunisia and #sidibouzid hashtags allowed us to follow the events for the whole month beforehand. January 14 [the day Ben Ali fled Tunisia] was the day we started believing in January 25.**

But much hard work went on *without* tweets, shares, and likes—because those platforms were soon penetrated and manipulated by security forces. On the third day of demonstrations an elaborate twenty-six-page paper manual circulated widely showing where to form up, how to deploy, what to wear, and tactics to use. Above all, it warned, stay off Twitter or Facebook: "They are monitored by the Ministry of the Interior. Distribute by e-mail or printing or photocopying, especially if you own an office or store."

These commercial social web platforms—corporately owned, without passion or accountability—proved dangerous. Anyone—state security or netizen—could operate on the Facebook and Twitter platforms. State security gamed Facebook's Terms of Service, flagging partisan content as offensive and triggering automatic removals, which employees at Facebook would take weeks to review. Facebook's Terms of Service forced page creators like El Shaheed to own up to his true identity—a revelation not especially conducive to staying out of the clutches of the state. Even before January 25 Wael Ghonim had to hand off "We Are All Khaled Sa'id" to a compadre who, safe on American soil, could own it in her real name. Ghonim remained anonymous and protected by "special arrangement" with Facebook. That's no way to run a revolution.

With the downfall of Mubarak, and the promise of a new day for Egypt, Facebook use soared by five thousand new accounts daily. In Saudi Arabia, still awaiting its "spring," web denizens grew wiser: Facebook use plunged by 25 percent over the same period.

Behind the worlds of both tradition and bureaucracy, of netizen and Facebook and Twitter, were people riven with fear, possessed of aspirations, some wishing for a future much like yesterday, others desperate to make tomorrow different at any cost.

From them arose leaders by the thousands in seconds. This was no "leaderless" revolution. But the digital world gave mass to a multiplicity of leaders, all carrying light armament like smart phones, using platforms like Facebook, quick to find and message networks of networks, a consistent vision moving all to action: "The people . . . want . . . to overthrow the regime!"

Traditional leaders like Mubarak were too slow to grasp this digital wave. ElBaradei struggled to be seen through the millions of texts; not being part of the digital wave, it is impossible to understand it.

New leaders like Wael Ghonim popped up however reluctantly, anointed by al-Jazeera and mainstream media searching for figureheads. Some new leaders were durable; some receded. Though only a few would step forward, setting themselves ablaze, someone else pops up on YouTube and says, "People, have some shame. I, a girl, am going down to Tahrir Square and I will stand alone, and I'll hold up a banner. Perhaps people will show some honor. . . ." And millions did.

This is the new leadership, where retweets and page views count, where "shares" and "likes" count. In the networked world, everybody gets social media, good guys and bad. Digital and kinetic collide. Best practice, if there is one, is never to repeat what you did yesterday, but constantly reinvent your digital moves: yesterday's "hacks" can get you killed.

We can say that the day of the great autocrats is imperiled—whether they are men and women in government, or in industry, or even in our communities and families. The networked world creates too much visibility for such tyrannies to go on without questioning.

Few are prepared for this sometimes blinding light. In Egypt, society soon began its jagged new march toward healing, restoring the rule of law, and rebuilding civic institutions that Gamal Abdel Nasser, Anwar Sadat, and Hosni Mubarak had each in turn eviscerated. That is the hard march to a nation of laws, perhaps the greatest collaboration of all, given name by Abraham Lincoln at Gettysburg: "government of the people, by the people, for the people."

In May 2011, crime waves swept Egypt. With their station houses destroyed and their leaders in prison, the police were standing down. The situation was at once worse and better than imagined. Worse because having maintained order by brute force for many years, the police were at a loss to understand the new demands of civil policing. What laws should they enforce, and how? Better because both the police and Egyptian society were confused and conflicted about the role of policing—and in their crisis perhaps available for change. As the Egyptian military slipped in to fill the void and signaled a worrisome return to the "bad old days" of just months earlier, would new police leadership emerge to rebuild policing in Egypt, not as a cornerstone of repression but as a guarantor of freedom? What will become of the Arab Spring?

We cannot say for sure. But the basis for collaboration is there. "What pace the political summer may keep with the natural," Thomas Paine wrote in *Common Sense*, "no human foresight can determine. It is, however, not difficult to perceive that the spring is begun. Thus wishing, as I sincerely do, freedom and happiness to all nations, I close . . ."

Acknowledgments

We start at the beginning—our author's representative, Alice Martell, who saw the power of the idea and the collaboration between us; and Roger Scholl, our editor at Random House, who said, "Let's go!" and gave us our charge: story-driven narrative. Into the grind of the writing itself, we acknowledge Karen Holt, who knew stories when she saw them and helped us frame each so the message and the characters finally welcomed every reader. Our wives, Rikki Klieman and Laura Barbieri, were our collaborators and editors throughout. Mary McKnight, Michael John, and Jack Papp helped us mobilize the power of social media and marketing to reach every possible reader. Alexandra Rigby provided invaluable bibliographic assistance.

We are indebted to the men and women who helped us bring their stories of collaboration to the reader. Over the years, and intensively during the past two, they filled our hearts and minds with their passion, courage, and stories—lots and lots of stories. We thank those principals whom we interviewed at length and directly: Doug Hull, Bill Johnson, Mike Krieger, Paul O'Neill, Steve Ellis and Richard Kovacevich, Claudia Costin, Harry Spence, John Halamka, Pete Kilner, Beverly Donohue, John Linder, Chuck Wade, and William Brownfield. To a man and to a woman, each bridled at the thought they would be featured; each protested mightily, "It was the team." So here we acknowledge those teams—and we spoke with many directly. But we make no apologies for declaring: these were the men and women who made it happen. Special thanks, also, to Gerald Chaleff, Michael Hillmann, and John Miller, who helped bring the LAPD accounts to light and to life.

Sprinkled throughout the book is the wisdom of teachers past and present. We owe a special debt to Harvard professors and colleagues Mark Moore, Jerry Mechling, Steven Kelman, Malcolm Sparrow, Stephen

Goldsmith, Thomas Eisenmann, John Gourville, Venkatesh Narayana-murti, Tommy Vallely, Frank Hartman, Tad Oelstrom, Andrew McAfee, and Raymond Goldberg for their gifts of insight and support. Teachers come in all shapes and sizes—and ranks. For their service and years of battling the headwinds of the go-it-alone mindset, ultimately achieving greatness in collaboration, we thank the men and women of the Boston Police Department, the New York City Transit Police Department, the New York Police Department, and the Los Angeles Police Department.

At the end of the day it comes down to two men writing, with friends, colleagues, and families critiquing and cheering them on. We thank you all.

Bibliographical Sources

Note: a complete bibliography is available online at
www.brattonandtumin.com.

Our principal sources are provided below.

Chapter 1: The Case for Collaboration

THE HUNT FOR TEN RED BALLOONS: See @geohot's website, Dudeitsaballoon.com; DARPA's Networkchallenge.darpa.mil; MIT and Georgia Tech team websites; and online accounts from *Popular Science, Scientific American, InformationWeek,* MSNBC, and others.

RESTORING AN EMPIRE STATE OF MIND: BILL BRATTON TAKES NEW YORK: See *Turnaround,* by William Bratton, and *The Crime Fighter,* by Jack Maple. Additional sources include articles by Malcolm Gladwell (*The New Yorker*) and Heather Mac Donald (*City Journal*); Harvard Kennedy School case studies on CompStat by John Buntin; and articles in the *New York Times, New York Daily News,* and *New York Post.*

COLLABORATION BY DESIGN: See accounts on Local-motors.com and its YouTube channel, YouTube/Localmotors.

COLLABORATION AVERTS COLLISION: We spoke with Jim "Crash" Blanton. There are useful accounts in the *Wall Street Journal,* and good background information is available from the US Strategic Command at Stratcom.mil.

COLLABORATION RISES FROM THE ASHES: Steven J. Spear has an excellent account in his book *Chasing the Rabbit.* See also Toshihiro Nishiguchi and Alexandre Beaudet in the *MIT Sloan Management Review,* and a series of articles by Valerie Reitman in the *Wall Street Journal* and by Michiyo Nakamoto in the *Financial Times.*

NO MORE EMPTY SHELVES: See Doug Henschen's article in *InformationWeek* online.

PLATFORM TO A SUCCESSFUL COLLABORATION: We spoke with DNDO's Robert DiLonardo, Thomas Tullia, Joseph Wileman, and William Wright, and consulted numerous web resources. Zach Tumin's research on DNDO has been published by the US government, unattributed, as *The DHS Domestic Nuclear Protection Office Goes NIEM.*

YES, WE CAN COLLABORATE: Joe Rospars's public presentations, panel discussions, and speeches were all helpful and are widely available on the web. We consulted David Plouffe's book *The Audacity to Win* and Larry J. Sabato's *The*

Year of Obama: How Barack Obama Won the White House. Numerous bloggers posted insightfully: Jose Antonio Vargas in the *Washington Post;* Tom Rosensteil on Stateofthemedia.org; Alexis Matsui on PBS.org; "Hyatt" on Politicsandthe newmedia.commons.yale.edu; and "dday" on D-day.blogspot.com.

Chapter 2: Blue-Sky Vision

THE INTERNET COMES TO CANADA: Doug Hull was generous with his time in interviews. Web and online database searches provided numerous additional sources of material. We consulted an unpublished case by Zachary Tumin, "Connecting Canadians: Canada's Community Access Program. A Case Study of Government Strategic Investment on the Internet."

IT: THE FIRST PLAY YOU RUN: In addition to Zach Tumin's own recollections, Art Warbelow and Benn Konsynksi's Harvard Business School case study, "The Brooklyn DA's Office: Client Contact Systems" was a helpful reminder. The *New York Times* carried numerous stories on Holtzman's reform efforts, op-eds written by Holtzman, and her letters to the editor, which we happily rediscovered and consulted. Aadya Shukla, a fellow at the Belfer Center for Science and International Affairs of Harvard's Kennedy School, was kind enough to share her formulation of Aadya's Law mentioned in chapter 2.

REFERENCE PROJECTIONS: You can find Ackoff's discussions in his numerous articles and books; we have enjoyed *The Art of Problem Solving* over the years and return to it from time to time for his wisdom. Grove's comments appeared in his op-ed on Bloomberg.com, "How to Make an American Job Before It's Too Late." Mirchandani's excellent account of innovation at General Electric appears in his book *The New Polymath: Profiles in Compound-Technology Innovations.*

A BLUE-SKY VISION FOR REFORM: We have listened to, gained insight from, and spoken with Harry Spence in many venues over the years, and draw from those encounters here. Many of Spence's colleagues kindly spoke to us as well. We source data on Spence's efforts from various news accounts in the *Boston Globe* and *Boston Herald*, especially those written by Patricia Wen and Dave Wedge, respectively. Stephanie Gould's Harvard Kennedy School case study *Jerome Miller and the Department of Youth Services* helped frame the historical setting; Salvador Minuchin's book *Families and Family Therapy* helped frame the theoretical perspective. Numerous governmental and corporate reports provided further documentation, as did Zach Tumin's unpublished case "Word Is Love: Harry Spence and the Tyranny and Promise of IT."

Chapter 3: Right-Size the Problem

COLLABORATION ON THE SEAS: The account of the Cuban gunboat docking in Key West can be found in J. J. Hysell's "Cuban Patrol Boat Returned," on KeysNews.

com. The account of the Iran simulation is found in Thom Shanker's *New York Times* article "Iran Encounter Grimly Echoes '02 War Game," published on January 12, 2008. Mike Krieger, Frank Petrovsky, and John Shea were among those who contributed their views and, by interview and discussion, helped us grasp this enormously complicated topic. We used a variety of additional sources, including John Frittelli's reports on maritime and port security for the Congressional Research Service; Stephen Flynn's book *America the Vulnerable: How Our Government Is Failing to Protect Us from Terrorism*; and Zach Tumin's unpublished case "Maritime Domain Awareness: A Case Study in Cross-Boundary Information Sharing Among the United States Navy, Coast Guard, and Department of Transportation."

BILL BRATTON IN LOS ANGELES: For those wishing additional information on the Skid Row Safer City initiative there are useful accounts in the *Los Angeles Times,* on the LAPD blog, and on ACLU.org. Heather Mac Donald has provided additional insight in *City Journal.* William H. Sousa and George L. Kelling's "Police and the Reclamation of Public Places: A Study of MacArthur Park in Los Angeles," in the *International Journal of Police Science and Management,* explores its implications in detail. Contrary views are offered by Gary Blasi in his report "Policing Our Way Out of Homelessness? The First Year of the Safer City Initiative on Skid Row."

FOUR TESTS OF READINESS FOR COLLABORATION: *The Character of Harms: Operational Challenges in Control* and *The Regulatory Craft,* by Malcolm Sparrow, provided useful theoretical and practical perspective.

TOMATOES, TRACEBACKS, AND SALMONELLA: David Acheson provided us with insight and wisdom in numerous venues, discussions, and interviews, as did Jeff Farrar, Edward Beckman, David Gombas, A. Martin Ley, Ana Hooper, and others in government and industry. Michael Osterholm's research and Jim Prevor's blog, *Perishable Pundit,* were helpful throughout. The best overall statement of the issue and its prospects can be found in the Institute of Food Technologists' "Task Order No. 7 Final Report: Revised Tracing Systems: An Exercise Exploring Data Needs and Design," published in 2009.

Chapter 4: Make a Clearing

BUILDING A PLATFORM TO EDUCATE A CITY: Claudia Costin was gracious with her time and views; in addition, we consulted and drew from Costin's own website, ClaudiaCostin.com.br, and from an unpublished research report by Zach Tumin and Archon Fung, "From Government 2.0 to Society 2.0."

PLATFORMS: THE ARCHITECTURE OF COLLABORATION: Thomas Eisenmann's work on platforms is found in articles such as "Managing Proprietary and Shared Platforms," in the *California Management Review;* "Strategies for Two-Sided

Markets" (with Geoffrey Parker), in the *Harvard Business Review*; and "Platform Envelopment" (with Parker and Marshall van Alstyne), in the *Harvard Business School Working Knowledge Series*. We also drew from Thomas H. Davenport and Laurence Prusak's "The Promise and Challenge of Knowledge Markets," in their book *Working Knowledge*.

LA-JRIC: BUILDING AN ANTITERRORISM PLATFORM: John Miller, Michael Downing, and Gary Williams all shared their recollections by interview. We consulted Zach Tumin's unpublished case study "LA-JRIC: The Los Angeles Police Department and the Global War on Terror."

A BAND OF EQUALS: HOW A COLLABORATION PLATFORM TRANSFORMED THE CREDIT CARD INDUSTRY: Hock's book, *Birth of the Chaordic Age,* is essential reading for the early days of Visa. David Stearn's PhD dissertation for the University of Edinburgh, " 'Think of It as Money': A History of the Visa Payment System, 1970–1984," contains riches for the researcher, based on Stearn's own exhaustive research. J. Stewart Dougherty and Robert G. Eccles Jr. wrote an illuminating Harvard Business School case study, which we drew from: *Visa International: The Management of Change.*

CAN YOU HEAR ME NOW? RESTORING THE US NAVY'S UNDERSEA ADVANTAGE: William M. Johnson gave generously of his time in interviews, discussion, and presentations. We consulted numerous sources of testimony, speeches, memoranda, and reports by government officials, including those of Ashton B. Carter, Malcolm I. Fages, Edmund P. Giambastiani, Michael G. Mullen, and John J. Young. We drew from the presentations and findings of research in reports by the US Air Force Scientific Advisory Board; the US House Armed Services Committee Panel on Defense Acquisition Reform; the Advisory Panel on Submarine and Antisubmarine Warfare to the House Armed Services Subcommittees on Research and Development, and Seapower and Strategic and Critical Materials; and the Defense Science Board Task Force on Integrating Commercial Systems into the DOD, Effectively and Efficiently. Summaries, presentations, and reports by Owen R. Cote, Greg Duckworth, David N. Ford and John T. Dillard, Laura J. Heath, Norman Polmar, John Schuster, and Bob Zarnich further shaped our understanding and views. We relied on news accounts from the *New York Times* and the *Los Angeles Times*, and articles in magazines and journals such as *Undersea Warfare, Jane's Navy International, Defense Daily,* and *The Submarine Review.*

Chapter 5: Make It Pay

WHEN COLLABORATION FAILS: Andrew McAfee's "Mastering the Three Worlds of Information Technology," in *Harvard Business Review*, called our attention to this story. His Harvard Business School case study (with Sarah M. MacGregor and Michael Benari), *Mount Auburn Hospital: Physician Order Entry*, provided further depth. David W. Bates, Troyen A. Brennan, Lucian L. Leape, and Amy C. Edmonson, collaborating with many coauthors, published numerous foundational reports that we drew from.

THE 10X FACTOR: John T. Gourville's "Eager Sellers and Stony Buyers: Understanding the Psychology of New-Product Adoption," a *Harvard Business Review OnPoint* article, provides the heart of the matter; Gourville's presentations and our discussions with him furthered our understanding. You can read more about the economics of horses, penguins, and lemmings in Joseph Farrell and Garth Saloner's essay of the same name. Andrew McAfee's blog post, "The 9X Email Problem," captured our attention.

AUTOMATE OR PERISH: We became aware of these events through interviews and conversations with many in the U.S. Customs Service, none more important than Robert Ehinger, Lynne Gordon, and Robert Nolle. We sourced this further through hundreds of trade and newspaper accounts of the time, notably from *American Shipper*, the *New York Times*, *Government Computer News*, the *Los Angeles Times*, the *Washington Post*, *Women's Wear Daily*, *San Diego Union Tribune*, PR Newswire (for US Customs announcements), and the Bureau of National Affairs, Inc.'s *Daily Report for Executives*.

FREE ISN'T CHEAP ENOUGH: John D. Halamka's thoughts are richly available on his blog, *Life as a Healthcare CIO*, which we consulted freely. Halamka further shared his views with us in speeches and interviews, as did many others. We also consulted sources including *Federal Computer Week*, *InformationWeek*, and Zach Tumin's research on the topic, published by the US government (without attribution), *NIEM and the HHS Meaningful Use Sprint*.

IBM INNOVATIONJAM: Information is widely available on the web. See, in particular, Gaurav Bhalla's blog posts on GauravBhalla.com; Osvald M. Bjelland and Robert Chapman Wood's "An Insider's View of IBM's 'Innovation Jam,'" in the *MIT Sloan Management Review*.

COMPANYCOMMAND: Pete Kilner gave us his time and views by interview and discussion on several occasions. David Axe, reporting for Wired.com's *Danger Room* blog, filled in many details. Dan Baum's account, "Annals of War: Battle Lessons," in *The New Yorker*, was especially helpful.

INNOCENTIVE: We consulted Gaurav Bhalla's "Oslo Innovation Clinic Offers Treatment for Ideas," in the *Harvard Business Review*, and, in the same journal, Karim R. Lakhani and Lars Bo Jeppesen's "Getting Unusual Suspects to Solve R&D Puzzles." Dean Takahashi's reporting in Venturebeat.com and David Wessel's in the *Wall Street Journal* were helpful.

THE APP STORE: Among other sources, we relied notably on Tomi T. Ahonen's "Full Analysis of iPhone Economics—It Is Bad News. And Then It Gets Worse," appearing on the blog *Communities Dominate Brands*. We scooped up further details from stories and releases on Apple.com, BBC.co.uk, the *New York Times*, Endgaget.com, Reuters, and other sources.

WAITING FOR VERIZON: We relied on numerous interviews, news sources, and document reviews. Reporting by Steve Marlin in *InformationWeek* and Shane Kite and Isabelle Clary, among others, in *Securities Technology Monitor* helped greatly. Remarks and presentations by Jill Considine, Donald F. Donahue, and Harvey L. Pitt helped clarify events. We draw from reports by the staffs of the Federal Reserve Board, the Federal Reserve Bank of New York, and the Securities and Exchange Commission; the Assuring Telecommunications Continuity Task Force of the Federal Reserve Bank of New York; the Computer Science and Telecommunications Board; and the SIAC itself. Chuck Wade gave us his time and thoughts in further bringing forward the essential facts.

Chapter 6: Add People; Stir

Although we are all fans of Mr. T, the A-Team concept in this context was introduced to us by our colleague Rick Webb. Harry Spence and Beverly Donohue both provided detail on the era of Galaxy development by interview. To augment this information, we reviewed and drew from numerous accounts and reports, especially those of Dorothy Siegel and her colleagues on performance-driven budgeting published by New York University's Institute for Education and Social Policy. The report by Steven Kelman, "Changing Big Government Organizations: Easier Than Meets the Eye?," caught our eye, as did his book *Unleashing Change: A Study of Organizational Renewal in Government*. Bo Cowgill and colleagues' "Using Prediction Markets to Track Information Flows: Evidence from Google" told us a lot about Googlers and ourselves.

Chapter 7: Performance

SHOW ME THE MONEY: Much has been written about Gary Loveman. We were drawn to the story originally by Thomas H. Davenport and Jeanne G. Harris's treatment of the Loveman era in their book *Competing on Analytics: The New Science of Winning*. From there we turned to cases, whether from Harvard Business School—Rajiv Lal's "Harrrah's Entertainment, Inc."—or Stanford—Kamram Ahsan and colleagues' "Harrah's Entertainment Inc.: Real-Time CRM in a Service Supply Chain," and Victoria Chang and Jeffrey Pfeffer's "Gary Loveman and Harrah's Entertainment." Loveman's own "Diamonds in the Mine," appearing in the *Harvard Business Review*, and John M. Gallaugher's "Data Asset in Action: Harrah's Solid Gold CRM for the Service Sector," on his website, illuminated much. David O. Becker in *McKinsey Quarterly*, Christina Binkley in the *Wall Street Journal*, Meridith Levinson on CIO.com, and numerous writers in *eWeek*, *Information Age*, *InformationWeek*, *CIO Insight*, and the *New York Times*, among other journals, magazines, and newspapers, all helped us better understand the history and the story.

THE LINDER METHOD: You can read more about John Linder in William Bratton's book *Turnaround*. Chris Smith's story in *New* York magazine, "The NYPD Guru," and an unattributed account of Linder in Baltimore, titled "Believe," that appeared in *SmartCEO* magazine, helped us build Linder's story here. Linder was generous with his time and frank with his views in numerous interviews for this book.

PAUL O'NEILL AND ALCOA: Steven J. Spear's account of O'Neill at Alcoa, in his book *Chasing the Rabbit,* and Ron Suskind's book *The Price of Loyalty* captured our attention. We turned as well to Harvard Business School case studies on O'Neill at Alcoa, also by Spear, and a Harvard Kennedy School case study by Pamela Varley, "Vision and Strategy: Paul H. O'Neill at OMB & Alcoa." We drew from numerous news accounts and profiles: Dana Milbank's in the *Wall Street Journal,* Dave Johnson's in *Industrial Safety & Hygiene News,* and Michael Lewis's in the *New York Times Magazine* were especially important. Alcoa's reports and website helped us fill in Alcoa's history. O'Neill has published and given speeches widely, many of which are available on the web. Lastly, Paul O'Neill gave generously of his time and views to us by interview.

Chapter 8: Politics: The Glue and the Grease

A BRUISING IN SAN DIEGO: Diane Ravitch's chapter "Lessons from San Diego," in her book *The Death and Life of the Great American School System,* is a powerful entrée to the events there. Maureen Magee's reporting in the *San Diego Union-Tribune* was helpful for additional detail. Anthony Alvarado's interview by Hedrick Smith on PBS.org offers rich further insight into Alvarado's thinking and personality.

A PLACE IN THE SUN: Spend some time with Philip B. Heymann's *The Politics of Public Management* or Richard E. Neustadt's *Preparing to Be President: The Memos of Richard E. Neustadt,* and you will find yourself in the presence of giants of strategy and political management. Add David Steven, a new thinker on the scene whose essay "After the Vote: Negotiate First with Your Base" you will find on the web at *Global Dashboard,* and your quest to stay in the headlamps of political support will be richly rewarded.

TAKEOVER: Steven Rattner's *Overhaul: An Insider's Account of the Obama Administration's Emergency Rescue of the Auto Industry* tells the story of the rise and fall of GM, and rise again, from an investment banker's perspective. Malcolm Gladwell takes Rattner to task for all this in "Steven Rattner and the Rescue of General Motors," his essay in *The New Yorker.* In between there are reams of exciting and interesting sources: Jonathan Alter's book *The Promise: President*

Obama, Year One; the reporting of Micheline Maynard, Sheryl Gay Stolberg, and Bill Vlasic in the *New York Times*; and of Nick Bunkley in *USA Today*. We relied on them all and more for this section.

THE (NOT SO) GREAT PHILIPS FIRE: Almar Latour's "Trial by Fire: A Blaze in Albuquerque Sets off Major Crisis for Cell-Phone Giants," in the *Wall Street Journal*, was one of the first and most comprehensive accounts of the Philips fire. Amit S. Mukherjee wrote of it further in the chapter "The Fire That Changed an Industry: A Case Study on Thriving in a Networked World," which appeared in his book *The Spider's Strategy: Creating Networks to Avert Crisis, Create Change, and Really Get Ahead*. Yossi Sheffi offered theoretical and practical perspective to all in *The Resilient Enterprise: Overcoming Vulnerability for Competitive Advantage*. We drew insight and understanding from each of these sources and numerous other news accounts.

BILL BRATTON ON SWAT: You can find the official LAPD report of the SWAT Board of Inquiry on the LAPD website. The author is Richard M. Aborn.

Chapter 9: Leadership

BILL BRATTON: MACARTHUR PARK: Studying and incorporating frequent mentions of *Los Angeles Times* reports permit us to stand back and see the world through the eyes of its reporters and editors. Andrew Blankstein, Patrick McGreevy, Tim Wooten, Duke Helfand, Marc Cooper, and Richard Winton are among those we draw from and cite. We took advantage of national reporting by Daniel B. Wood of the *Christian Science Monitor,* Connie Bruck in *The New Yorker,* and others to augment our own perspectives. The report on the day by Michael Hillmann and Gerald L. Chaleff—*Los Angeles Police Department Report to the Board of Police Commissioners: An Examination of May Day 2007*—can be found on the LAPD website. Both Hillmann and Chaleff sat for interviews.

THE BILLION-DOLLAR BET: At the heart of our story are interviews with Steve Ellis, Richard Kovacevich, and Danny Peltz. We refer to Italo Calvino's *Six Memos for the Next Millennium* and Jim Collins's *Good to Great: Why Some Companies Make the Leap . . . and Others Don't*. We relied on many journals and magazines such as *Bank Technology News, Computerworld, Fortune,* and *GT News,* and the reporting of seasoned financial industry technology writers such as Steven Marlin at *InformationWeek*, J. Nicholas Hoover at *Wall Street & Technology* and *Bank Systems & Technology*, and John Beck for his profiles of Ellis in *The Banker*. You can find information on Conway's Law in *Wikipedia*.

Chapter 10: Out of Egypt

We discovered that hundreds of blogs, dozens of online journals and newspapers, and a handful of exceptionally talented writers around the world can all contribute to a single story told (we hope) as if by one voice. Among the many we found, learned from, and relied upon were Shahanaaz Habib, who wrote in TheStar.com that in Tunisia a "Fruit Seller Ignites a Revolution." We relied upon al-Jazeera (English) and accounts by reporters such as Yasmine Ryan, Paul Amar, Tarak Barkawi, Mary Joyce, and Jillian C. York, and Cairo's *al-Masry al-Youm* and reporters Heba Afify and Alastair Beach. Mona El-Ghobashy, writing online for the *Middle East Research and Information Project,* provided an electrifying account of the days around January 25 in her article "The Praxis of the Egyptian Revolution." Mona Eltahawy contributed to the record of these times with reports such as "Mubarak Is Our Berlin Wall: Egyptian Columnist Mona Eltahawy on How the Youth Drove the Uprising in Cairo and Implications for Democracy in the Region," appearing on the Democracy Now! website. We discovered the young scholar David Faris in reporting by Trey Popp in "Anatomy of an Uprising," an astonishing assemblage of voices and images appearing in the *Pennsylvania Gazette.* Thereafter we followed David Faris's writing for the Meta-Activism Project website, and Eric Trager's writing in TheAtlantic.com. Ethan Zuckerman's writing on Globalvoicesonline.org and his blog, *My Heart's in Accra,* gave us further insight into events. *New Yorker* editor David Remnick's "The Dictator Is the Last to Know" no doubt left many wishing they'd said it first—but few see things as Remnick does. Many YouTube videos later we feel as though we know activists Asmaa Mahfouz and Wael Ghonim well, though we don't at all. Lastly, one of the most gratifying encounters was with a blogger, Sarah Carr, writing on her blog *Inanities,* whose voice and pen surely trumped all by a mile and brought the world close-on to the nights and days of the Egyptian upheavals as no others did.

To all, we are indebted.

Index